PENGUIN BOOKS
WOMEN AND CHILDREN LAST

Ruth Sidel is a professor of sociology at Hunter College in New York City. A frequent speaker throughout the country on women's issues and social policy, Sidel is the author of many books, including *On Her Own: Growing up in the Shadow of the American Dream* and *Battling Bias: The Struggle For Identity and Community on College Campuses*.

WOMEN AND CHILDREN LAST

THE PLIGHT OF POOR WOMEN IN AFFLUENT AMERICA

Ruth Sidel

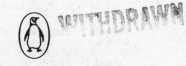

PENGUIN BOOKS

PENGUIN BOOKS

Published by the Penguin Group
Penguin Books USA Inc.,
375 Hudson Street, New York, New York 10014, U.S.A.
Penguin Books Ltd, 27 Wrights Lane,
London W8 5TZ, England
Penguin Books Australia Ltd, Ringwood,
Victoria, Australia
Penguin Books Canada Ltd, 10 Alcorn Avenue,
Toronto, Ontario, Canada M4V 3B2
Penguin Books (N.Z.) Ltd, 182-190 Wairau Road,
Auckland 10, New Zealand

Penguin Books Ltd, Registered Offices:
Harmondsworth, Middlesex, England

First published in the United States of America by
Viking Penguin Inc. 1986

Published in Penguin Books 1987
This revised edition with a new foreword and afterword
published in Penguin Books 1992

7   9   10   8

LIBRARY OF CONGRESS CATALOGING IN PUBLICATION DATA
Sidel, Ruth.
Women and children last: the plight of poor women in affluent
America/ Ruth Sidel.—Rev. ed.
p.   cm.
Includes bibliographical references and index.
ISBN 0 14 01.6766 8
1. Poor women—United States.   2. Public welfare—United States.
3. Family policy—United States.   I. Title.
HV1.S49   1992
362.83' 0973—dc20   91–21102

Printed in the United States of America

to the memory of my father
Maxwell B. Grossman
whose love, wit, and commitment to family
will never die

The test of our progress is not whether we add more to the abundance of those who have much; it is whether we provide enough for those who have too little.

—Franklin Delano Roosevelt
Second Inaugural Address
January 20, 1937

FOREWORD

According to the Children's Defense Fund, the following were some "Moments in America" in 1991:

- Every 35 seconds an infant is born into poverty.
- Every 2 minutes an infant is born to a mother who received late or no prenatal care.
- Every 2 minutes an infant is born at low birthweight.
- Every 14 minutes an infant dies in the first year of life.
- Every 64 seconds an infant is born to a teenage mother.
- Every 14 hours a child younger than 5 is murdered.
- Every 5 hours a 15- to 19-year-old is murdered.[1]

Since the original publication of *Women and Children Last*, the United States has done little to address these critical problems. Women and children still constitute the majority of poor people in the United States. Single-parent families, particularly those who are members of minority groups, are still at greatest risk of poverty. The child-care and health-care systems are still shamefully inadequate to meet the needs of American families, particularly poor families. During the past several years, moreover, living conditions for the poor have deteriorated markedly: many cities have been gripped by increasing violence; the plague of AIDS has become an ever-present threat for many Americans, particularly for poor people of color; and hunger and homelessness seem to be permanent features of life during the final decade of the twentieth century.

While women and children still appear to be last in the priorities of the United States and much that was written in the original edition of this book is tragically all too relevant today, it seemed necessary and important at this time to reexamine the status and quality of life of the millions of women and children living in poverty. Since *Women and Children Last* was originally published, the United States has elected a new president, one who promised to lead us toward a "kinder, gentler nation"; we have moved into the last decade of the twentieth century and are looking ahead to the challenges and opportunities of the next hundred years; and we have witnessed a profound shift in world politics—the end of the Cold War and the virtual dismantling of socialism all over the world. This is, I believe, a particularly crucial moment for reflection and for reevaluation of our national priorities and goals. It is in this spirit that this new edition of *Women and Children Last* is offered.

While the original book has been left largely intact, the Introduction has been substantially revised to include the most recent poverty data and issues that have emerged as critically important since the mid-1980s. In an Afterword written specifically for this edition, I reexamine and bring up to date several of the issues discussed in the original edition and evaluate the progress (or lack of progress) that has been made around the development of a family policy. It is my hope that this edition of *Women and Children Last* will help to illuminate and clarify the exceedingly difficult and complex problems of poverty among women and children and will move many to press for urgently needed solutions during this decade.

My appreciation, as ever, to those who have encouraged my work over the years: my students and colleagues at Hunter College, particularly at the Center for the Study of Family Policy and people across the country who have read *Women and Children Last* and generously shared their comments and criticisms. To Mindy Werner and Janine Steel at Viking Penguin and to Vic Sidel, my special thanks.

ACKNOWLEDGMENTS

This book literally could not have been written without the active cooperation and support of many, many people across the country. To all of them I want to express my deep appreciation.

To the women who shared with me their often-painful lives, their hopes, their feelings of inadequacy and their successes, my profound gratitude. They are the heart of the book. I cannot, unfortunately, thank each woman by name since I have attempted to preserve their privacy by giving them pseudonyms. Their willingness to participate in this project, their warmth and generosity, their genuine concern about the urgent problems of women and children in poverty, are vivid expressions of the "sharing and caring" that so many of them feel is necessary for survival. They are models for us all.

To all of those who gave time, energy, and encouragement, who arranged for me to interview others, who met with me and shared their knowledge and their views, my sincere appreciation. Special thanks to Barbara Burke-Tatum, Naomi Chase, Lee Chelminiak, Carole Dane, Magdalen Daniels, Flora Donham, Mariann Edgar, Jean Eller, Austin Ford, Theresa Funiciello, Vera Galeas, Gloria Garcia, Maria Garcia, Esta Gutierrez, Margot Haas, Eileen Hayes, Karen Hymbaugh, Dorothy Johnson, Henry Kahn, Jeanne Keller, Judith Kitzes, Laurie Kramer, Becky Lamey, Betty Levinson, Mimi Marchev, Kathleen McConnell, Peggy McDonald, Kim McLoughlin, Brina Melemed, Sherry Mofield, Mary Murphree, Anne Nichols, Jeanne O'Day, Frances Pauley, Jan Poppendieck, Sandra Robertson, Dina Romero, Kevin Sidel, Mark Sidel, Julia Soto, Milton Terris, Karren Thomas, Shirley Trussell, Gladys Valdivieso,

Mary Vallo, Sara Voorhees, Lanelle Ward, Barbara Warren, Phoebe Weber, Robin Yager and Michael Zubkoff.

To Elisa Petrini, my appreciation for her meticulous work on the manuscript and to Pat Mulcahy, my editor at Viking Penguin, my gratitude for her intellectual acuity, her creative suggestions about both substance and style, her constant support, and her ever-present good humor.

And finally to Vic, who listens to every new idea, reads every draft, fights with the word processor when it won't do its thing, and always takes time, even when he doesn't have any, my thanks and my love.

CONTENTS

INTRODUCTION

High in the crow's nest of the New White Star Liner *Titanic*, Lookout Frederick Fleet peered into a dazzling night. It was calm, clear and bitterly cold. There was no moon, but the cloudless sky blazed with stars. The Atlantic was like polished plate glass; people later said they had never seen it so smooth. . . .

Suddenly Fleet saw something directly ahead, even darker than the darkness. At first it was small . . . but every second it grew larger and closer. Quickly Fleet banged the crow's-nest bell three times, the warning of danger ahead.[1]

For the next thirty-seven seconds Fleet and fellow lookout Reginald Lee watched the iceberg draw closer and closer. The ship did not turn until the last second, when "the berg towered wet and glistening far above the forecastle deck." Finally the ship steered clear and "the ice glided swiftly by." It seemed as though they had narrowly avoided certain disaster. But within the next few seconds, people all over the glittering, gleaming ship—which was on its maiden voyage from Southampton, England, to New York—felt "a faint grinding jar [that] seemed to come from somewhere deep inside the ship."[2]

During the next two and a half hours, between 11:40 P.M. on April 14, 1912, and 2:20 A.M. the following morning, the "unsinkable" *Titanic* would go down in the frigid waters of the Atlantic and more than 1,500 lives would be lost.

On this magnificent ship, four city blocks long, were a French "side-walk cafe," the finest band on the Atlantic, a Turkish bath with a mosaic floor, blue-green tiled walls, and gilded beams—

but a mere twenty lifeboats with room for only 1,178 of the 2,207 passengers and crew members on board.[3]

Women and children were, indeed, the first to be saved that dreadful night. Women were persuaded to climb into the lifeboats, leaving their husbands standing by the railing; a few refused to do so and remained together to the end. Most men played by the rules, but some had to be forcibly removed from the boats, one or two at gunpoint. All this is well known; less well known is the fact that the percentage of women and children saved in first and second class was far higher than the percentage saved in third class, known in those days as "steerage." Indeed, the vast majority of first- and second-class women and children survived; the majority of women and children in steerage did not.

In all, only 4 of the 143 first-class women (3 by their own choice) and 15 of 93 second-class women—a total of 8 percent—drowned that night; 81 of the 179 women in steerage—that is, 45 percent—died. The children's statistics are even more dramatic: only one child of 29 first- and second-class children, or 3 percent, died; but 53 of the 76 children in steerage—70 percent—perished.[4]

There were many reasons, of course, that first- and second-class passengers survived in such great numbers. Access to the lifeboats was from the first- and second-class decks; the barriers to keep those in third class from going onto other decks were not removed during the disaster, and many could not find their way or, if they did, could not get through. Moreover, little effort was made to save the people in steerage; indeed, some were forcibly kept down below by seamen standing guard.

The United States of the 1980s surely glittered and gleamed; it was considered by many to be unsinkable. Even during the leaner years of the early 1990s, the wealth of many Americans is truly incredible; many others, less dramatically wealthy, are nonetheless doing very well. They can afford home computers, VCRs, expensive cars, college and graduate school for their children. But despite our sidewalk cafes, our saunas, our luxurious boutiques, we too lack lifeboats for everyone. When disaster strikes—be it a severe economic recession, a burgeoning divorce rate, or the epidemic of teenage pregnancy—many survive; but survival in any meaningful sense for millions of women and children is denied. As on the

Titanic, the United States is filled with locked gates, segregated decks, and policies that assure that women and children will be first—not the first to be saved but the first to fall into the abyss that is poverty.

This paradox—between great wealth and opportunity on the one hand and the barest survival on the other—is seen most vividly if we look at what has happened to the status of women over the past quarter century. During the past twenty-five years, the lives of many American women have been remarkably transformed. In this short span of time—a single generation—women's roles, men's roles, even the very nature and functions of the family have been questioned, reevaluated, and, in some instances, have undergone substantial change. Women have entered the workforce in ever-increasing numbers. In 1950 barely a third of women worked outside the home; in 1989 69 percent of American women were in the civilian labor force.[5] In recent years women have entered the elite professions of law and medicine in astonishing numbers, they have been moving into business and banking, setting up their own firms, and making headway in artistic fields such as film directing and publishing. They have even moved into blue-collar jobs that were once considered taboo, and they are gradually being accepted into the male-dominated bastions of police work, fire-fighting, and even, in certain capacities, the military.

Women's lives have changed significantly in other ways as well. Women have demanded and been at least partially successful in obtaining some control over their bodies. Contraception is more widely available. Despite strong efforts to reverse the 1973 Supreme Court decision and apparent success in limiting access to abortion for poor women, abortion remains legal in the United States. Physician- and technology-dominated childbirth has been challenged, with the result that today many women have child-bearing options that they did not have a generation ago.

Notions about female sexuality have altered radically. Both women's and men's awareness of the nature and legitimacy of female sexuality has grown markedly, and while we still have a long way to go before we understand how to achieve true intimacy, the sexual gains for women have been real.

But amid these positive developments, this remarkable reevaluation of the roles, responsibilities, and rights of women, other developments, equally prominent and far more devastating, have occurred. Even as some women have graduated from Princeton, pursued their M.B.A., passed the bar exam, taken a residency in surgery, or moved up the corporate hierarchy, vast and ever-increasing numbers of women have been living in poverty.

In 1990, 13.5 percent of all Americans—33.6 million people—were officially classified as poor—that is, as living below the poverty line. In that year the poverty level for a family of four was set by the federal government at $13,359. The number of poor people and the poverty rate have declined somewhat since 1983, when over 15 percent of all Americans lived below the poverty line, but the number and rate rose sharply in 1990. Between 1989 and the recession year of 1990 2.1 million additional Americans particularly children and the elderly fell into poverty. Moreover, the composition of poor families has changed significantly over the past twenty-five years. While the number of people living in poverty in white, male-headed families declined markedly in the 1970s and rose moderately during the 1980s, the number of people in poor families headed by women has risen dramatically. In 1959, 23 percent of all poor families were headed by women; by 1989 that figure had risen to 51.7 percent. Today nearly 40 percent of the American poor are children and over half of them are part of female-headed families.[7]

Moreover, poverty statistics for families headed by black and Hispanic women are even more bleak. The data for 1989 demonstrate clearly that female-headed families, particularly black and Hispanic female-headed families, continue to be at greatest risk of poverty. Among poor black families, nearly three quarters, or 73.4 percent, were headed by women with no husband present; among poor families of Hispanic origin, nearly half, 46.8 percent, were headed by women.[8]

In comparing the poverty rate of married-couple families with that of female-headed families, the significant differences in economic status and therefore in life chances become clear. Among white married-couple families, the poverty rate in 1989 was 5 percent; among white female-headed households, the poverty rate was five times higher, or 25.4 percent. While the same differentials are apparent among black families and among families of Hispanic origin, these groups suffer from the additional burden of significantly higher poverty rates for all households. Among black families, for example, 11.8 percent of married-couple families lived below the poverty line in 1989, while 46.5 percent, nearly half of female-headed families, lived in poverty. The statistics for Hispanic families are equally disturbing: 16.2 percent of married-couple families lived in poverty, compared to 47.5 percent of female-headed families.[9]

The poverty rate for children continues, as it has since 1975, to be higher than that of any other age group. In 1990 the poverty rate for all children under 18 was 20.6 percent. In other words, over 13 million—one out of every five American children—lived below the poverty line. In 1989 14.2 percent of white children, 34.9 percent of Hispanic children, and 43 percent of black children lived in poverty.[10] Among children under the age of six, over five million, or 22.5 percent, were officially poor.[11]

Since the mid-1980s, several critical, often life-threatening problems that particularly afflict poor women and children have become apparent. During the second half of the decade, substance abuse was recognized as a significant threat to the well-being of mothers and their children. While cigarette smoking and alcohol consumption are associated with severe health problems for both mother and child, the use of crack cocaine by pregnant women has captured the attention of both professionals and the media. Anna Quindlen writes about one hospital in New York City:

> The future of America's cities is lying in isolettes in the neonatal intensive care unit of Bronx-Lebanon hospital. The bright room is filled with baby misery: babies born months too soon; babies born weighing little more than a hardcover book; babies that look like wizened old men in the last stages of a terminal illness, wrinkled skin clinging to chicken bones; babies who do not cry because their mouths and noses are full of tubes.[12]

Since 1985 when crack cocaine first appeared on the streets of New York, the number of "crack babies"—babies exposed to the drug when their mothers used it during pregnancy—has grown alarmingly. One recent nationwide survey of women indicated that

11 percent of the respondents admitted using illegal drugs during pregnancy; many experts believe, however, that the number of pregnant women using drugs is far higher.[13]

The National Institute on Drug Abuse estimated that in 1988 five million women of childbearing age used illegal drugs.[14] There is general agreement on the serious, frequently disastrous effects of drug use during pregnancy on the infant. Crack babies are often born with low birth weights, may have suffered from damage to the brain or intestinal tract due to loss of blood supply to those organs, or may suffer from more subtle problems such as unresponsiveness, hypersensitivity, irritability, or, in later life, serious learning disabilities and emotional problems.[15]

The relationship between substance abuse during pregnancy and poverty is less direct, particularly if all drug use is investigated. Drug use during pregnancy, particularly if alcohol is included, seems equally prevalent among white middle-class women and low-income women of color. Nevertheless, poor African-American women are far more likely to be prosecuted across the country for the "prenatal crime" of delivering drugs to the fetus than more affluent white women. As critics have pointed out, poor women are often in close contact with government agencies; their drug use is therefore more likely to be detected and reported than would be the drug use of middle-class women. Moreover, the toxicological testing of newborns, which is the government's primary source of information about prenatal drug use, is performed almost exclusively by public hospitals that serve poor minority communities. Furthermore, the prosecution of poor black crack addicts, "women whom society views as undeserving to be mothers in the first place," makes prosecution of pregnant women more palatable to the public and diverts attention from poverty, racism, and a grossly inadequate health-care system to "bad acts of individual mothers." As one professor of law has stated, "Poor black mothers are thus made the scapegoats for the black community's ill health. Punishing them assuages the nation's guilt for an underclass of people whose babies die at rates higher than in some third world countries."[16]

The problems of drug-abusing mothers and their children continue, of course, past childbirth and infancy. Drug-abusing mothers, particularly poor mothers, have serious difficulty finding and being accepted in drug treatment programs, are at significant risk for problems such as homelessness, may well lose their children to the foster care system, and often have great difficulty getting them back. The number of children in foster care in New York City, for example, has risen from 16,000 in 1984 to 45,000 in 1991;[17] a substantial number of these placements are thought to be due, directly or indirectly, to the mothers' drug use.

Among young people, particularly among casual users,[18] college students,[19] and other middle-class users, the use of cocaine may have peaked during the late 1980s and early 1990s,[20] but during the same period, the age of crack users and dealers has been declining and the level of violence in the lives of these young people has escalated dramatically.[21]

With the passage in 1973 of the so-called "Rockefeller Laws" in New York, which mandated a severe prison term for anyone over the age of eighteen convicted of possession of an illegal drug, drug dealers have been employing teenagers, and some children as young as ten years old, to function as intermediaries between themselves and their customers. In his revealing book *The Cocaine Kids*, Terry Williams delineates the role of teenagers in the drug trade in New York City.[22] These young people, many of whom, according to Williams, are using the drug business to obtain their piece of the American Dream, often have responsibilities for thousands or even hundreds of thousands of dollars worth of drugs and are at great risk of becoming addicted themselves and of being caught both by the police and by the violence that is endemic to the drug business.

But the violence of the drug trade has permeated neighborhoods, schools, and the lives of young people far beyond the boundaries of crack houses and street-corner drug deals. Weapons of violence, particularly guns, are ubiquitous. During the summer of 1990, in less than two weeks four children were killed in New York City by bullets meant for someone else. One child was asleep on her mother's lap when she was killed; another, a nine-month-old Bronx boy, was "playing in a walker in his grandmother's apartment when a hail of bullets crashed through the door."[23]

Buying or borrowing handguns in some neighborhoods of

Washington, D.C. and parts of Prince George's County in Maryland "has never been easier," according to police officials in the Washington area.[24] Many experts feel that "some of the children growing up in settings that have been rife with violent turf battles over drugs have come to believe that guns are a necessary tool for survival, even if they do not have an appetite for using or selling drugs."[25] The threat of dying a violent death at a young age, particularly in our poorest neighborhoods, has become almost commonplace, particularly among black males. Recent data from the Federal Centers for Disease Control indicate that the homicide rate among black men between the ages of fifteen and twenty-four rose by two-thirds between 1984 and 1988. According to a youth worker in Los Angeles, "Young blacks are an endangered species. They are dying out, like the condor, out there in the streets."[26]

Among the most devastating problems that disproportionately afflict poor women and children are surely human immunodeficiency virus (HIV) infection and AIDS. From 1981 to 1989, 8,556 AIDS cases were reported in women aged fifteen to forty-four. Over half (57.2 percent) of the cases were related to intravenous drug use and another 20.2 percent to sexual relations with an intravenous drug user. AIDS is a serious problem among children under sixteen, although fewer than a third of the children of HIV-infected women are thus far known to develop AIDS.[27] Black and Hispanic children are disproportionately afflicted with AIDS. Black children make up 15 percent of the U.S. population younger than age fifteen but account for 52 percent of reported AIDS cases in that age group. Children of Hispanic origin represent only 9 percent of the pediatric population but account for 25 percent of pediatric AIDS cases.[28] The number of new AIDS cases is increasing faster among women and newborns than among most other groups. Between 1988 and 1989 the number of AIDS cases in women increased 11 percent, and there was a 17-percent increase in the number of cases transmitted from mother to newborn.[29]

Homelessness has become yet another national problem that has increased in scope and severity during the 1980s. Today families with children comprise approximately a third of the nation's homeless population. Estimates of the number of children who are homeless on any given night range from 61,500 to 500,000. According to the Children's Defense Fund, at least 100,000 American children go to bed homeless each night. Two-parent families are afflicted along with single-parent families, but the latter, most often headed by women, represent an estimated three-fourths of all homeless families nationwide. Young families are much more likely to be homeless than older families; consequently, young children make up a significant proportion of clients in shelters for the homeless. Recent studies indicate that 50 percent of the children in family shelters in Oregon in 1988 were younger than five, and, in the same year, 35 percent of children in shelters in Colorado were younger than three.[30]

According to a recent Children's Defense Fund publication, "Homelessness is a devastating experience for families, parents and children alike. It disrupts virtually every aspect of family life, damaging the physical and emotional health of family members, interfering with children's education and development, and resulting in the damaging separation of family members."[31] Homeless children have a significantly higher infant-mortality rate than housed low-income children, homeless mothers are far less likely to receive prenatal care than low-income pregnant women who are housed, and their children are far more likely to be born at low birth weight than housed low-income children. Homeless children are at significant risk of suffering from poor nutrition and hunger, of receiving grossly inadequate health and medical care, and of having their education severely disrupted.[32] Moreover, the violence many families experience in shelters and "welfare hotels"—the fights, the drugs, the constant threat of robbery, the rapes, the murders, and, above all, the treatment of human beings as though they are subhuman—is truly traumatizing.

And what of the stigma and the self-hatred spawned by these conditions? In his book *Rachel and Her Children*, Jonathan Kozol describes the feelings of women placed by New York City in the infamous Martinique Hotel in the mid-1980s:

Self-hate is common among many women here. If a woman feels she is despised, and has no recognition of the forces that demean her, perhaps it is inevitable that she will feel despicable. If nothing can affirm her dignity (if she is . . . forced to beg and sweat and tremble in the hallway of the Martinique, hiding her children in a tiny room for fear of being cast out on the street) it seems understandable that she may see herself as worthy of contempt.[33]

Women and Children Last is about these women and their children; not about the newly trained doctors and lawyers or the newly promoted bankers and corporate executives, but about women living at or near the edge of poverty: who they are and how they got there, what poverty does to them and their children, and how they cope with being poor in one of the richest countries in the world.

One of the goals of this book is to provide a glimpse of the people behind the statistics and the sociological terms that so often distance us from the day-to-day reality of being poor in America. Statistics, it has been said, are "people with the tears washed off." So long as we think of individuals in terms of percentages or as members of "female-headed households" or the "new poor," we do not need to see them as real people, very much like ourselves, with hopes and dreams, frustrations and fears. Just as we dehumanize the enemy during wartime in order to kill with minimal guilt, so do we depersonalize and dehumanize the poor in order to justify our society's inhumane treatment of them. Perhaps these women can help us look behind the pat phrases and stereotypes in order to understand more clearly, more intimately, their lives and their needs and those of people in similar circumstances. Perhaps we can even feel some of their pain.

The interviews I have conducted in many parts of the country with poor women, and with professionals who work with them and their children, indicate that very few American women are really protected from poverty. A happily married New Hampshire mother of eight sees her income drop in a matter of weeks from $70,000 a year to $7,000 when her husband leaves her for another woman. Formerly affluent widows in Palo Alto, California, find themselves counting pennies for food as the cost of living vastly outstrips their fixed incomes. A former welfare worker in the Bronx finds herself a welfare mother of three when her husband becomes addicted to heroin and alcohol. A bright, articulate Maine mother of two who is pregnant with her third child must choose between a husband who threatens to kill her and destitution.

I have been fortunate to be able to observe both aspects of the dramatic changes in the lives of women: both the enormous advances for some and the increasing problems for many others. As a psychiatric social worker, I worked first with families who were trying to cope with economic problems, emotional conflicts, and the results of overt and covert racism. I saw firsthand the damaging effects of an insensitive, hostile, incredibly shortsighted welfare system that inevitably disrupted families and maintained women and children in abject poverty. I later worked more intensively with parents and children who were suffering with severe emotional problems; and finally, with families in the Bronx who were trying to provide a healthy environment for their children against almost overwhelming odds.

More recently I have had an opportunity to look at these issues from a broader, more theoretical, sociological perspective. In attempting to teach child welfare to my students at Hunter College, I have tried to deepen my own understanding of how the system actually works and, more specifically, what it really means to be poor in affluent America. I have also had the good fortune to be able to visit several other countries—countries as disparate as China and Sweden—and to observe in some depth how they have dealt with issues of family policy, women's rights, and the well-being of children.

I have attempted in this book to use all of these experiences, plus interviews with almost one hundred poor women and professionals in twelve states from coast to coast, to describe the lives of poor and near-poor women and children in the United States. I have attempted to analyze the forces that have propelled millions of women and children into poverty and work to keep them there. And finally, I have put forth a family policy that will, I believe, begin to provide the lifeboats so necessary for all women and children, not only in times of trouble but also before disaster strikes. In the years that have elapsed since the original publication of this book all too little has changed in the lives of the poor. As the 1990s began, both the number of people living in poverty increased and life for many became even more desperate. The fundamental reality of widespread, cruel and disabling squalor in a land of often astonishing affluence remains unchanged. The United States *can* provide a humane environment in which families can thrive and children can grow. It is in the interest of all of us to make sure that our society provides that environment.

WOMEN AND CHILDREN LAST

1
WHO ARE THE POOR?

> Despite the widespread misperception that women are achieving economic equality, their economic status has deteriorated sharply since the late 1960s. . . . Poverty in the United States has always been disproportionately concentrated among minorities, but the convergence of gender and class is unprecedented in American history.[1]
>
> —*Barbara Ehrenreich and*
> *Frances Fox Piven*

Barbara, a lean, dark-haired woman in her mid-thirties, comes from a middle-class, New England background. She describes her early adult years:

> I came from a terrific family and when I graduated from high school I decided to go to college. During my first semester I found that I was pregnant by the boy I was engaged to. I got married in December and when our daughter was six weeks old my husband left for Vietnam. He came back a year and a half later a different man—real quiet, withdrawn. He wouldn't talk about Vietnam then; he won't even talk about it today.

Shortly after Barbara's husband returned from Vietnam, they invested in a home. He returned to school but soon felt that he could not handle "the whole scene," and left. Barbara then took her daughter and "with no resources and no inner strength," moved into an apartment, enrolled in a local university, worked evenings, and received supplementary welfare. She had become a female head-of-household living in poverty.

Virginia Rowan, a handsome, part Cherokee, part black, seventy-three-year-old widow, lives in Tucson, Arizona. When she was in her early thirties, her husband died; she then worked for over twenty-five years as a domestic and part time as a hairdresser in order to support herself and her daughter. She worked until she needed to be hospitalized because of severe diabetes. Following hospitalization, she was transferred to a nursing home and has recently moved to a community setting for the elderly. She currently receives a total of $302 per month from Social Security and Supplementary Security Income (SSI), a yearly inome of $3,624. After working most of her adult life, Virginia Rowan has joined the ranks of the poor.

Maria Garcia (her real name), a serious young woman with dark wavy hair and lovely dark eyes, grew up in the Williamsburg section of Brooklyn. When she was very young, her mother became ill with a heart condition; shortly afterward her father walked out. Consequently, from the age of five or six, she was placed in a series of foster homes. Maria recalls, "Every time somebody was going to adopt me, my mother would take me with her for a few months." She felt that her mother did not want her but did not want anyone else to have her, either. "My mother threw me out because she couldn't handle me and I wouldn't let her keep me locked up in the house any more. We couldn't talk to each other. It got worse as I started to fill out and get a figure."[2] She was eventually placed in a series of group homes and, in one of them, met the young man who fathered her child. By the time she had given birth, he had disappeared; she and her daughter went on welfare for the next three years. Maria had become a poor, single, teenage parent.

These are the poor: young and old; black, white, and Hispanic; once married, never married; urban and rural; those who are part of the labor force, and those who are not. They have varied backgrounds and life experiences, but the one thing they have in common is that they are women. For as American women move into the last decade and a half of the twentieth century, millions of them are moving into a world of poverty.

Of poor people in the United States today, the vast majority are women and their children. According to the Census Bureau, in 1984, 14.4 percent of all Americans—33.7 million people—lived below the poverty line. From 1980 to 1984 the number of poor people increased by 4½ million. For female-headed households in 1984, the poverty rate was 34.5 percent, a rate five times that for married-couple families. The poverty rate for white female-headed families was 27.1 percent, for black female-headed families, 51.7 percent, and for Hispanic families headed by women, 53.4 percent. The poverty rate for the elderly, most of whom are women, was 12.4 percent in 1984.[3] Two out of every three poor adults are women, and the economic status of families headed by women is declining.

The impact of women's poverty on the economic status of children is even more shocking. The poverty rate for children under six was 24 percent in 1984; in other words, nearly one out of every four preschool children lived in poverty.[4] In the same year the poverty rate for children living in female-headed households was 53.9 percent. Among black children, the poverty rate was 46.3 percent; among black children living in female-headed families, 66.6 percent. Among Hispanic children, 39.0 percent were poor; among Hispanic children living in female-headed families, the poverty rate was 70.5 percent.[5]

What are the factors that are responsible for this "feminization" of poverty? In an era in which so many gains have been made by so many women, in a country as rich as the United States, why do millions of women and their children live without adequate resources for food, clothing, and shelter? Before discussing these issues, let us first examine how poverty and the number of people living in poverty are officially determined.

In 1795, according to the records of economist Bruno Stein, a group of English magistrates decided that "a minimum income should be the cost of a gallon loaf of bread, multiplied by three, plus an allowance for each dependent."[6] The poverty level today is set in much the same way. In 1963 Mollie Orshansky and her colleagues at the Social Security Administration set the "official" poverty line by using, according to Michael Harrington, a "minimal diet—just sufficient to hold body and soul together—as the base."[7] Since U.S. Department of Agriculture studies in 1955 indicated that the average American family spent approximately one-third of its net income on food, Orshansky took a low-cost food budget prepared by the USDA, multiplied it by three, and came up with a "poverty line" for a family of four. And thus, the first U.S. poverty line was established in 1964 at $3,000.[8]

Between 1965 and 1974, the cost of the USDA Economy Food Plan was used in determining the poverty line; since 1974, a new Thrifty Food Plan has been the standard. It is important to note, as one observer has stated, "The USDA does not consider the Thrifty Food Plan to be nutritionally adequate for long-term use, a fact that is simply ignored in setting the poverty line."[9] Today, the U.S. government poverty line still equals the cost of a Thrifty Food Plan for a family of four, multiplied by three, with adjustments for family size and for changes in the consumer price index. In 1984 the poverty line for a family of four was set at $10,609.

There is considerable controversy over this line. Many analysts feel that the number of people in dire need is underestimated because the poverty line is set too low and that it is virtually impossible for an urban family of four to meet their basic needs of food, clothing, and shelter on less than $11,000 per year. Others, most notably officials in the Reagan administration, believe that the number of poor people is exaggerated because noncash income, such as the value of food stamps, public housing, Medicare, and Medicaid, is not included when calculating the number of Americans living in poverty.

If we look closely at what the poverty line means for a family of four, we see that families at this level are indeed barely surviving. If, as the basis for calculation of the poverty line assumes, a family of four spends one-third of its income on food, a family living at the 1984 poverty level of $10,609 would have $3,536 per year for food and $7,073 for everything else. This would mean that family members would have $68.00 a week or $2.43 per person per day, to spend on food. The remainder, $589.40 a month, would have to cover rent, utilities, transportation costs—including automobile maintenance—clothing, medical and dental bills, educational expenses, entertainment, and taxes. As one analyst has stated, "In the real world, individuals who live at or below the poverty line live poorly, and they do so absolutely; they have considerable and persistent difficulty getting enough to eat, finding adequate shelter (with heat and light), securing appropriate clothing, and obtaining medical care."[10] Moreover, most poor families live well below the threshold of poverty. If an employed adult is paid the minimum wage of $3.35 an hour, he or she will only earn $6,968 a year, far below this line as well. Aid to Families with Dependent Children (AFDC) recipients are maintained far below the poverty line. In fact, in 1982, of all families living below the poverty line, the average poor family had a cash income of $6,477.[11]

But beyond the statistics, what is the meaning of poverty in an affluent society? What does it mean to be poor in a country as rich as the United States? When we think of poverty in poor countries, we think of emaciated or swollen-bellied children starving to death in Ethiopia, people dying by the side of the road in prerevolutionary China, large families huddling together in the squatters' settlements that exist in most Latin American cities, children begging outside opulent tourist hotels in countries as dissimilar as India and Haiti.

But what are the images of poverty in America? Being poor in the United States surely means standing in line for food in soup kitchens; it means living in welfare hotels; it means a homeless woman sleeping in a doorway, her possessions all around her; it means television programs about families in winter with no heat. These images are stark and real. This is absolute poverty.

But there are other forms of poverty in affluent countries. What does it mean, to others not quite so desperate, to be "poor" in a society as wealthy as this one? What constitutes poverty when every few minutes television advertisements drum out versions of the "good life"—middle-class families in comfortable homes keeping in touch by calling one another long distance; a young couple celebrating the building of their new home by drinking high-priced, high-status beer; sleek cars, invariably accompanied by the sleek women? What does it mean to be poor when magnificent photography, knowing voice-overs, and music that triggers just the right emotions have conditioned us to believe that it is our birthright to own that car; to experience the joy that is supposed to come with the good life and a good beer; to be able to buy this season's hottest, newest jeans—and, of course, have the body to go into them? For, while we have created a never-ending demand for goods, we have also created a group of outsiders who can only watch and long to be part of that golden world.

Singer Tina Turner articulates the anger felt by some of these outsiders:

> *A Night In Television Wonderland*
> *Another Fairytale About Some Rich Bitch*
> *Lying By The Swimming Pool*
> *It's The Golden School*
> *Living's Easy When You Make The Rules . . .*
>
> *Try To Get On Board, You Find The Lock*
>   *Is On The Door*
> *Well, I Say "No Way . . .*
> *Don't Try To Keep Me Out Or There'll*
>   *Be Hell To Pay . . ."*[12]

It may be clear what poverty means in Biafra, but what does it mean to a family in Youngstown, Ohio, whose primary bread-winner has been unemployed for eighteen months; or to a mother who is trying, on the salary of a chambermaid in a Boston hotel, to raise her children? What does it mean to a battered wife in Maine who is afraid to leave her husband because she knows she cannot possibly support their children herself; or to an elderly widow in Tucson who does not receive enough from Social Security to get through the month? And what does poverty mean for all those parents who are just getting by but know their children are not getting their share of the American dream—are not getting adequate medical and dental care, are attending inferior schools, have no money for the extras that mean so much to children? What does it mean to be poor in a rich society?

"Absolute poverty" and "relative poverty" must be distinguished. Absolute poverty means living below the official poverty line; absolute poverty is not having money for adequate food, clothing, and shelter. But relative poverty is much more difficult to define. Is not having a telephone in this society relative poverty? Is not having a car in rural Vermont relative poverty? Is relative poverty not having the money to buy the kind of sneakers, or running shoes, as they are now called, every other twelve-year-old boy in the community is wearing? Is relative poverty not having the money to buy your fourteen-year-old daughter designer jeans? And in a society in which what we consume defines who and what we are, what does living outside mainstream America do to people?

A beautiful, well-dressed black woman in her mid-thirties who supports her two children by working for a voluntary agency in northern California talks about the stresses of trying to manage on a limited budget:

> There are very few pleasures. In the summer I have to struggle to see how I can get my children to summer camp. I have to apply for scholarships. I have to beg. . . .
>
> I feel as though I am overburdened. I am constantly stressed. I am never relaxed—never feel quite secure. I break down often with crying jags. I worry constantly. I worry about race relations, about prejudice becoming more blatant, about money, about everything.

A Bronx welfare recipient feels that her children are deprived. "I want a nursery school for my middle child but I cannot afford it. Maybe next year? I don't know how I'll manage." She feels trapped in a one-bedroom apartment with three children. She feels she has no privacy. There is no where to go. She has resisted fixing up the apartment because she is thinking she is going to move, but she is unable to do so. "My life and my marriage don't say who I am. My apartment does not say who I am." In a letter she writes:

> On Sunday I'll be 38. I notice that I'm struggling with the sin of envy. Suddenly those around me are moving away, buying houses, finding life easier economically. I don't begrudge their successes but find life in an ancient, one-bedroom apartment noisy and chaotic. We intrude on each other. My oldest son needs a quiet, private place of his own and I'm unable to provide it for him.

The furnishings are all so decrepit that I could leave tomorrow leaving most everything behind. I have a certain status and respect in my community which is somehow undone by my shabby surroundings. I've stopped inviting people over.

This woman is experiencing what one community worker in San Francisco has termed, a "thirst for loveliness." Moreover, her son needs a private place of his own and she is "unable to provide it for him." It is not her husband's drug addiction that makes it impossible for her son to have that quiet place, or a welfare system that provides too little money to live on; in her head *she* is the one unable to provide for her children.

Over and over, the theme of self-blame emerges. Somehow it is "my fault." "I should be able to do better." The battered woman feels guilty that she's been beaten up. The wife whose husband walks out for another woman blames herself. Those who get by but aren't really living the American dream wonder what is wrong with them. A bright, engaging woman in California wonders if somehow she's not smart enough to make it and plans to take an IQ test to check herself out. A savvy Brooklyn welfare mother and activist feels that poor people, and especially welfare mothers, are told by a variety of institutions in society:

You're in the position you're in because of something you didn't do right in the first place. If you're not attached to a man, something must be wrong with you. If you can't get a job, the newspapers, TV, your parents, your friends are telling you something is wrong with you. If you don't have Sasson jeans, something is wrong with you.

If your life does not fit the middle class, or even better, the upper middle class, image that appears on TV, something is wrong with you. For, if you are poor in America, you are an outsider and it's your own fault. If you are blind, disabled, or old, there is some excuse; you are one of the worthy poor. But if you are a welfare mother, you must be doing something drastically wrong.

If you live surrounded by poor people, you may feel some solidarity and mutual support, but you will also feel cut off from working, buying America. A Brooklyn mother discusses the trade-offs of living in a poor neighborhood versus moving to a working-class neighborhood:

In the last few years I have worked my way across Brooklyn. Where I lived before everyone had the same problems. In Flatbush [where she now lives] people don't all have the same problems. Where we used to live my children could not see anyone get up in the morning and leave home to go to work. They did not see anyone who looked like they were supposed to look, like on TV.

I wanted them to live in a place where some people are working-class people. Where they would see a different image, different role models. But in moving I lost the supports I had. Before when I lived in the neighborhood and was like everyone else I didn't feel as much how society viewed welfare mothers. Now when I feed my children I feel I am taking money out of the pockets of my working neighbors.

In either case the poor are isolated; they are outsiders. In the ghetto, surrounded by poor people, they are isolated from mainstream America, but in a working-class community they are still isolated—isolated by the stigma of being poor; by the stigma of being "on welfare"; by the disdain of many working Americans; and by their own sense of guilt, guilt for not making it, guilt for "taking money out of the pockets of my working neighbors."

Being poor in America in the 1980s is seen as being different, deficient, almost unclean. It is perhaps not hyperbole to state that the poor American, particularly the poor welfare mother, is the modern leper. Instead of a bell to warn the healthy to keep their distance, the semimonthly welfare check alerts—indeed, warns—landlords, merchants, teachers, neighbors, health workers, all those with whom the recipient comes into contact, that she is somehow different, even deviant, and ultimately guilty of bringing on her own misfortune.

To be poor in America is to let America down—to let that Pepsi image down; to let the American dream down; to not do your share, carry your weight, lift up your corner of the flag. The poor, simply by being, are besmirching that sunlight-on-a-tree-lined-street America, that wheat-blowing-in-the-breeze America, that we-can-do-it-no-matter-what America. And they know it.

According to the Canadian Council on Social Development, the concept of relative poverty

a more humane calculation

> defines poverty, or deprivation, in terms of whether a household has considerably less income than others. This method views low income as entirely relative to other incomes in the community. If surrounding incomes are generally high, then the poverty level will also be high. To do otherwise, to maintain serious income distortions, is to make some households "stand out" by their more frugal lifestyles and deny their members roughly the same opportunities that average- and higher-income households have. The relative income approach springs more from the principle of equity than it does from a concern to provide simply for the basic necessities of life.[13]

In the 1980s we don't hear much about equity in relation to the poor. The Bureau of Labor Statistics calculates the minimum income necessary for a family of four to participate in life in the United States at a "lower level," an "intermediate level," and a "higher level." In 1981, the last year that this figure was calculated, the "lower" income level for an urban family of four was $15,323. In the same year the poverty line was $8,450 for a nonfarm family.[14] It is clear that the poverty line is the demarcation of absolute poverty in the United States—even though many economists, sociologists, and social welfare experts question whether that figure is indeed adequate—and the Bureau of Labor Statistics's "lower level" figure is the demarcation of relative poverty. The family trying to survive at this lower level is "poor relative to the rest of the population" but still "only one emergency or one accident away from truly dire straits."[15]

If the United States were to estimate poverty in relative terms, we would clearly have a far higher percentage of our population officially designated as poor. In any case, counting only cash income, the number of Americans officially living in poverty rose from 26.1 million in 1979[16] to 33.7 million in 1984, an increase of nearly 30 percent. In 1979, 11.7 percent of the U.S. population was classified as poor[17]; in 1984, 14.4 percent were classified this way.

The number of Americans living in poverty had increased to 35.5 million, 15.3 percent of the population, in 1983. This rise in 1983 to the highest level since the early 1960s was in large part caused by the 1982–1983 recession, which produced a sharp increase in the number of unemployed Americans. Between 1983 and 1984 the poverty rate deceased almost one percentage point. While the number of female-headed families living in poverty declined somewhat between 1983 and 1984, the drop in the poverty rate in 1984 was due largely to white male workers returning to the labor force. Nearly three-fourths of the families who escaped poverty were male-headed white families.[18] The 1984 reduction in poverty is surely a positive and welcome development, but it is clear that all groups are not benefiting equally from the economic recovery. Female-headed families and children, particularly non-white children, remain especially vulnerable to poverty.

Except for 1982 and 1983, the 1984 poverty rate is the highest Americans have suffered since 1966. Moreover, the gap between rich and poor was wider in 1984 than at any time since the Census Bureau began collecting these statistics in 1947. According to the Center on Budget and Policy Priorities, a Washington-based research and advocacy group, the poorest 40 percent of U.S. families received just 15.7 percent of the national income in 1984, again the lowest percentage since 1947. In contrast, the top 40 percent received 67.3 percent of the national income, the highest percentage ever recorded. The median income for families in the poorest 40 percent of the population was $470 *lower* in 1984 than in 1980; the median income for families in the most affluent 40 percent was $1,800 *higher* in 1984 than in 1980. Furthermore, the number of families who might be described as the "poorest of the poor," those with incomes below $5,000 a year, has increased 43 percent since the late 1970s.[19]

Who are the 33.7 million people who remain poor? Many Americans have a stereotype of a "typical" poor person. The poor are commonly thought of as black, urban females who have been dependent on welfare for many years and whose children will, in all likelihood, also be dependent on welfare. Many aspects of this stereotype are false. The poor, particularly the adult poor, are indeed typically female, and the majority are urban, because our society is overwhelmingly urban; but what is often not recognized is that "persistent poverty falls disproportionately on . . . those living in rural areas and in the South."[20] The other components, rooted in racism, in misinformation, and in an ideology that seeks to cast the poor in the least favorable light in order to justify our often heartless treatment of them, are far from the truth.

First, it must be stated that the poor are overwhelmingly white. Approximately four-fifths of all Americans are white; consequently, the majority of the poor, approximately two-thirds, are white. It is indeed true, however, that a far larger percentage of nonwhites are poor than are whites. For example, in 1984, 11.5 percent of whites were poor, while 28.4 percent of Hispanics and 33.8 percent of blacks were officially designated as poor.[21]

Perhaps the most deeply rooted stereotype, however, is that the poor today are a different breed from the rest of us and from the poor of earlier generations. It is commonly thought that those who were poor when they first emigrated to this country eventually worked their way out of poverty into the working class or even beyond. Popular notions about the poor today are that they are a little-changing group caught in a never-ending cycle of poverty, early childbearing, inadequate job skills, and hopelessness. While this characterization is true for many poor people, it is not a valid description of the majority of poor Americans.

According to a recent study conducted by the Survey Research Center of the University of Michigan, "an astonishing amount of turnover takes place in the low income population." This study, conducted over a ten-year period, found that "only a little over one-half of the individuals living in poverty in one year are found to be poor in the next, and considerably less than one-half of those who experience poverty remain persistently poor over many years."[22] The researchers found that only 2.6 percent of the population could be called "persistently poor" over the ten-year period from 1968 to 1978—*persistent poverty* was defined as being poor eight of the ten years. This means that among the poor who in 1978 made up approximately 12 percent of the population, only 2.6 percent had been poor during the previous decade.[23]

Who are the "persistent poor"? One-third are elderly; approximately one-third are rural, and rural poverty seems to be "much more persistent than is urban poverty."[24] And, overall, "The persistently poor are heavily concentrated into two overlapping groups: black households and female-headed households."[25]

And who are the "temporarily poor"? This question becomes extremely important since the number of people who are only intermittently poor is substantial and the number who are persistently poor is considerably smaller. According to Greg Duncan, the author of the Michigan report, *"The temporarily poor do not appear to be very different from the population as a whole, appearing to differ from nonpoor families only in that they have one or two bad years.* [Italics mine.]"[26] The study found that the demographic characteristics of the temporarily poor are much more similar to those of the population as a whole than to those of the persistently poor.[27]

Several women whom I interviewed are examples of the "temporarily poor." A Maine mother of two, for example, was forced after her marriage broke up to go on welfare and to obtain food stamps; she managed to outwit the welfare department long enough to return to college and obtain her BA—it is illegal to attend a four-year college while receiving AFDC. Eventually she was able to earn her own living as a family-planning counselor. A Massachusetts mother of one found herself living in poverty after the death of her husband; she is in the process of training herself to be a plumber.

Sandra Wittaker is a black woman in her mid-thirties:

I was born in Boston, the oldest of four children. My mother was a single parent; she worked in a meat market so we always ate well. We were considered well-off compared to the people around us.

During high school I was part of the "Upward Bound" program which was located in a small Catholic school in the suburbs. It's a small college, pretty, all women, and when they asked where I would like to go to college I said, well, I'll go here. I did not know any other college. I had wanted to go to Howard but my mother did not want me to go out of town. I had a full four-year scholarship, partly because of their recruitment of minority students. I graduated and then became a teacher.

Sandra taught first in a day-care center, earning $8,000 a year ("It was much more than my mother had ever earned in her entire life") and then first grade in a Boston public school. She had married during this time; her daughter was born in 1971. A second child, a son, was born two years later, shortly after she and her husband moved to California.

My husband was a disc jockey in Boston and when we moved to California he could not get a job because he didn't have the connections out here. I went back to work; one child was in day care and the other was with a baby sitter. In November of 1974 we broke up and I went back to Boston, but I returned to California because I thought the kids should be with their father. By the end of the year we had broken up again; I asked him to leave. We broke up primarily over finances; he wasn't applying himself.

Following the breakup, Sandra couldn't find work and went on welfare and food stamps. The following September, after being on welfare for six months, she started teaching in the San Francisco school system, earning $10,000 a year. Aid to Families with Dependent Children had tided her over following her separation until she was able to find work again. Today she works for a voluntary agency outside San Francisco and earns approximately $20,000 a year. As the Michigan study states, Sandra is not "very different from the population as a whole" but went through a brief period of time when she needed help.

While the Michigan report confirms that blacks, the elderly, women, and children are at greatest risk of poverty, it disputes the commonly held idea that if the poor had more positive attitudes, they would climb out of poverty much more rapidly.[28] These findings are extremely important, not only for our understanding of the issue of poverty in America but also for the formulaton of a social policy that will effectively meet the needs of the poor. But, first, why do women and children make up the overwhelming majority of poor people today?

The feminization of poverty, a phrase originally coined by sociologist Diana Pearce,[29] has been caused over the past fifteen years by a convergence of several social and economic factors. These include the weakening of the traditional nuclear family; the rapid growth of female-headed families; the continuing existence of a dual-labor market that actively discriminates against female workers; a welfare system that seeks to maintain its recipients below the poverty line; the time-consuming yet unpaid domestic responsibilities of women, particularly child care; and an administration in power in Washington that is systematically dismantling or reducing funds for programs that serve those who are most in need. Broader social, political, and economic aspects of life in the United States in the waning days of the twentieth century, such as unemployment; continuing discrimination on the basis of race, class, and age; and the changing nature of the economy also contribute to the increasing impoverishment of women and children. One additional factor that must be mentioned, and will be discussed at a later point in some detail, is the continuing notion on the part of women that they will someday be taken care of by a man, that they do not really need to prepare themselves to be fully independent. This lingering remnant of another era is really an example of "culture lag," an idea, a set of beliefs that has lasted long after the conditions that produced them have changed dramatically. This core of dependency is, of course, fostered by almost all the social institutions of our culture, so that breaking out of the traditional role becomes extremely difficult.

What is particularly disturbing about poverty in the United States over the past twenty years is that there have been two simultaneous trends: The percentage of Americans who are poor has decreased, only to rise again during the Reagan administration, and the percentage of poor women and children has sharply increased. This means that as Americans as a whole were moving out of poverty, women and children were moving in.

Beginning in the 1960s the proportion of the population that was defined as poor decreased markedly. The poverty rate for male-headed families, however, declined much more sharply than for female-headed families. In addition, the number of female-headed families increased significantly. As a result, by 1981 the number of persons in poor families headed by women *increased* 54 percent, in contrast with the nearly 50 percent *decrease* in the number of persons in poor families headed by white men.[30] Due to economic conditions, starting in the late 1970s the poverty rate among two-parent families began to climb rapidly once again, but female-headed families are still five times more likely to be poor than two-parent families.[31]

In families headed by minority women, the statistics are even more disturbing. Data for Hispanics, available only since 1972, indicate that between 1972 and 1981 the number of poor Hispanics living in female-headed families doubled; between 1959 and 1981 the number of blacks living in poor, female-headed families more than doubled as well. As a recent report of the United States Commission on Civil Rights stated, "As a group, female-headed households are sheltering an increasing percentage of poor persons, and this trend shows no signs of abating."[32]

One of the significant social phenomena of the 1970s and the early 1980s was the proliferation of female-headed families. Between 1970 and 1984 the number of families maintained by women mushroomed from 5.5 million in 1970 to 9.9 million in 1984, an increase of 80 percent. In 1984 single-parent families, 89 percent of which were headed by women, accounted for 26 percent of all families with children under 18.[33] Women who headed families in 1970 were likely to be older women who had been widowed and had grown children who could provide some financial support; women heading families in the 1980s are far more likely to be several years younger, to have never married or to be divorced, and to have young children whom they need to support.[34] Why did the number of female-headed families grow so dramatically during the 1970s?

According to the Michigan study, the "single most important factor accounting for changes in family well-being was a fundamental change in family structure: divorce, death, marriage, birth, or a child leaving home."[35] The study indicates that women are far more affected by changes in family composition than men; it shows, furthermore, that women who remain married show improved economic status while women who divorce show a significant decline.

Over the past fifteen years, the divorce rate has soared. Nearly one out of every two marriages in the United States now ends in divorce, and the figures are even higher for teenage marriages. Between 1970 and 1981 the divorce rate more than doubled; the rate may be leveling off, however, for since 1981 it has declined for three consecutive years.[36]

The impact of family disruption on the well-being of children is clear. Children who live in families that are disrupted by divorce or separation experience "severe drops in economic well-being. . . .":

These children . . . carried a disproportionately large burden of economic misfortune, mirroring and magnifying the . . . devastating economic effects of divorce or separation on the mothers with whom they usually lived. The situations of these children are striking evidence of the far-reaching, unsolved economic problems posed by family disruption.[37]

Furthermore, having and keeping a child outside of marriage has become far more acceptable during this period. During the 1970s families headed by never-married mothers climbed to 3.4 million, an incease of 356 percent.[38] In 1983, almost 70 percent of families headed by never-married mothers were poor.[39]

Among single mothers the number of births to teenagers has risen explosively since the post–World War II period. While out-of-wedlock births increased in all groups, since 1950 unmarried teenagers have exceeded all other age groups in out-of-wedlock births. During the 1970s, however, the birth rate for teenagers actually declined, in part because the number of women in that age group declined, but the birth rate of unmarried adolescents has continued to rise.[40] In 1982 over 14 percent of all babies born in the United States and 37 percent of all out-of-wedlock births were born to teenagers under 20.[41] Much of the available literature indicates that there is a direct correlation between teenage pregnancy and economic adversity. The education of the teenager is almost invariably interrupted by pregnancy and the birth of the baby, and that circumstance, combined with the absence of day care, virtually guarantees that the teenage mother will, as she moves into adulthood, remain unskilled, unemployed, and often unemployable. As a result of these factors, by 1983 20 percent of all American children lived with one parent.[42]

As significant as the increase in female-headed families is for the population at large, the implications for black families are that much greater. While white female-headed families with no spouse present and with children under the age of eighteen increased from 8.9 percent of all white families with children under eighteen in 1970 to 17.3 percent in 1984, black female-headed families in the same circumstances increased from 33 percent to 55.9 percent. Over 50 percent of all black families with children under eighteen are headed by women![43]

Similarly, the divorce rate for blacks has soared over the past decade and a half. Between 1970 and 1981 the divorce rate for Hispanic women rose 80 percent, the white female divorce rate doubled and the black female divorce rate nearly tripled.[44] Moreover, the number of out-of-wedlock births to unmarried black females ages fifteen to nineteen doubled from 1940 to 1972 and by 1977 was over six times the rate for white teenagers.[45] During the 1970s, however, the birth rate for unmarried black adolescents declined significantly.[46]

The number of separated and divorced black women, combined with the number of never-married black mothers, substantially increases the risk of black women and children living in poverty. Black children are three times more likely to live in poverty than white children, and black children in female-headed families are far more likely to do so. In fact, in the early 1980s 74.2 percent of all black children under the age of six living in female-headed families lived below the poverty level.[47]

Another significant factor in the feminization of poverty is the perpetuation of the dual labor market. Occupational segregation, sex discrimination, and racism still combine to limit women's income and economic mobility. Women today work for the most part in service, sales, and clerical jobs that often pay meager wages. The median income for women in 1983 was $6,320, while the median income for men was $14,630, over twice as much.[48] Women who work full-time, year-round still earn only 64 percent of what men earn, and furthermore, men even earn substantially higher wages when they are working in traditionally "female" occupations such as nursing and social work. While women have recently entered a few of the male-dominated blue-collar occupations, they have frequently encountered significant resistance, social isolation, and sexual harassment.

In addition, unemployment contributes both directly and indirectly to poverty among women. While the unemployment rate has dropped from a high of 10.7 percent in December 1982, when nearly 12 million Americans were officially unemployed, to 7.2 percent in February 1985, over 8 million people were still officially classified as jobless in the total labor force, including both the civilian and military sectors.[49] A significant percentage of the unemployed are, of course, women—women with few skills; women in the service sector who were employed under government-funded auspices but whose jobs were abolished when federal funding was cut; women in male-dominated occupations who were the last to be hired and therefore the first to be laid off. Male unemployment is a major factor in the poverty rate among women and children, for when the man is the unemployed worker in the family, family stability is significantly undermined. Studies have shown a clear correlation between unemployment and family violence, desertion, separation, and divorce.

Yet another major factor that contributes to the high level of poverty among women and their children is a welfare system that segregates and stigmatizes dependent children and their mothers and, as a matter of social policy, maintains these families below the poverty level. Moreover, many women are forced to combine welfare with mindless, low-paid, low-status work that offers essentially no chance for advancement; when they are laid off, many women are not eligible for unemployment compensation, and the welfare check becomes their unemployment check.

The cutbacks in human services since the 1980 election of Ronald Reagan have further exacerbated the poverty rate among women and children. Since 1980 there have been significant cuts in Medicaid, in maternal- and child-health programs, and in funds for community health centers and for family planning programs. Aid to Families with Dependent Children has been slashed a total of over $2 billion.[50] Child nutrition programs were cut drastically in 1981. The food stamp program was cut sharply in the 1982 fiscal year and in fiscal 1983 as well; total cuts exceeded $2 billion a year.[51]

Federal funds for day care were cut in the fiscal year 1982, and Title XX, under which federal funds paid for all or part of licensed child-care centers and homes, was replaced by the Social Services Block Grant. Funding was reduced 21 percent, and the requirement that the states supply $1 for every $3 in federal money was eliminated.[52]

In the area of employment, the Reagan administration has eliminated all training and employment programs under the Comprehensive Employment and Training Act (CETA), reduced funding for the Youth Employment Demonstration Projects Act by 80 percent, for the Summer Youth Employment Program by 20 percent, and added "workfare" requirements under Aid to Families with Dependent Children.[53]

The cutbacks initiated and implemented by the Reagan administration have had a major impact on the nation's poor, particularly on its women and children. While the shocking increase in the number of poor women and children took place primarily during the 1970s, the cutbacks and the overall economic policies of the Reagan administration have exacerbated the already vulnerable position of these groups.[54] According to a recent study conducted by the nonpartisan Congressional Research Service, budget cuts alone increased the number of poor people in 1982 by at least 557,000. Moreover, the recession of 1981–1982 caused an even larger number, 1.6 million people, to fall into poverty. While the recession had greatest impact on working-age adults and married-couple families, changes in social welfare progams clearly had greater impact on female-headed families. In addition, the study found that, because of budget restrictions, the number of poor children had increased by 331,000. These children account for more than half of the total number forced into poverty because of the cutbacks.[55]

A New York City study by researchers at Columbia University determined that working mothers were particularly hurt by Reagan administration policies. It was found in this sample that the reduction or elimination of AFDC support caused the percentage of working mothers living below the poverty line to more than double.[56]

Many studies have indicated that blacks have suffered perhaps more than any other group under these policies. A study done by the nonpartisan, nonprofit Center on Budget and Policy Priorities found that blacks were worse off in 1984 than they were in 1980 by almost every measurement—income, poverty status, and unemployment levels.[57]

The recent economic recovery has clearly not "trickled down" to the poor. For example, in New York City, whose economy generally reflects national trends, the 1983–1984 economic recovery has meant a booming business for the tourist industry, for real estate, for small businesses, and for financial institutions. In 1984 the number of jobs in the city was the highest in a decade. And yet 40,000 more people were forced onto the welfare rolls in 1984 than in 1983, a total of approximately 930,000 out of a population of 7.1 million. More people are said to be hungry and homeless than at any time since the Great Depression, and the high-school dropout rate is almost 40 percent. New York is described as "two separate and unequal cities—one for the haves, largely whites, and one for the have-nots, largely nonwhites."[58] According to investment banker and chairman of New York State's Municipal Assistance Corporation, Felix Rohatyn, those "who have a place in the mainstream are being pushed along by the tremendous wave of technology and the rapid accumulation of wealth. But those who are out of the mainstream, for one reason or another, are falling further behind." He went on to say, "I don't believe a healthy democracy allows those gaps to widen."[59]

But perhaps the most serious result of the Reagan administration's economic policies, particularly the cutbacks in human services, has been the legitimization of the negative attitudes held by many Americans toward the poor. The ideology that the poor are poor because they are "lazy"; that if they only worked harder they could make it like the rest of us; that they are "free-loaders" and don't really need their benefits; that they are corrupt, collect double rent checks, don't need food stamps and, when they unjustly receive them, sell them in order to buy liquor; and, above all, that if only we didn't provide them with so many benefits, they would get a job—which is there for the asking—work hard, and become upstanding citizens like every real American has been a part of American ideology since colonial times.

During more liberal periods of our history, this ideology has been countered by some recognition of the social, economic, and political forces that create poverty; but President Reagan's ability to express the point of view, in a mild, amiable tone of voice, that the poor are poor primarily because of their own shortcomings has, I believe, permitted significant numbers of Americans to move their prejudices from the back of their consciousness to the fore-front. The very existence of large numbers of poor people in this country can open to question the heart of the American dream—that anyone, with enough hard work, can surely make it to the middle class and perhaps beyond. In order to reaffirm our faith in the American Dream, particularly for ourselves, we must blame the poor for their poverty. With extraordinary cleverness, the Reagan administration has manipulated this belief to justify its economic programs. The perpetuation, the revitalization, of this peculiarly American mythology is perhaps Mr. Reagan's most significant and most pernicious accomplishment.

There is currently significant discussion about whether the phenomenon we are seeing—increasing numbers of women and children making up the ranks of the poor—is really the feminization or the "minoritization" of poverty. There is no question that the economic situation of many blacks in this country—men, women, and children—remains bleak. In summer 1983 the Center for the Study of Social Policy, a private research group headed by a former Nixon administration official, released a report based on data from the 1980 census, stating that while the median family income has increased for blacks and for whites in the twenty-year period, the income gap between blacks and whites is as wide today as it was in 1960. In 1960 black median income, measured in 1981 dollars to account for inflation, was 55 percent of white median income—$9,919, compared to $17,259 for whites. By 1981 black median income was $13,266 and white median income was $23,517. During the 1960s the disparity between black and white median income decreased slightly, so that by 1970 black income was 61 percent that of whites; but by 1981 it was back down to 56 percent.[60] In 1984 the median income for black families was $15,430; for white families it was $27,690.[61]

This alarming gap between black and white income is primarily due to two factors that are themselves interrelated—the number of black men who are unemployed, and the rise in the number of black, female-headed families. According to the center's report, titled *A Dream Deferred:* "Since black, female-headed households are the most rapidly increasing proportion of all black families, the fact that they have not gained economic ground has more than offset the increases made by other types of black families."[62] In fact, the income of black families in which both parents work has risen significantly over recent years. In 1968 black families in which two parents worked had an income 73 percent as large as white families in which both parents worked. By 1981 those black families were earning 84 percent of comparable white earnings.[63] But they were by far the exception. In 1981, while over 54 percent of all black families had income levels below $15,000 a year, only 28 percent of white families had incomes that low.[64]

One of the most startling findings of the report was the educational gains blacks have made over the past twenty years. By 1981, for example, the median level of schooling for blacks, both males and females, was over twelve years, and the difference between black and white years of schooling was only a half a year. Furthermore, the illiteracy rate for blacks has dropped significantly, until there is now little difference between black and white ability to read; and, at the other end of the educational spectrum, rates of college enrollment for blacks have increased dramatically.[65] But the financial rewards for education, according to the report, are far different for the two groups. Black college graduates tend to earn the same income as white high school graduates. In 1981, 47 percent of blacks with four or more years of college earned $20,000 to $40,000 a year, the same income earned by the same percentage of whites with no more than a high school education.[66] These statistics suggest that black income is more related to the availability of job opportunities for blacks than to levels of education—in other words, blacks are being widely discriminated against in the workplace.

For those blacks lucky enough to be employed, the number who hold professional, technical, managerial, and sales jobs has increased significantly; but the number of blacks—particularly black men—who are unemployed is astronomical. It is estimated that approximately 45 percent of all black men do not have jobs, including not only those officially classified by the Census Bureau but also those who are counted as "discouraged" and no longer looking for work.[67] In addition, according to a statistician with the Children's Defense Fund, approximately 15 to 29 percent of black men aged twenty to forty could not be found by the Bureau in 1980. They are presumed to have neither permanent residences nor jobs. If they are added to the number of unemployed, the number of black men without jobs can be estimated to be well over 50 percent.[68]

Clearly, this shockingly high rate of male unemployment has had a direct bearing on the dramatic rise in black female-headed families. We still look for the "causes" of the rise in black female-headed families, debate whether the welfare system encourages their proliferation, blame the mothers for having babies outside of marriage—but largely ignore the impact of male unemployment on family life.

The recent study by the Center on Budget and Policy Priorities details the continuing erosion of the economic status of blacks during the Reagan administration: From 1980 to 1983 the income of the typical black family, after allowing for inflation, fell 5.3 percent, a larger decline than for any other population group; 9.9 million black Americans, nearly 36 percent of all blacks, lived in poverty in 1983, the highest rate since the Census Bureau began collecting data on black poverty in 1966; from 1980 to 1983 the proportion of blacks who joined the ranks of the poor was almost twice as large as the proportion of whites who fell into poverty; and black unemployment is significantly higher in 1984 than it was in 1980.[69]

The answer to the question, therefore, of whether we are seeing the feminization of poverty or the minoritization of poverty must, I believe, be that we are seeing both. While there is no question that vast numbers of blacks continue to be discriminated against economically, socially, and politically—and that this discrimination translates into a far higher rate of poverty for blacks and for other nonwhites than for whites—women are also a particularly oppressed group, no matter what their color.

Another criticism that has been raised about the feminization-of-poverty analysis is that it falsely treats all women as members of an oppressed class. Critics point out that not all women are vulnerable to poverty.[70] Many women of the upper and upper-middle classes have the financial resources, education, and skills to support themselves handsomely, even in their older years, even if a prolonged illness should strike, even if left without a man. The notion that all women are more or less at risk is, it is felt by some, an incorrect and misleading analysis that will inevitably lead to inappropriate political action. While there is clearly much truth to the statement that race and class have been major determinants of poverty in this country, women as a group, including middle- and sometimes even upper-middle-class women, have recently become far more vulnerable to poverty or near-poverty than their male counterparts.

The feminization-of-poverty argument has been criticized, in addition, for ignoring the vast numbers of poor men in this society—the unemployed, the elderly, the homeless, and particularly nonwhite men who have spent most of their adult lives without work, without hope, almost without identity. Poverty is, of course, not confined to women and children alone. Men are victims of an unjust economic system that builds into its structure unemployment, early "retirement," and mechanization that makes workers superfluous. But statistics indicate that the fastest growing population living in poverty today is made up of women and children. This does not mean that we can ignore poor men or the fact that nonwhite poor and working people are most at risk. It means that we must examine the entire picture and attempt to develop a social policy that will eliminate, insofar as possible, these inequities, which inevitably fall hardest on the most vulnerable.

Finally, it is clear that some of the key causes of poverty among women are fundamentally different from the causes of poverty among men and that the same remedies cannot, therefore, be implemented exclusively. The lives of the vast majority of women reflect a very different reality. Women's lives are inextricably bound up with caring for others. While it is recognized that women spend much of their lives caring for children, what is less often recognized is the time and effort that they spend caring for men, for elderly parents, for grandchildren, for friends, and sometimes even for distant relatives. For, it is women, for the most part, who weave the bonds that connect us. In a society that rewards "productive" labor, these "nonproductive" activities inevitably reduce the time and energy that might be spent in earning a living. Women have, in addition, primary responsibility for domestic work within the home. The combined hours spent by women on childrearing, or caring for other family members, and on cooking, cleaning, and managing the home are, of course, unpaid hours of work. A recent study has shown that if the work done at home by married women were compensated, the family's income would be increased by more than 60 percent.[71] Any analysis of poverty among women must, therefore, take into account societal expectations that women will fulfill these roles; the fact that American society has offered few alternatives to women performing these functions; and that women have, for the most part, been socialized to accept these tasks as a natural and central component of their identity. This book will explore the ways society can redistribute its caring functions to relieve women of some of that burden and how it can, at the same time, utilize women's caring qualities, or "different moral sense," as Carol Gilligan has termed it,[72] to help to humanize society itself.

In summary, recent evidence indicates that the poor in the United States are, for the most part, women and children, blacks and other nonwhites, the very young and the old. There are clearly two groups of poor people—the temporary poor and the persistent poor—and, contrary to commonly held popular ideas, the persistent poor make up considerably less than one-half of the poor overall. Life events such as birth, death, separation and divorce, and economic conditions—a high rate of unemployment, recessions, and cuts in welfare benefits and human services—are the primary causes of Americans falling into poverty. The ultimate question is how we as a society can most effectively protect people against economic hardship and, at the same time, provide supports to individuals and to families that will enable them to live rewarding and productive lives. We will explore other aspects of poverty, particularly with respect to women and children, and return to this question in the final chapter of this book.

2
THE NEW POOR

> Within a few weeks the family's income dropped from $70,000 a year to just over $7,000. . . . I was devastated. I became suicidal. My self-esteem was a big, black zero.
>
> —*Doreen Cullen*

Doreen is a lively, overweight, forty-six-year-old Catholic woman whose dark hair is streaked with gray. She lives in a small city in New Hampshire. In twenty-three years of marriage, she had thirteen pregnancies; eight children survived.

She and her husband were both eighteen when they married. They had their first child one year later. According to Doreen:

My husband was a devoted husband and father but we had very separate roles. He took care of everything outside of the home and I took care of everything inside the home. He handled all the financial matters. When I told him I wanted to get a job after twenty years of marriage, he didn't understand and told me everything had to be done around the house the same way even if I worked. No routines could be interrupted; all the meals must be ready on time and supper must be on the table at five o'clock every day.

Meanwhile, I was losing myself. Not having my hair done. I had gained weight. I was losing myself and I didn't know it.

On their twenty-third anniversary Doreen's husband sent her flowers for the first time since she had given birth. Shortly afterward he took her dancing—another first. Within the next few weeks he told her he wanted to talk with her, and over coffee at McDonald's he told her he had fallen in love with a twenty-eight-year-old woman, and that he was leaving her. His exact words, according to Doreen, were: "I love you and I love the kids; but I just can't live without Sandy."

In addition to a precipitous drop in Doreen's self-esteem, the family's income dropped from $70,000 a year to just over $7,000. Her husband paid no child support because he walked away from his job at the same time he walked away from his family. Doreen was working part time as a homemaker/health aide and earning the typically low salary of human service workers.

Even when she took her husband to court and he was ordered by the judge to pay her $125 per week, he rarely complied. By November of that year she was out of heating oil. She sold her dishwasher and anything else she could do without. She lost their house because the bank foreclosed on the mortgage. By the time he had been gone a year and a half, her husband owed her $10,576. When she went to court for her divorce, the judge waived the $10,000 because her husband had no job. Doreen and the children have been struggling economically ever since.

Doreen is a member of the "new poor," a group of people, largely women, who were not born into poverty but who have been forced into it by recent events in their lives. These precipitating events include unemployment; illness; and, particularly for women, the disruption of a marriage, especially following the birth of a child, or childbirth outside of marriage.

The new poor or "nouveau poor," as they have been called, are mostly women whose descent into poverty begins, as Barbara Ehrenreich and Karen Stallard have stated, "with single parenthood—becoming single or becoming a parent, whichever comes first."[1] None of these women would have been poor without this combination of factors. On their own, they could have managed; with children to care for, they have virtually no way to manage without outside help.

The limited choices of the vast majority of American women

may come as a shock to regular consumers of American culture. The inordinate emphasis of television on the very rich (*Dynasty*, *Dallas*, *Falcon Crest*, *Knot's Landing*, or, for those who consider themselves a bit more intellectual, the many *Masterpiece Theatre* presentations); the focus by most popular magazines on the lives of celebrities; and many newspapers' obsession with the daily habits of young urban professionals—what they eat for breakfast, what they wear, how they exercise, what singles bars they frequent, whether they are into sushi or enchiladas—lead us gradually, insidiously, to believe that the majority of Americans are upper-middle-class professionals with few, if any, financial problems or office workers like Mary Richards, the original and quintessential yuppie, of *The Mary Tyler Moore Show*. Poor and working-class people are rarely depicted realistically on television. They are either Archie Bunker types, comic characters, criminals, neglecting or abusing mothers or, occasionally, maids. It takes a Jane Fonda or a Cicely Tyson to portray a poor woman positively, and then they are heroic characters.

When the *New York Times Sunday Magazine* does an article on the working mother as role model, it features a "busy and successful general dentist;"[2] when it does an article on women trying to make it in the male world, it features a thirty-eight-year-old first vice-president at E. F. Hutton & Company who has a live-in housekeeper and volunteers in her spare time behind the information desk at the Metropolitan Museum of Art and organizes dinner parties for subscribers to the Yorkville Ball.[3] Aren't waitresses, secretaries, saleswomen, and nurses' aides role models for their children? What of the women without live-in help and a successful husband? How do they make it?

For, most American women do not choose between law school and medical school, do not postpone marriage and childbearing in order to pursue a "career," are not climbing the editorial ladder at a publishing house or the corporate ladder at a Fortune 500 company. The vast majority of American women, despite what the media would have us believe, still define themselves by the men they marry and by the children they bear.

While traveling around the country interviewing women, I could not help but note their automatic assumption that they should become mothers. Becoming a mother is viewed—particularly by those women who do not have the opportunity to go on to higher education and do not live in a social or economic environment that tells them that anything is possible professionally—as a crucial aspect of becoming a woman. Usually but not always tied to the assumption that motherhood is essential is the assumption that the woman will have a man alongside her—either in marriage or in a long-term relationship. But even when a woman has, for one reason or another, written off the possibility of a permanent, stable relationship with a man, her image of herself as a mother persists.

A recent segment of the CBS evening news discussed the new phenomenon of "bachelor" mothers. When working-class or poor women have a child outside of marriage, they are called "unwed" or "unmarried" mothers; when middle- and upper-middle-class women have children outside of marriage, they are called bachelor mothers. Presumably, a term that is usually used to describe men gives added prestige and panache. Moreover, the stigma of having had sex outside of marriage, which is so strongly connected to the term "unwed" mother, is absent from the new phrase. After all, it's always been all right for bachelors to have sex outside of marriage.

The women described by CBS had consciously decided to have a child even though they had no steady, long-term relationship with a man. They became pregnant either through artificial insemination or when "a friend did me a favor." As one of the women, an attractive woman about thirty with a good job and a comfortable apartment said, "Why shouldn't I have it all?"[4]

Many women, moreover, consciously use childbearing as a way to solve problems in their lives—to hold a marriage together, to have someone to love, or to acquire a certain defined role and status in society. For childbearing is one area over which women have some control. Still, vast numbers of women have little control over their own childbearing because of lack of information about birth control, inaccessibility of birth control information and materials, and above all, societal expectations.

The centrality of childbearing to women's lives and to the problems confronting poor women is elucidated by Becky Lamey, director of Family Planning Services and Women's, Infants and Children's Services (WIC) for the Southern Kennebec Valley in Maine: "Childbearing and childrearing are central to women's image of growing up and to their conception of their ongoing role as women," she states. "Most women are not aware that they have any choice about their lives. There are scads of women who don't know that it's okay not to have a baby every year."

Nancy Chodorow, anthropologist and author of *The Reproduction of Mothering*, observes, "Women mother. In our society, as in most societies, women not only bear children. They also take primary responsibility for infant care [and] spend more time with infants and children than do men. . . ."[5] She goes on to connect women's childbearing and childrearing functions to their broader roles in society: "Women's mothering is central to the sexual division of labor. Women's maternal role has profound effects on women's lives, on ideology about women, on the reproduction of masculinity and sexual inequality, and on the reproduction of particular forms of labor power."[6] Chodorow points out that women's childcare responsibilities have consigned them in virtually all societies to the domestic or "private" sphere of life, while men's primary affiliation and activity have been in the "public" sphere, in society itself, which is generally defined as masculine.

The fact that women identify with the domestic sphere and spend their time and energy primarily in this arena means that they are particularly vulnerable when they find themselves the sole support and caretaker of the family: For society's expectations that women will play the domestic role is exactly what places them in a dependent, secondary position. While it is true that more and more women are entering the labor market, they are most often entering the secondary labor market, in low-paying jobs with little opportunity either for advancement or gratification. Simone de Beauvoir carries the analysis even further:

> Generally speaking, motherhood today is still a form of slavery. If a woman's main task is baby-making, then she's not going to get involved in politics, in technology, and she won't oppose male supremacy. . . . Since you can't tell women that it's sacred to scour pots, you tell them it's a sacred task to bring up children.

But having children has a lot to do with scrubbing pots, since the way the world is today, it forces her to stay home. It's a way of sending woman back to her position as a relative being, a secondary being.[7]

Motherhood as a form of slavery—a harsh indictment? A gross overstatement? Perhaps not, in a society that provides few supports for the mother and child, particularly the mother and child who are left to make it on their own. Often women have few marketable skills, and must work in jobs that do not pay a living wage. These are women for whom the society provides few services.

Ann is a plump, attractive young woman in her late twenties who lives in rural New England. She has two children, ages six and two. Ann married when she was nineteen, her husband twentytwo. "It was not a healthy marriage," she states. "We were into long hair and the whole drug scene and I worked my way out but he didn't." They were living on a commune when she moved out with her child. (She had one at the time.) She planned to go to college, but she knew no one, had no money and no car—she lives in Maine, where a car is essential. "It was a very humbling experience."

Elizabeth Cameron is a slim, blond woman in her early thirties who speaks in a quiet, thoughtful, mild tone of voice. She lives in a very neat, sparsely furnished, three-room apartment in the Bronx with her three children, ages nine, three, and one. Her comment, "The choice of marital partner a woman makes is crucial in her future life," is borne out by her story:

I originally came from Ohio and went to Ohio State. After graduation I came to New York. I got married ten years ago and it was a marriage into poverty. I married someone who came from poverty, someone who was Hispanic, a welfare client, *my* welfare client.

I worked for five years in a welfare office in the Bronx and I was confused and lonely. I was away from my family structure and fell apart. I couldn't find a place for myself here. So I ended up with him, a good guy, a basically decent, loving man but one with insurmountable handicaps. He has little education, a drug problem, and an alcohol problem.

After eight years of marriage—of physical abuse to her and psychological damage to the children—Elizabeth changed the locks on her doors, applied to the welfare department (the same office in which she used to work), and lived apart from her husband for six months while he was in a treatment program. After six months, "I weakened"; but eventually he "switched back to drugs and became hooked on heroin. Then we separated again so I could survive economically."

None of these women were poor as children. All of them became poor as a result of their marriages. They had children to care for, and none of them had the financial resources or skills to be able to support themselves and their children at a decent standard of living.

The problems of attempting to raise a child alone are, of course, greatly magnified if the child has any significant physical or emotional problems. Margaret is a soft-spoken, auburn-haired woman of twenty-nine who lives in a medium-sized city in Maine. At twenty she became pregnant, got married, and had her first child when she was twenty-one. When her baby was two months old, she left her husband because he had severe emotional problems. He has since committed suicide.

From birth the child had multiple problems—cerebral palsy, epilepsy, mental retardation. When she first left her husband, Margaret got two jobs waitressing because she did not want to go on welfare, but she did not really have adequate care for her son, and had to quit. Next she lived with an uncle in return for cleaning his house. She never slept more than two hours continuously during day or night because the baby never slept more than two hours at a time. She became "a wreck, a total wreck." She finally decided she had to institutionalize her son for a while because she was "ready to toss him out the window." With the help of a state social worker, she placed him in a hospital diagnostic center. She would hitchhike to see him once a week and found after the first two weeks that he was receiving such inadequate care that he had bedsores. Her comment was, "He never had bedsores with me!" He was also losing weight, becoming lethargic, not smiling. Against the advice of the social worker, she removed him from the hospital, looked long and hard for an alternative, and finally placed him in a private nursing home.

Margaret feels that there were few people to help her when she needed it, and that the social workers whose job it was to help were hostile and grossly insensitive. The combination of having to cope with a severely damaged child, with no job skills that could both support her and pay for adequate care for her son, cost Margaret many years of anguish.

Being bright, intellectual, and ambitious is not sufficient to avoid membership in the ranks of the new poor. Margot Danziger is a breezy, tall, blond, heavyset woman who lives in Tucson, Arizona. She has two master's degrees, one in Oriental Studies and one in Russian, and two daughters, one eighteen and one fifteen. She first married at the age of seventeen. "My first mistake was getting married and my second mistake was getting pregnant." She, her husband, and baby moved to Japan, and while they were there she left her husband—"ditched him," as she puts it. "I came back to this country and that's when I hit rock bottom and had to start on welfare." While receiving welfare benefits, she managed to go to college and get her bachelor's degree.

A few years later she remarried but found out afterward that her second husband was on drugs. "He walked out almost a year ago, and it was then that I learned he had been molesting the girls for several years." She is currently "on poverty row" even though she managed over the years to buy a nice house in Tucson. She is having trouble selling the house, but once she does she hopes to move to Tokyo in order to run a school there. Until then she is working at minimum-wage jobs and barely getting by. What is so striking about Margot is how little she has been able to accomplish materially and professionally considering her intelligence, her drive, and her outgoing personality. Margot feels that a central problem for her and many other women is that women are taught from the time they are five that they have to have a man. "A woman does not fit into society if she does not have a man. In order to be normal in this society, you have to have a man. Women must be taught," she states emphatically, "that they can be independent and whole people even if they don't."

Joyce Morrison, a thirty-five-year-old, extremely intelligent, Vermont mother of two agrees:

Women are afraid to live their lives by themselves and society has put us in this position. Women are taught that you can't take care of yourself no matter how intelligent or how strong you are, but that's a myth. More marriages end in divorce or death, so if you can't see that early enough, you are going to end up on welfare. Or in a loveless marriage or being beaten up just because you are afraid to take care of yourself.

My father always told me some man's going to take care of you. He used to say, "I don't have to fix your teeth; your husband will fix your teeth for you." My father let us know that we might be intelligent, we might get good grades but someone had to be there to take care of us.

But, more and more, that someone is not there. All too often, when the marriage breaks up it is the man who walks out. A Maine mother of four reported that her husband walked out on Mother's Day. "He said, 'I'm going to the store and I'll be right back,' and that was it." According to her, "He left because he couldn't take the pressures"—several small children close in age and an older child with serious medical problems. She survived by working in a textile mill and receiving supplementary welfare. Her hope is that "my children will know there is a better life."

The group of women whose lives are perhaps most seriously affected by motherhood are teenagers, particularly those who have not completed their high school education. Early childbearing significantly increases the likelihood that the mother and her children will require AFDC. According to a recent study, "Almost half of all AFDC expenditures go to households in which women bore their first child as teenagers. Sixty percent of all teenage mothers receive welfare at some time."[8] These statistics include women who have children out of wedlock as well as teenagers who are married at the time of the birth of their first child. Because the divorce rate is so high among teenage marriages—estimated at 60 to 72 percent after six years of marriage—most teenage mothers become single parents eventually whether they marry initially or not.[9]

Many of these women are not, of course, part of the new poor; many of them came originally from poor families. Many others, however, come from fairly well-off families, and become part of the new poor only when they become single parents.

Among those teenagers who become single parents, some consciously choose to have a child; some discover they are pregnant and are so reluctant to have an abortion that they are, in a sense, forced to have the child. Most of these women do not foresee the extraordinary difficulties of both caring for a child and working to support it. Clearly, changing social attitudes about premarital sexual activity, and about single women having and raising babies outside of marriage, have made it possible for these women to consider raising their children alone.

Janet, a bright, articulate woman in her early thirties, came from an Irish-Catholic working-class family in New York's South Bronx. She was the first member of her family to attend college but felt "so inferior" when she got there that she avoided going to classes. Instead, "I read voluminously to try to catch up and see what it was all about." Her second year she learned she was pregnant, had an abortion, and then soon became pregnant again. When she became pregnant the second time, she began to wonder why she had let this happen, that maybe she really wanted to have a child. She resisted her boyfriend's urging to have a second abortion and decided to have the baby.

While she was pregnant, Janet applied for welfare and spent the next several years caring for her child, finishing college, working at part-time jobs such as cleaning people's houses and typing at home, and being a welfare recipient. Janet had entered the ranks of the poor.

For some women, having a baby is a way of changing the direction of their lives. Sarah Gold, a thirty-three-year-old, extremely overweight, Jewish woman with a very pretty face, pale skin, and lovely, long reddish-brown hair, lives in a once elegant seventy-year-old gray-stone apartment building in the Bronx. When Sarah and I first talked on the telephone to arrange our interview, she said that she is a "new breed" because she "chose" to go on welfare, but now she's "stuck in it." Later we talked in her kitchen where tacked up on the bulletin board along with her daughter's artwork was a quote from Albert Einstein: "The fairest thing we can experience is life's mystery." She describes her background:

I come from an upper-middle-class family, first in Queens and then on Long Island. My father was a furniture salesman and my mother was a housewife who became a political hack for the Democratic party. I am the oldest of five. One of my brothers is a dentist, another is in the air force, and my sister is married and is an office worker.

Sarah got married at the age of nineteen to a graduate student who was working toward his PhD in English. She supported him by working at a variety of jobs, from serving drinks in a bar to running an EEG machine in a local hospital. They separated in 1976 because of "resentment and money." "He thought his mind was 100 percent important and that subsistence was not important." She feels he was a "selfish, dependent little boy."

The next two years she worked for a state agency, rising to a fairly responsible position; then she got pregnant. She decided to have the baby to "get off the D train." In fact, she had wanted to have a baby during much of her marriage, but her husband had been opposed. As it was, she had a child with somebody who was "not going to threaten my independence." The father of the child was "not for me. He was a nice person to make love with but not someone to talk with." She never considered having an abortion, and he never offered to take responsibility for the child. Her plan was to obtain unemployment compensation and then look for a job.

After the baby was born, "I tried to get unemployment but I was discriminated against because they saw the baby and didn't think I was willing to work. I didn't feel like appealing and going through that bureaucratic red tape, so after three months I went to the welfare office."

Sarah receives $350 a month plus $100 in food stamps. She had her telephone disconnected because she couldn't afford to keep it up. She says it is impossible to live on what the welfare system gives her. Furthermore, "My mother does not help me because she does not like having a daughter on welfare." She continues, "Pride goes before the heart. The Jewish people pride themselves on getting on their feet," and therefore, she feels, they don't have much use for people like her. She tells her mother that money cannot buy love, but her mother says it can buy tricycles. "I'm poor and I know it, and," she admits, "it hurts sometimes." She would like to go back to school to get her bachelor's degree and wants to be working by the time her daughter is in school. She does not want her daughter to suffer the stigma of being a welfare recipient.

Unemployment, particularly male unemployment, can propel a two-parent family into poverty. Julia Soto, director of Patient Services at the El Rio Santa Cruz Neighborhood Health Center in Tucson, Arizona, describes a group of new-poor women who are now alone because their marriages have broken up as a direct result of their husband's unemployment. In the Tucson area most of the copper mines have been closed, and thousands of copper miners have been laid off since the early 1980s. There is little else for copper miners to do in this area, and according to Soto, many of the families are separated because the husbands cannot adjust to not playing their usual role as provider for their families. Others are away from home either looking for work or being retrained. Or the wives are working but not making nearly as much as their husbands used to earn. In any case, there are significant strains on these marriages, due to separation or role reversal, and always due to economic difficulties. "Homes and cars are being lost and this is the new poor, people who are not used to poverty, people who don't know how to cope."

Illness can suddenly precipitate a previously self-supporting mother into real economic need. Debbie White is a very attractive twenty-two-year-old with long, blond, curly hair. She lives in a pleasant, modern apartment in a small New Hampshire suburb with her two-year-old son. Debbie describes her current situation:

I am totally single. I was almost twenty when I had Matthew. I was out of high school and working full time, waitressing. I thought briefly about marriage but Matthew's father was a "mountain man." He was twenty-two, had a lot of things he wanted to do, and was into hiking, mountain climbing, and things like that. He didn't want financial responsibility and certainly didn't want family responsibility.

Debbie grew up in Los Angeles and feels she "grew up faster than she should have." When she became pregnant, she thought about having an abortion—drove around for two hours thinking about it but "just couldn't do it." She had always wanted a family and thought it would be very easy taking care of one child. "I was making good money at the time, had a new car, a nice apartment, all the clothes I wanted, and I didn't think it would be any problem."

Debbie was lucky; she had parents who were willing to help her, and whose help she was willing to accept. Before she had the baby, she moved home with her parents, had the baby, and was back at work in six weeks. She worked an evening shift in order to be with the baby during the day, and her mother watched him in the evenings. She lived at home for eight months while she was looking for a place of her own. "I have always been independent; I have been independent since I was seventeen." She then moved to her current apartment and hired a sitter to care for Matthew while she worked as a cocktail waitress from 5 P.M. to 11 P.M. She earned nearly $300 a week in tips.

Approximately eight months ago, she started not feeling well. She had tests to see what was wrong, and since she has no health insurance from her job, the cost of the tests "really set me back." The doctors thought her appendix was the cause of her symptoms, but when they operated to remove it, they found the appendix was fine but that her fallopian tubes were blocked and inflamed. They had to remove her right tube and are treating her left one. The doctors say she has a fifty-fifty chance of ever having more children. She had wanted four. Her comment is, "Thank God I had Matthew!"

Debbie has already been out of work for several weeks because of the surgery, must stay out several more to recuperate, and has no money. Before she became ill, she lived from week to week and was able to save essentially nothing. She has no money to meet her car payments, to pay her rent, to buy food. She does not want to borrow from her parents because they are retired and living on a limited income, and because she has too much pride. She does not want to ask the state, either. "I'm so used to having money that I really don't want to ask anyone for it." Furthermore, she is "totally against welfare" and "would dishwash before I would go on welfare."

In all likelihood, Debbie will find a solution that will tide her over until she can work again—if there are no complications. If she has complications, if she needs further medical care and cannot return to work fairly soon, she will be in even deeper financial difficulties. Already, a week in the hospital plus surgeon's and anaesthesiologist's fees and other expenses have amounted to several thousand dollars, which she will have to pay off in the coming months. For even those single mothers who are living a relatively comfortable life, one disaster, one illness can make for some very hard times.

In addition to the precipitating events of separation or divorce, and the all-too-real hazards of single parenthood, especially among teenagers, many women are also suddenly faced with poverty if and when they decide to leave their battering husbands. Being battered is often a trade-off for economic security, particularly when children are involved. And when, finally, the battered woman has the strength to leave, she is confronted not only with the social and psychological problems that stem from leaving her husband and living on her own but also with the day-to-day problems of finding a place to live, earning a living, and caring for the children.

The decision to leave is often a most difficult one. According to Mimi Marchev, director of the Family Violence Project in Augusta, Maine, "Battered women are particularly isolated. They are isolated by their husbands often because of their extreme jealousy. And they isolate themselves; they are isolated by their shame. Battered women may not see people outside the family for months at a time."

Furthermore, the battered woman often feels responsible for the battering. She frequently has low self-esteem, feels she is supposed to take care of her husband and their children, and has somehow failed. It seems, according to Marchev, that "being battered is intrinsic to women's and men's roles in our society. Men grow up thinking they must be strong and that violence is an acceptable way to exercise control." Women are socialized to be more passive than men and to believe they will be taken care of by men. Moreover, in reality, women's inadequate earning power, coupled with their feelings of responsibility for the children, make it seem as though they have few choices but to remain in situations that are frequently intolerable.

Willie, a black teenager in Gloria Naylor's novel *Linden Hills*, describes to his friend, Lester, his mother's options when faced with her battering husband:

> My mom got beat up every night after payday by a man who couldn't bear the thought of bringing home a paycheck only large enough for three people and making it stretch over eight people, so he drank up half of it. And she stayed, Les. She stayed because a bruised face and half a paycheck was better than welfare, and that's the only place she had left to go with no education and six kids.[10]

Joan is a twenty-nine-year-old former Texan who has transplanted herself to New England:

> At twenty I met my first husband, lived with him and decided to get married. I never should have married him. He used to beat me up, he drank a lot, but I stayed with him. I thought a baby would make the marriage better so our first child was born on our second anniversary.
>
> He spent a lot of money drinking and wouldn't support us so I had to. He became violent when he was drinking, but I saw the good in him when he was not. He would smash things; he almost choked me a few times. The only time he would leave me alone is when I pretended I was dead, or when I was pregnant.

After four years together, Joan finally "kicked him out." She then became involved in a second disastrous marriage by which she had a second child. Joan is now receiving AFDC, food stamps, and WIC.

Marilyn, a bright, serious, articulate, thirty-five-year-old mother of two, is pregnant with a third child. Her husband is now in jail; they separated several months ago and she went on welfare at that time. She describes her husband, a six-foot-eight-inch, 250-pound man who has a black belt in karate:

My husband, he's off his rocker. He liked to punch holes in walls. If he saw blood, he loved it. He once tried to strangle me. He was into drugs and drinking but he was in a better mood when he was drinking.

One night when he broke down the door, chased her around the apartment, terrorized the children, and threatened to kill her, she called the police but was told that, since they were not divorced, he had the right to break the door down and there was nothing they could do. She then called the Family Violence Project; while talking with a worker there, she realized, "You mean, I don't have to put up with this?" Shortly thereafter her husband beat up his partner at work; the man had fourteen broken ribs and was left in a pool of blood at the bottom of an elevator shaft. Marilyn's comment: "That could have been me."

Roberta Fielding is a twenty-one-year-old divorced woman who lives with her two-year-old daughter in a small New England city. She is a waitress at a local Howard Johnson's making $2.01 an hour plus tips. She earns approximately $85 a week for twenty-four hours of work and is also receiving food stamps and WIC. Every night she brings her daughter to her parents' house and then goes to work from 9 P.M. to 3 A.M. She sleeps from 4 P.M. to 9 A.M. Her parents bring her daughter home at seven in the morning on their way to work, and then she and her daughter go back to sleep for an additional two hours.

My husband left this past January. We had been married three years. He was twenty-three when we split up. Things had started getting bad. First he wanted a baby and then after the baby was born he resented her, he started drinking and was getting abusive. He started hitting me. He always called me names. I was afraid he would really beat me.

Roberta finally decided she would be better off without him, and when he left she obtained a divorce. She hopes to get another job, a better job; she wants to move out of her apartment and to get a car, but she has "gotten involved with a series of violent guys" and is currently trying to work out these problems through counseling. In passing she mentions that her father also "beat up" both her mother and the children while she was growing up.

Battered women can themselves be driven to violence, as the recent cases of women murdering their husbands have indicated. Mary Giovanni is a bright, lively young woman in her mid-thirties who currently lives in Tucson. The middle child of five, she came from a middle-class family. Her father was an aeronautical engineer; her mother was a nurse. They were divorced when she was eleven. Mary dropped out of high school at sixteen, went to San Francisco, and "did the drug thing." She didn't marry until she was thirty, when she was working as a sorter in a thrift shop for the minimum wage, $3.35 an hour.

She describes her husband as a "a real con" and feels she was in a vulnerable situation financially and emotionally when she met him:

> I had no idea that he had been in prison for rape before I met him. During the four years we were together he chased me around the country from Anchorage to Houston and back. He tried to blow up the house. When I said I wanted a divorce, he couldn't handle it and said "I have a gun; I even have bullets" and let me know that he would kill me rather than let me divorce him. He tried to choke me; he broke my ankle.

After her husband threatened to kill her, Mary took his truck, loaded what she could on it and left.

> I knew I was going to kill him. I knew I was not going to be pushed anymore. I'd been pushed beyond my limitations of caring for another human being. I would never take another person's life but when I felt I could pick up a gun and blow out someone's brains, I couldn't believe the point my mind had been pushed to. I couldn't believe that I had been conditioned like that. It is a terrible thing for any woman to go through.

Mary talks about why it is so hard for battered women to leave:

> Most women are basically too afraid to leave. They're uneducated and it's mostly economic. Battered wives are kept barefoot and

pregnant by their men and are afraid to leave. Ninety percent is due to economic fears. If a woman goes on AFDC in Texas she receives $80 a month. It is the U.S. of Texas, and you can quote me.* Most women feel no hope even if they get away. There are no agencies and no help. Most have to turn to be barmaids or prostitutes and the most you can get is a $3.35 an hour job. A select few get into grocery stores. There is no help for women in the state of Texas. Your husband owns you.

Because families are so reluctant to admit that battering is occurring, the number of battered wives can only be estimated. Some researchers conclude that "violence is a startlingly common problem in American families. According to a 1976 national survey, at least 1.8 million American women are beaten each year in their homes." Many researchers, however, believe that this figure "substantially underrepresents the extent of violence in American families, perhaps by half."[12] Others estimate that physical assault occurs in nearly one-third of American families.[13] Lenore Walker, author of *The Battered Woman*, holds that "as many as fifty percent of all women will be battering victims at some point in their lives."[14] Furthermore, researchers agree that "battering of women crosses all socioeconomic, geographical, and religious distinctions. It occurs in all age brackets, regardless of one's ethnic group, state of sobriety, or education."[15]

Why does the battered woman stay with the batterer? As Mimi Marchev of the Augusta, Maine, Family Violence Project points out, "Each battered woman has her own reasons for staying, but in general, there is little support in our society for her leaving. Our institutions, agencies, and most individuals she comes in contact with pressure her directly or indirectly to stay." Other experts note that the battered woman is often unable to support herself financially, has nowhere to go, and, if she is a mother, she may be reluctant to split up the family. Lenore Walker holds that when the incidence of domestic violence reaches the levels we have been

_____

*While this amount has been increased somewhat in recent years, in 1985 Texas AFDC paid a three-person family only 30 percent of the amount the state itself had determined such a family needed in order to survive. This was the lowest percentage of "need" paid by any state.[11]

discussing, "We are dealing not with a problem of individual psychology but with a serious social disorder."[16] R. Emerson Dobash and Russell Dobash, authors of *Violence Against Wives*, conclude that wife abuse is deeply rooted in our culture:

The seeds of wife beating lie in the subordination of females and in their subjection to male authority and control. This relationship between women and men has been institutionalized in the structure of the patriarchal family and is supported by the economic and political institutions and by a belief system, including a religious one, that makes such relationships seem natural, morally just, and sacred.[17]

Society's attitudes toward male/female relationships within the family are perhaps best seen in the response of the police or criminal justice system to the abuse of women. For example, the 1979 Ohio Attorney General's Report on Domestic Violence states, "Police rarely file reports on domestic violence and even more rarely arrest men for battering. In Cleveland, Ohio, during a 9-month period in 1979, police received approximately 15,000 domestic violence calls. Reports were filed in 700 of these cases, and arrests were made in 460 cases."[18] Until recently rape was not considered a crime if it occurred while the man and woman were legally married. This is perhaps an extreme consequence of the belief that a wife is really her husband's property.

This institutionalization of male authority and female subordination has led to what one researcher has termed "learned helplessness." According to Walker, "Early in their lives, little girls learn from their parents and society that they are to be more passive than boys. Having systematically trained to be second best, women begin marriage with a psychological disadvantage." Furthermore, while men frequently feel powerless to control their environment, Walker claims that "the very fact of being a woman, more specifically a married woman, automatically creates a situation of powerlessness."[19] This inherent powerlessness combined with repeated batterings "diminish the woman's motivation to respond. She becomes passive . . . more prone to depression and anxiety."[20] The combination of women's economic, psychological, and physical subordination offers the battered woman few alternatives, particularly if she has children to care for. But the question, Why does she stay? is a particularly insidious form of "blaming the victim." Most women who manage to leave are risking social censure, further violence, perhaps their lives, and, in many cases, poverty.

For women, whether single, divorced, or separated, to lift themselves and their children out of poverty generally takes extraordinary stamina, commitment, and courage. Usually without financial resources, with few marketable skills, with little self-esteem and less community and family support, these women must wend their way through the maze of social service agencies—many of them hostile; of job training programs—most of them leading nowhere; of public opinion that holds that a woman, particularly a woman with children but without a man, is clearly a failure—and somehow make a life for themselves.

Barbara, for example, who described herself at the time her marriage broke up as having "no resources and no inner strength," had, in reality, considerable reserves of both. Over the past dozen years she has been trained as a medical-outreach worker and worked for Project Head Start as a social-work aide. Six years ago she started working in the field of family planning. Now thirty-four years old, Barbara currently earns $12,500 annually—not a munificent salary but enough to live on—and knows she should go back to college but is frightened. "Having a child at nineteen puts you into a tunnel and I feel I've gotten sucked along." Once there, it's very difficult to find daylight at the other end and walk off in another direction.

Ann, the Maine mother of two, despite the proscription of AFDC that recipients not be supported while attending a four-year college, enrolled in the University of Southern Maine and majored in communications. In addition to going to school and caring for her first child, she worked part time at school. The first year was "really awful." She was using private babysitters and would come home and find her child parked in front of the TV. Finally her son turned three and was able to go to day care.

She also needed AFDC and food stamps in order to survive, and while she was more bothered by the stigma of receiving welfare than by the welfare workers, she found the food-stamp workers "abusive and condescending" and finally refused to accept any more. Ann feels that one of the problems with the food-stamp program is that it doesn't make allowances for someone who is trying to make it.

By her last years of college Ann was "feeling real good" about herself. She had an apartment, a car, friends. She bought a stereo and a camera, and felt that these acts were "survival techniques." As she puts it, "I felt I had to have something nice, some kind of reward, some material thing for plodding along day after day." Ann even knew enough to get a babysitter in order to go out once a week with her friends. If need be, she would not pay a bill that week in order to be able to get out—to be with adults and away from children. When asked how she knew that that was an important thing to do, her response was, "I'm smart and I'm introspective and I can figure out what I need. Also I belong to a woman's group and got lots of support. And, don't forget, I was in college." Needless to say, most single women trying to raise children while living at the poverty level are not in an atmosphere that recognizes their needs and rights as human beings.

Ann is, of course, highlighting one of the central problems of being poor in an affluent society, especially when one is newly poor: Not being able to consume in a society that worships material goods can be extremely debilitating and can even cause a form of depression. For the new poor, who have known middle-class life, falling into poverty is almost like falling from grace. The usual solutions no longer work; the world seems restructured in an odd, unfamiliar way. These women often need to learn a new set of coping mechanisms and are further hindered by feeling personally devalued by their new status. For to be poor, single, and female with children to support, is to have very few options in an exceedingly harsh world.

3
WOMEN AND WORK

Now the Lord spoke to Moses saying, "Speak to the children of Israel, and say to them: 'When a man consecrates by a vow certain persons to the Lord, according to your valuation, If your valuation is of a male from twenty years old up to sixty years old, then your valuation shall be fifty shekels of silver, according to the shekel of the sanctuary. If it is a female, then your valuation shall be thirty shekels.' "

—*Leviticus, 27:1–4*

Women are known as "secondary" workers. What is the meaning of this term? Are they of less importance than other workers? Is women's work not as urgent, as serious, as necessary as men's work?

It used to be said that women worked for "pin money," but we know today that the vast majority of women work because they need to—either to support their families singlehandedly or to work together with other family members to do so. But, according to economist Bettina Berch, "The myth of the woman worker as less permanent, less typical, and less real is extremely pervasive, even if there is no logical reason for it."[1]

Throughout American history women have been in a subordinate role to men, particularly with respect to work. Moreover, the importance of the family, and of women's role within the family, has been a significant contributor to women's economic subordination. In colonial New England, according to historian Alice Kessler-Harris, "The family was the centerpiece of the economic system."[2] Within the family, women worked hard and worked equally but generally performed domestic chores inside the home; and while the Puritans recognized the importance of domestic work, "The role of the wife was distinctly secondary to that of the husband."[3]

The only women who could properly be called wage earners were domestic servants, and even among them male servants were considered more valuable than female ones. Women, of course, could work as farmers, and often did so successfully. But, while they could inherit land from their fathers, the law stipulated that after marriage a woman's property went to her husband. In an agrarian economy, "Long-term land deprivation imposed a heavy burden. It deprived women of economic independence, control of a household, and political influence. Without these advantages, colonial women as a group remained at the mercy of fathers and husbands or government authorities."[4]

During the postrevolutionary period from 1780 to 1830, women and children entered the wage labor force in significant numbers. Often the intermediary step between domestic work and wage labor was home work, which has once again become an issue in the 1980s. During much of the eighteenth century, women worked in their homes stitching boots and shoes and making straw hats. As these industries became concentrated in central locations, women went out to work into textile and other factories. By 1840, "Women constituted half of the total and sometimes as many as 90% of those employed in shoe factories, textile mills and millinery shops."[5]

During the early part of the nineteenth century, class distinctions sharpened between affluent women who could afford to remain at home until marriage and those who needed to support themselves or to help support their families; a more subtle distinction developed between women who worked in occupations such as teaching or writing and those who worked in factories. A response by a woman teacher to a newspaper series titled, "A Factory Girl," indicates the strong feelings women had about these class differences: "I do claim to be superior to the vulgar herd with which

our factories are stocked and I do consider them unfit to associate with me, or to move in the same society to which I belong."[6]

The distribution of jobs and the unlikelihood of upward mobility
in the mills in Lowell, Massachusetts, forewarned of conditions
for working women in this country—conditions that have continued for the most part until the present time. Kessler-Harris describes work in the mills:

> Jobs . . . were distributed according to sex. Men supervised, did
> the heavy work, and were the skilled mechanics. Women spun,
> wove, carded, dressed, and did everything else. Women could
> move up the economic ladder only within those occupations de-
> fined as theirs. Normally, increased earnings came from increased
> productivity through experience at the same job. So women
> achieved peak earning capacity quickly and maintained a plateau
> until they left the mills. If men moved up they did so by achieving
> supervisory positions.[7]

In the nineteenth century, women's relationship to work continued to show patterns that we have come to know well in the
twentieth. The depressions of 1837–1839 threw large numbers of
workers out of work, including women. The continued development of factories discouraged home production; increasing numbers of immigrants contributed to the labor supply; and by 1860
no more than 15 percent of all women were in the paid labor
force.

During this period an ideology that we still grapple with today
began to take root in American society: the "domestic code" holding that the home required the presence, the care, and the special
concern of women. As production became divorced from domestic
life, significant numbers of men went out to work in impersonal
settings over which they had little control; now women were needed
to run the household and to make it into a sanctuary for the
besieged men. There emerged "the concept of the home as a sanctuary or retreat, beyond the pale of the outside world, where the
husband might soothe his harassed spirit and breathe fresh life
into his benumbed faculties."[8] Or, as Christopher Lasch has stated,
"During the first stage of the industrial revolution, capitalists took

production out of the household and collectivized it, under their own supervision, in the factory."[9] This process, "the socialization of production," was quickly followed by the "socialization of re-production."[10]

In fact, this is an extremely apt designation, because motherhood was to become the linchpin of women's activity in the home. Since men spent many hours each day away from the home, rearing the children was left predominately to the women. As the historian Bernard Wishy describes the ideology of this period, "The mother was the obvious source of everything that would save or damn the child—the historical and spiritual destiny of America lay in her hands."[11] As it was the male's role to go out and earn a living to support his wife and family, so it was the wife's role to remain in the home and make it a "haven in a heartless world." The model of womanhood came to be the "lady" who remained in the home, not making an economic contribution to the household. Families that could not live up to that standard were clearly seen as deficient.

By the time the Civil War broke out, approximately half of all women were not entering the labor market at all; two-thirds of the remaining half worked until marriage; and the remaining one-sixth of women were attempting to earn an income.[12] As Kessler-Harris movingly describes:

> Wage work became the refuge of immigrants, the desperately poor, and those without male support. . . . In place of the proud mill girl, women in this group became what they had never been before: objects of pity and subjects of sympathy. Women had risen to the challenge of wage work out of a proud independence; but those who continued to work did so largely out of desperate necessity.[13]

As the men went off to fight during the Civil War, new job opportunities opened up for women, particularly in clerical work, nursing, and war industries. During the post–Civil War period technological advances led to increased mechanization of produc-tion and, ultimately, to the assembly-line factory. With mecha-nization, skilled male workers could be replaced by less skilled women, immigrants, and emancipated blacks—at lower wages. In 1887 Samuel Gompers, president of the American Federation of Labor (AFL), clearly indicated the concerns of labor organizations: "We know to our regret that too often are wives, sisters, and children brought into the factories and workshops only to reduce the wages and displace the labor of men—the heads of families."[14] In 1906 Gompers put forth labor's position in greater detail stating that women made their greatest contributions to the family by "attending to the duties of the home" and that there was no necessity for the wife to contribute to family income through wage labor.[15]

Gompers's statement reflects the economic ideas of this period, particularly the notion of the "family wage." Some theorists suggest that the subordinate role of women to men in the workplace is largely a result of a family-wage system, under which men were presumed to earn enough to support a wife and children. The family wage was "an important victory of the late 19th and early 20th century labor struggles" but, at the same time, "helped to thwart women's aspirations for higher wages, particularly in typically female occupations."[16] Of course, many women were not supported by men, and many men did not earn an adequate family wage; but the concept nonetheless led to women's being viewed as "secondary" workers, working primarily to supplement a husband's primary earnings.

While the unions' overall policies were to protect the jobs of white males against the encroachment of women, blacks, and immigrant workers, some unions, particularly in those trades in which women made up a significant percentage of the work force, moved to restrict women's competition in another way—through "protective legislation." The rationale for this was clearly stated in a 1908 U.S. Supreme Court decision:

> . . . woman's physical structure and the performance of maternal functions place her at a disadvantage in the struggle for subsistence. . . . [Since] healthy mothers are essential to vigorous offspring, the physical well-being of woman becomes an object of public interest and care in order to preserve the strength and vigor of the race.[17]

As Kessler-Harris points out, there were basically two different kinds of protective labor legislation. There was legislation that attempted to provide safe, clean conditions for all workers; to minimize health hazards; to establish a minimum wage; to shorten hours, and, eventually, to compensate workers for job-related accidents. These laws, which differed from state to state, affected all workers, male and female. The second type of protective legislation attempted to exclude some workers from certain jobs and to restrict their time and place of work. These laws applied primarily to women, and their effect on women's ability to earn a living was substantial. "Protective legislation divided workers into those who could and could not perform certain roles. It therefore bears some of the responsibility for successfully institutionalizing women's secondary labor force participation."[18]

The first protective legislation law was passed in 1881 in California. It denied women the right to work in places that sold alcoholic beverages. Later laws prevented women from working in mines, or as messengers, elevator operators, letter carriers, and taxi drivers. Some states passed legislation limiting the number of hours women could work, or preventing women from working at night. By 1914, twenty-seven states had passed some kind of protective legislation, even though the laws in some states hardly "protected" the workers. In North Carolina, for example, women could only work eleven hours per day, six days a week; and in Vermont, New Hampshire, and Tennessee, only ten-and-a-quarter to ten-and-a-half hours![19]

Despite the plethora of "protective" laws, conditions under which women worked were far too often abysmal and extraordinarily dangerous:

A muffled explosion at about 4:30 in the afternoon was the first warning anyone had that March 25, 1911, would be different from any other Saturday in industrial history. Smoke billowed from the eighth floor of the Asch Building on Greene Street and Washington Place, the middle floor of the three which housed the Triangle Shirtwaist Company. One passerby saw what he took to be "a bale of dark dress goods" being thrown out of a window. Another who saw it thought the factory owner was trying to save his cloth from the fire. But then the screams began. It had not been a bundle of cloth, but a human being, leaping from the window. Then came another, and then another.[20]

The Triangle Shirtwaist Company fire of 1911 was an unforgettable tragedy in the history of the American working class and particularly in the history of American working-class women. One hundred and forty-six workers, most of them girls and women, suffocated, were burned, or jumped to their death in New York that day. The doors to the factory had been locked to "keep the women in and the organizers out"; there was no sprinkler system; no fire drills had been held.[21] Protective legislation was clearly not protecting these workers.

As America moved into the twentieth century, notions about the role of women had markedly changed from those during the labor-scarce colonial period. In a labor-surplus economy women were seen as weak, in need of protection by the state; their roles as homemakers and mothers were viewed as primary. Some women, of course, welcomed protective legislation because it made it a little easier for them to handle their double burden of home and job. And now, since the functions of the family had changed significantly—from a unit of production to a unit of consumption— a central role for women was one of consumption. A 1909 article in the *American Journal of Sociology* pointed out that the family had become

conservative because it is the natural unit not of production but of consumption, and consumption is not easily revolutionized. For the purpose of using its resources society is less effectively organized than for creating them, since it does not recognize the management of consumption as a validly accredited career.[22]

If women were to be limited in the twentieth century in their roles as producers, they surely were not to be limited in their roles as consumers. As the United States became more and more industrially productive, focusing much of its productive capacity on consumer goods, women—particularly middle- and upper-class women—were to become the managers of consumption, par excellence.

During World War I women were able to move into jobs previously denied to them—banking, the chemical industry, automotive manufacturing, iron and steel—but at the end of the war, these jobs, for the most part, reverted to male control.[23] But while women suffered losses in manufacturing during the postwar period, they were moving steadily into what had become known as "white-collar" jobs—as telephone operators, clerks, bookkeepers, and into the fields of advertising and sales as copywriters, saleswomen, buyers, and decorators. By 1920, 25.6 percent of employed women worked in white-collar jobs, compared to 23.8 percent in manufacturing, 18.2 percent in domestic work, and 12.9 percent in agriculture.[24]

The 1920s brought a further increase in the number of office jobs, jobs that were seen as good training for the permanent, lifelong job as wife. Other careers considered consistent with women's role in the home also emerged: Nursing, library work, teaching, and social work were seen to utilize women's special interpersonal skills and to complement their roles at home. Nevertheless, one-third of all wage-earning women continued to work in factories.

During the depression women were given a double message. On the one hand, their low wages often permitted them to keep their jobs while their men lost theirs, and women's wages many times kept families going. On the other hand, women were urged, for the sake of the men and for the sake of family unity, to avoid wage work. Popular media contributed to the pressure on women to stay home and help their husbands cope with their economic problems by portraying "Husbands who endlessly hunted for jobs, while wives sat by poignantly wringing their hands in despair."[25] Women were also exhorted to remain at home to fulfill their urgent responsibilities toward their children. According to one study published in 1931, "Truancy, incorrigibility, robbery, teenage tantrums, and difficulty in managing the children" all stemmed from a "mother's absence at her job."[26] Perhaps Norman Cousins stated it most succinctly in 1939: "There are approximately 10,000,000 people out of work in the United States today. There are also 10,000,000 or more women, married and single, who are jobholders. Simply fire the women, who shouldn't be working anyway, and hire the men. Presto! No unemployment. No relief rolls. No depression."[27]

The economic situation changed dramatically for women with the outbreak of World War II. Between 1940 and 1944, over 6 million women entered the paid labor force, an increase of 50 percent.[28] The most dramatic gains were in the "war industries" such as metals, chemicals, and rubber, in which female employment rose 460 percent. The percentage of women in the auto industry jumped from 6 percent in 1940 to 24 percent in 1944[29]; in electrical manufacturing it rose from 32 percent to 49 percent during the same period.[30]

By the end of the war all union restrictions barring women from membership had been dropped, and female union membership rose to 3.5 million in 1944. While this accounted for only 15 to 20 percent of all women in the labor force at that time, it was, according to one observer, "an unprecedented achievement."[31] In addition, by the end of the war most unions supported equal pay for equal work. Women, of course, often did not do the same work as men, and a 1944 study found that men's hourly wages were 50 percent higher than women's, 20 percent higher on unskilled jobs. Moreover, many union contracts did not even guarantee the same starting salaries for women as for men.[32] The war had, nonetheless, made a significant difference in women's labor force participation. As Ruth Milkman points out:

> Not only were women integrated into what had previously been "men's jobs," but they were organized into unions to an unprecedented degree, and the unions had come out in strong support, self-serving as it may have been, of their rights to equal pay. There were certainly many instances of discriminatory treatment toward women, but the war conditions had nevertheless transformed women's relationship both to paid work and to the organized labor movement. The possibility, indeed the partial reality, of eliminating job segregation by sex appeared to exist for the first time in the twentieth century.[33]

This possibility did not, of course, come to pass. In the transition to a peacetime economy, the elimination of many war-related jobs, the exercise of seniority rights by veterans returning to civilian jobs, and the failure of Congress to pass full-employment legislation combined to cause massive layoffs immediately after the war;

women were laid off at a 75 percent higher rate than men. While women supported veterans' seniority rights, they lost ground still further by the reclassification of many jobs as "men's jobs." Milkman states that it is "indisputable" that "union–management collusion in this area was common in the postwar period." She further indicates that conditions at the local level were even more discriminatory, and that while women's participation in the labor force continued to grow, their union membership in the postwar decades declined.[34]

Over the past three hundred years, black women have had, of course, a very different experience. As Barbara Wertheimer has stated, "One group of women, from the start of their life in America, worked outside their homes on a full-time basis: slave women."[35] While the family responsibilities of white women were seen as preeminent, "The slave woman was first a full-time worker for her owner, and only incidentally a wife, mother, and homemaker."[36] Furthermore, contrary to popular misconceptions, slave women did not work primarily in the "big house" as cooks, maids, or mammies but rather as farm workers. Girls and women were sent to the fields, where they labored alongside the men planting and harvesting tobacco, rice, and cotton, and cutting cane. As Angela Davis has stated, "For most girls and women as for most boys and men, it was hard labor in the fields from sunup to sundown."[37]

Pregnancy made little or no difference in work assignments unless perhaps a slave woman was the mistress of the plantation owner. A woman generally worked until the time of delivery sometimes "giving birth in the grass nearby."[38] After delivery she might have a lighter work assignment for a brief period of time before assuming her arduous schedule.

As ex-slave Lewis Clarke remembers women's work in the fields,

The bell rings at four o'clock in the morning, and they have half an hour to get ready. Men and women start together, and the women must work as steadily as the men, and perform the same tasks as the men. If the plantation is far from the house, the sucking children are taken out and kept in the field all day. If the cabins are near, the women are permitted to go in two or three times a day to their infant children. The mother is driven out when the child is three or four weeks old.[39]

Ex-slave and abolitionist leader Frederick Douglass writes movingly about how his mother's maternal role had to be sacrificed to her primary function as a field hand:

> I never saw my mother, to know her as such, more than four or five times in my life. . . . She was hired by Mr. Stewart, who lived about twelve miles from my home. She made her journeys to see me in the night, travelling the whole distance on foot, after the performance of her day's work. She was a field hand, and a whipping is the penalty of not being in the field at sunrise. . . . I do not recollect of ever seeing my mother by the light of day. She was with me in the night. She would lie down with me, and get me to sleep, but long before I waked she was gone. . . . She died when I was about seven years old. . . . I was not allowed to be present during her illness, at her death, or burial.[40]

As industrialization developed during the nineteenth century and white women's roles became increasingly those of "wife" and "mother," the domestic code had little relevance for black women both in the North and in the South. Forced to work out of economic necessity, they were nonetheless prevented from working at the same jobs as whites. Even in urban areas, where by 1860 approximately half a million free blacks lived, black women were "confined to the most onerous jobs"—as cleaning women, nurse-maids, laundresses, cooks, and chambermaids; some also worked as seamstresses and midwives.[41] And yet they were often vilified for not tending exclusively to their families. As Kessler-Harris has noted,

> The ideology that exalted home roles condemned the lives of those forced to undertake wage work. Sympathetic perceptions of women wage earners sacrificing for the sake of their families gave way to charges of selfishness and family neglect. So the small minority of women who continued to work for wages after their teenage years found themselves entirely without sympathetic support— almost an outcast group.[42]

While black women were criticized for entering the labor force rather than staying at home to care for their husbands and children, they were also looked upon with suspicion and fear by white workers. Few unions admitted blacks to membership, and few black women were eligible for union membership since they were seldom permitted to work in skilled occupations. In 1890 census figures indicated that 38.7 percent of black women worked in agriculture, 30.8 percent in domestic work, 15.6 percent in laundry work, and only 2.8 percent in manufacturing.[43] One black woman described working conditions for most black women in the post–Civil War South:

> I am a negro woman, and I was born and reared in the South. . . . For more than thirty years—or since I was ten years old—I have been a servant. . . . During the last ten years I have been a nurse. . . .
> More than two-thirds of the negroes of the town where I live are menial servants of one kind or another. . . . The condition . . . of poor colored people is just as bad as, if not worse than it was during the days of slavery. Tho' today we are enjoying nominal freedom, we are literally slaves. . . .[44]

This woman continues by describing her own working conditions:

> I frequently work from fourteen to sixteen hours a day. I am compelled . . . to sleep in the house. I am allowed to go home to my children . . . only once in two weeks, every other Sunday afternoon—even then I'm not permitted to stay all night.
> I not only have to nurse a little white child, now eleven months old, but I have to act as playmate . . . to three other children in the home. . . . If the baby falls to sleep during the day . . . I am not permitted to rest. . . . So it is not strange to see "mammy" watering the lawn . . . sweeping the sidewalk, mopping the porch and halls, dusting around the house, helping the cook, or darning stockings. . . . I don't know what it is to go to a lecture or entertainment or anything of the kind; I live a treadmill life. . . . You might as well say that I'm on duty all the time—from sunrise to sunrise, every day of the week. I am the slave, body and soul, of this family.[45]

During World War I black women were able to move into jobs previously closed to them, but by 1920, 75 percent of all black women were still employed in agricultural, domestic, and laundry work. Work remained rigidly segregated by race; white women were sometimes able to start work one hour later, and when amenities such as lunchrooms, fresh drinking water, and clean toilets were available, they were available primarily to white women. "The menial jobs, the dirty and heavy work, consistently went to black women along with foreign women of 'low grade.' "[46]

World War II brought a dramatic improvement in the working lives of black women. Approximately 20 percent of those who had been domestic servants moved into the jobs white women vacated when they moved into factory work. The combined pressure of the Fair Employment Practices Commission, created in July 1941, union pressure, and demonstrations on the part of black women resulted in a 15 percent drop in domestic work; the number of factory workers more than doubled and the number of clerical, sales, and professional workers increased substantially as well. Nevertheless, during this period black women were never able to move into some of the most lucrative jobs as riveters, ship fitters, or welders.[47]

Female participation in the labor force has risen significantly from 31.8 percent of women in 1947 to 53.5 percent in 1984. More than two-thirds of the women ages 25 to 54 are employed. Furthermore, three out of every five women with children work, 46 percent with children under age three and 52 percent with children under age six.[48]

But while we know that women are moving into the labor force in increasing numbers, what jobs are they holding? Have these jobs changed significantly over the years? In 1870 the ten leading occupations of women workers were, in order of numbers of women: domestic servants, agricultural laborers, tailoresses and seamstresses, milliners and dressmakers, teachers, cotton mill operators, laundresses, woolen mill operators, farmers, and nurses. Servants remained the largest category until 1950, when they dropped to fourth place and were replaced by stenographers, typists, and secretaries. In 1970 secretaries and various kinds of office workers comprised three categories out of the top ten; four out of the remaining seven—teachers, sewers and stitchers, nurses, private household cleaners and servants—had been on the 1870 list. The three remaining occupations were retail sales clerks, waitresses, and cashiers.[49] The major change over the hundred-year period was the shift from agricultural work and employment in textile mills to office work.

What has not changed is the existence of a dual labor market— one for men and one for women. The majority of women are clustered in 20 of the 420 occupations listed by the Bureau of Labor Statistics. While the number of women entering the prestigious professions has increased markedly over the past few years— for example, from 1962 to 1982 the percentage of females among all engineers rose from 1 to 6 percent; among physicians from 6 to 15 percent; among college teachers from 19 to 25 percent; and women, having entered law in unprecedented numbers, now make up 15 percent of all lawyers—approximately two-thirds of working women are employed in service and retail jobs or in state and local government.[50] Professional women may get the lion's share of media attention, but the reality is that five of the top ten women's occupations are clerical and sales jobs.[51] Moreover these occupations are characterized by low wages and little opportunity for advancement. For example, 99 percent of all secretaries are women; their annual median salary in 1983 was $13,000. Ninety-seven percent of all prekindergarten and kindergarten teachers are women, and their median annual salary is $14,000. Ninety-four percent of all bank tellers are women; their median annual salary, $10,500. Seventy-five percent of all food service workers are women; their median annual salary is $8,200.[52]

As recently as 1984 women working year-round at full-time jobs still earned only $14,780, 64 percent of the $23,220 that men working full time earned.[53] Women are, of course, less likely to work full time and year-round than men, so the real disparity is even greater.

One of the reasons that women's wages have remained low is that the vast majority of female workers in the United States remain nonunionized. Unlike employees in most other Western industrialized countries, only 20 percent of the total American work force is unionized; but a still smaller percentage, only 11 percent, of female workers belongs to unions. Historically, as we have seen, trade unions were not sympathetic to female workers and, indeed, saw them as a threat to male employment. But even when women did join unions in large numbers, as in the garment industry, those unions were for the most part directed and controlled by men. Little effort was made to encourage women to assume leadership positions.

Moreover, women have traditionally entered occupations that are thought to be particularly difficult to organize: jobs in small shops in which women were isolated from other female workers; clerical, secretarial or health-care jobs that replicate the patriarchal family structure; jobs that are seasonal, part-time or temporary. And women themselves have been thought to be particularly difficult to organize. Much of their socialization as females has encouraged them to be passive rather than active, less comfortable with the expression of aggression necessary to demand higher wages and better working conditions, and unsure of their intrinsic worth in the marketplace. Furthermore, while women have entered the labor market in recent years in unprecedented numbers, the structure of the family, the distribution of housework, and the care of children have changed very little. According to economist Nancy Barrett, "There is no evidence of sweeping changes in the division of labor within households coincident with women's increasing labor force participation."[54] Women, therefore, continue to see their work outside of the home as only half of their total workload, and often not the most important half. In addition, as Rosabeth Kanter's work has shown, women often do not expect promotion and higher wages because they have become conditioned by the reality of their work experience not to expect these improvements in their work status.[55] In other words, they have adjusted to reality.

Some of these issues became extraordinarily clear in the recent efforts of Local 34 of the Federation of University Employees, a unit of the Hotel Employees and Restaurant Employees International, to organize clerical and technical workers at Yale University. The workers involved were a diverse group—payroll clerks, library employees, hospital aides, laboratory technicians, computer and telephone operators, and secretaries—but what they had in common was that 82 percent of them were women.

Local 34 started its organizing drive in November 1980 and worked for two years before distributing membership cards and asking for an election. Kim McLoughlin, a full-time organizer for the union, describes the organizing process:

There were 2,700 workers involved and only 15 to 20 percent started out in any way pro-union. The rest were anti-union. They thought, "Big labor will take away our rights." They thought, "They're so good to me; they let me use the Yale swimming pool." Of course, it depended on whose secretary you were. If you were the secretary to the head of the department of surgery, you would most likely identify with your boss and enjoy the experience of having international visitors and that sort of thing; but if you were a shelver in the library, you would have different views about your job.

Most of these people are blue collar people with hopes and dreams for middle-class status. The union's organizing effort forced a lot of women to sit down and take a look at reality. They had to give up their hopes and dreams a little.

The union, according to Kim, used a new style of organizing. They believed that the union was its membership and that to organize properly they had to work "from the bottom up," finding indigenous leaders within the ranks of the workers themselves. They talked with the workers individually and tried to encourage the women to "talk about their opinions about themselves." Kim feels that many of the workers had a "basic lack of confidence." Once the organizers identified leaders, meetings were scheduled day after day to discuss, "What are we worth?" As Kim describes it, this process was reminiscent both of consciousness raising among women's groups in this country and of "Speak Bitterness" meetings in the liberated areas of China during the late 1930s and 1940s. Once leaders were identified in a Chinese village, the women of the village were brought together to hear one or two women speak about their bitter lives. The others would identify so intensely with the experience of other women that their own anger was mobilized and they could then perceive their own oppression all the more clearly.

The Yale election was held in May 1983; the union won by thirty-nine votes. Once the vote was taken, both sides—the union and the university—had one year to agree on a contract; and in April 1984, they signed an interim contract that settled many of the issues but not the economic ones, specifically pay increases and the salary structure. Clerical and technical workers at Yale at that time averaged $13,473 a year, and the union claimed that women and members of minority groups were systematically paid less than white males.

But there was more at stake at Yale than money. Connie Baker, a thirty-year-old black mother of two whose husband suffers from epilepsy and is unemployed, is a shelver in Yale's medical library. She has worked there for three-and-a-half years and earned $9,600 a year. She talked about her job: "We are called 'the shelvers.' This is nothing but a high-class repetitious job. We are like a human assembly line. And we're supposed to know everything, but if someone asks us a question, we're not supposed to answer. We're supposed to be dummies, use our hands not our mouths."

Connie liked working at Yale and hoped to stay, but she needed more money and wanted to be treated differently:

I am willing to go on strike. Sure, we get good vacations, but who can go on vacation without money? We have no dental plan; if I go to the dentist, I have to take out loans. Yale is a big prestigious university and everybody looks up to them, but they don't care about the workers. They only care about the money they get from their big donors. They would get better work if they treated the workers better, but Yale thinks we're pushovers because we're women.

Connie's final comments were "Yale's attitude is, 'You should be glad you're working at Yale,'" and, after a moment of thought, "The union gives me something worth fighting for."

Sherry Mofield is a member of the union's negotiating committee. She is a lively, articulate woman who was part of the union's efforts almost from the beginning. Sherry, who has been at Yale for four years and currently works as a secretary in the medical school, describes the union drive:

It was a matter of raising people's thoughts about themselves. People are worth a lot more than they thought, but they needed to question the roles they were put into. It's not just a matter of money; it's respect. People tended to look down on you because of what you did.

As an example, Sherry talked about a secretary in the obstetrics/gynecology department who had to play the role of "office wife" and make lunch every day for her boss, was called "stupid," and finally was hit in the head by him when she did something he didn't like. Sherry feels you have to overcome the mentality that says, "I'm okay; I'm fortunate to be working here; I'm not worth any more than what I'm getting; and the university will take care of me." She acknowledged, "It's hard for those who have been mashed down for so long to stand up," and said that some of the workers had been terrified of joining the union for fear they'd be fired or that their bosses would make their lives miserable. But, she stated, "Most of the women have overcome their fear and said, 'Enough is enough.' Now there's almost a cockiness because we're so unified, we're a group. People talk to each other so much more than they used to, and we're right there for them if they're having a problem."

Finally, Sherry talked about what involvement with the union at Yale has meant to her personally:

We've been leaders and I'm really proud of that. We've made history and shown it can be done. It is my life right now and I have grown so much. I don't take anything anymore. I really feel I'm worth a lot more.

It's a high—like a good love affair—and I always want that high. Even though I'm tired, tired of struggling with people, I'll never leave it behind. I'll always be involved in something. Because I learned to organize and I learned to care, now I can give that direction to others. I'll never sit back and take it again or watch someone else take it. It's like coming into your own.

On September 26, 1984, sixteen hundred of Yale's two thousand clerical and technical workers went on strike. They had sought wage increases of 26 percent over three years; Yale had offered 17.1 percent. The union offered to submit the dispute to binding arbitration; the university refused. The strike lasted for ten weeks.

The workers returned to their jobs in December and finally won and ratified a new contract on January 22, 1985.

In the spare but elegant New England–style Center Church on the New Haven Green, hundreds of clerical and technical workers, most of them women, applauded and cheered as the provisions of the new contract were announced by the chief union negotiator, John Wilhelm, himself a Yale graduate. These included a much improved pension plan and medical benefits for retired workers, a dental plan, maternity or paternity leave for both biological and adoptive parents, significant changes in job classification and in the provisions to ensure job security, and across-the-board increases in salary. Wilhelm stated that the total value of the wage increases over the next three-and-a-half years would be 35 percent. The long, complex effort has been termed "highly imaginative." During a period when many unions have been seriously weakened, the workers at Yale, mostly women, "showed immense solidarity, the kind often found today only in labor-history books."[56] As Wilhelm told the workers while the votes were being counted, "You have shown the country that people, a lot of them women, some men, who do the work you do can successfully demand economic justice." The vote was 890 to 2 in favor of ratification.

Women earn less than men at every level. Whether they work in professional fields dominated by men such as accounting, in which female workers comprise less than 40 percent of all workers and earn only 71.2 percent of what men earn; or in retail, in which women make up over 60 percent of the work force and yet earn only 67.4 percent of what men earn; or in occupations dominated by women, such as clerical and kindred jobs, in which women make up 78.4 percent of the work force and yet earn only 67 percent of what men earn; women consistently earn less than men. Even when we compare the 1981 figures for occupations in which men and women earned the highest median weekly earnings, we see significant discrepancies. Men working in the twenty occupations with the highest income earn significantly higher wages than women who work in professions that pay them the highest income. Male civil engineers (the lowest of the top twenty occupations for men by income) received a median income nearly $100 more per week than women in their most lucrative occupations.

Furthermore, the occupations that rank high for female earnings are not the so-called women's professions. On the contrary, the occupations in which women earn the most money are those that are male-dominated—operations and systems research and analysis, computer systems analysis, law, medicine, and dentistry.[57]

One way of combating the low wages of the "pink collar ghetto," therefore, has been for women to attempt to enter traditionally male-dominated blue-collar jobs in significant numbers. Over the last two decades the percentage of mail carriers who are female has risen from 3 to 17 percent; of butchers from 4 to 16 percent; of bartenders from 11 to 50 percent; and of bus drivers from 12 to 47 percent.[58] Between 1960 and 1970 the number of women working in skilled trades rose by nearly 80 percent. Women became carpenters, electricians, plumbers, auto mechanics, painters, and machinists. Their numbers had, of course, been so miniscule at the beginning of the decade that even doubling or, in some cases, quadrupling the number, has still left these occupations overwhelmingly male.

By 1981, for example, only 1.4 percent of carpenters, 1.7 percent of electricians, 0.7 percent of automobile mechanics, and 3.9 percent of painters were female. Interestingly, 12.4 percent of precision machine operatives and 31 percent of compositors and typesetters were female. The Bureau of Labor Statistics does not have data on women's earnings in many skilled fields because it does not collect data for occupations in which there are fewer than 50,000 workers. The data for craft and kindred workers in general indicate, however, that in 1981 5.6 percent were women, and that these women earned 66.5 percent of what men earned. An even smaller number of women (2.1 percent) worked as mechanics and repairers, and they earned an uncommonly high percentage (83.9 percent) of what male mechanics and repairers earned. This supports the conclusion that the higher the proportion of female workers in a given occupation, the lower their wages, relative to men's, will be. For example, women comprised 38.8 percent of all "operatives," such as assemblers and bottling and canning workers, and earned only 62.9 of what men in these occupations earned.[59]

It is clear, therefore, that women who enter male-dominated occupations are likely to earn considerably more than women who work in female-dominated jobs, both because the wages are higher and because women are frequently paid more equitably in these fields. But it takes women with certain characteristics to be able to "tough it out" in the male workplace. Mary Lindenstein Walshok, in her valuable study, *Blue-Collar Women: Pioneers on the Male Frontier*, analyzes the characteristics of women who choose welding, carpentry, mechanics, plumbing, machine work, and other occupations previously unheard of for females. She found that women who enter these occupations seem to be highly motivated. They value physical activity and enjoy working alone. They want autonomy and control over their work rather than direction and supervision; they see work as central to their lives rather than tangential.[60] She also found that these women had had early experiences that emphasized independence and responsibility, and that because of economic circumstances, they frequently needed to make financial contributions to their families. She found, furthermore, that many of these women had strong mothers as role models. As one woman stated, "We may have been poor, but mother really loved us and worked hard for us."[61] But in addition to strong, hardworking mothers, many of these women who were pioneers in making their way in blue-collar occupations had men during their childhood years who played an important role in the development of their special interests—fathers, uncles, or grandfathers who encouraged their nontraditional activities. A woman who is a pipe fitter and active in her union remembers: "I spent most of my time with my brother and we spent a lot of time— like chopping down trees and building little log structures. My grandfather was a carpenter and he would draw designs of kites we could build and then we would go out and build them and fly them."[62]

Another woman, a UPS delivery-truck driver, talks of enjoying athletics with her father:

> I was real close to my brother and I was real close to my father because of sports. He encouraged me in sports and I was a competitive speed skater, so we went to meets all the time and stuff. . . . My father spent a lot of time with the kids, took us places. I was also in softball. He basically worked every day and

then at night he'd come home and we'd go to a training session. . . . That's how I remember him.[63]

Clearly, it takes a strong, highly motivated woman to break new ground, to do the unusual, to face the disapproval of friends and family and the undisguised hostility of male co-workers. It takes someone who is a risk taker. June Lawton, for example, is a member of the International Alliance of Theatrical Stage Employees and Moving Picture Machine Operators. A slim young woman with long, ash-blond hair who works in the Sun Belt, she describes herself as a stagehand; she does lights and sound for live theater and "behind-the-camera work," electrical work and lighting for films. Although she is paid at the same rate as male members of her union who do the same work, she is rarely called for a job by her union. On qualification tests, she has scored 70 percent higher than the men in her union but she works one-quarter as much as they do.

Her union is dominated, she states, by Mexican-American males who feel that women should not be working in this field. When she questions why she isn't assigned jobs, she is told, "You don't have a family to support." She has been told many times that she should "quit, get married, and have babies." If she does manage to get a job, it is said that she slept with someone in order to get it. Actually, the story that makes the rounds is that she is a "lesbian screwing the business agent." The contradictions of that statement do not seem to bother the union members who spread it. It is an extremely hostile environment in which to work, she says, but she can't afford to turn down work since she earned only $3,500 during 1982.

She and another female union member have filed an official complaint with the county attorney about the union's discriminatory practices, and an investigation is in progress. June's hope is to move toward an equal referral system, and while she thinks it looks promising, she is not sure she can continue doing the kind of work she loves so much. She says with some anger mixed with sadness, "My work is constantly being undermined. I'm told I'm not any good. There's no hope of my work being respected."

Nancy Ohlsson is a muscular, wiry, thirty-year-old woman with a cheerful, straightforward manner. She and her younger brother grew up in the Boston area; their father was a mechanic for the transit authority, their mother an administrator for a human-service agency. Today she is an auto mechanic who loves her work but acknowledges readily that "it is really shitty work, too greasy, the bottom of the trades. It's the pits." Her roommate during her last year of college was a backyard mechanic; since she wanted to learn auto mechanics, and he was a good teacher, she "hung out with him." She had no shop, no tools. After graduation she went up and down the streets looking for someone to take her on as an apprentice and was finally hired at $3 an hour in a family business. "They taught me as I went along. You're an indentured servant for a couple of years, and those first years are a real struggle. It's very hard work physically—lifting, constantly taking nuts and bolts off—you need a certain amount of strength just to do the work." "Also," she continues, "you have to think about what you're doing. It's a whole new way of looking at things—a mechanical way of looking at things. It's very tiring mentally. You have to think of eight or ten different things at once. It's a form of problem solving. New worlds opened up for me. I had never felt quite so inadequate. They, the guys, have so much knowledge, so much information."

At this point, Nancy's friend, Jane Palmer, a widow in her mid-thirties and a mother of a five-year-old, joined the discussion. She said that her father, who repaired computers for a living, was a tinkerer at home and involved her in a lot of his activities. To be competent was of value in her family. In the rural community in New Jersey where she grew up, her high school counselor asked her, "What do you want to be? A teacher or a nurse?" She went to college to study nursing, dropped it to study French, and was working on her PhD when she realized she did not want a sedentary job.

After she moved to Boston and got a job teaching French to high school students, her Volkswagen started to fall apart and she found she enjoyed fixing it. An auto mechanics cooperative was starting at the time, and she went over to watch what they were doing. She took a carburetor apart and found she could put it back together. She became part owner of the cooperative with very little training. She is currently learning to be a plumber and is, at the same time, teaching a course in auto repair to women. "Getting dirty is half the battle. Women don't like to get dirty and they don't like to make mistakes. They have a general fear of machinery, a fear they're going to mess it up."

Jane and Nancy explain that auto mechanics and carpentry are the most accessible blue-collar jobs because everyone needs a car or house fixed, and you can enter these fields without special training. Both women felt that in these fields, as in other areas, men's skills are overvalued and women's skills undervalued—by men and women alike: "People listen to what men say differently; they bullshit better. Women are eventually pushed into the women's end of the work, which means talking to the customers and holding their hand."

Both women felt strongly that nontraditional jobs are not the answer to women's economic problems. "It is a limited answer for a limited number of women. The problem is that women must be given value in society and only then will women's work be given value as well."

Reports of sexual harassment and other expressions of hostility abound in the fire departments, police departments, construction sites, and coal mines in which women have gone to work. Carol Green, a tall, large woman with short, salt-and-pepper hair and a lively, easy manner, worked in a copper mine near Tucson, Arizona, until she was laid off. She describes the conditions under which she and other women worked:

> I worked in the copper mine for nine years. I started as a laborer, then worked in the mill as a regrind operator, then in the metallurgical lab, then in the warehouse as a counterperson, then as part of the changing crew, and then I was laid off. In 1974 the company had 850 workers, 52 of whom were women; now there is one left. The rest have been laid off.

She lost her job in summer 1982. According to Carol, there are no women in the trades and crafts because the unions will not let them in. The supervisor has said that "over his dead body" would women be allowed to work in the trades and crafts sections of the mine. Women were placed in the pit as truck drivers because, she thinks, there was, literally and figuratively, no place for them to go from there. "Once you're in the pit you're locked in; there's no chance for advancement."

Carol does not feel she will be called back to work: "They don't like me too much because I was real active in the union." She complained repeatedly because there were no bathrooms in the pits; if a woman needed to go to the bathroom, she had to ask her supervisor to be brought up to the top. In addition, some of the bathrooms were for both men and women, with the urinals right out in the open. "If I want to watch a man going to the bathroom, I can go home and watch my husband," she states flatly. She was particularly angry that there were no sanitary napkins available in the bathrooms. There were some in the foreman's office, but then the women had to ask for one! "I don't care for myself," she declared angrily. "I've had a hysterectomy."

Perhaps one of the most difficult dilemmas for women in the labor force is faced by women who are trained for service jobs during a period of expanding government involvement only to find that the jobs have been phased out during a period of retrenchment. Gwen Johnson, a calm, self-possessed, extremely articulate thirty-five-year-old black resident of Brooklyn, illustrates many of the problems of women in the secondary sector of the labor market. After growing up in East Harlem, she married at the age of seventeen, had her first child at eighteen and her second at nineteen, and then discovered that her husband was a drug addict. When he lost his job, they had to go on welfare and move to a low-rent apartment on the Lower East Side of Manhattan. She describes the apartment as "unbearable, a rat hole." "How could you send somebody to a place like that?" she asks. "But we had no choice; I had no job and he had no job. We had to take it."

Eventually she got involved with Mobilization for Youth, a community-action agency that was organized by the Office of Economic Opportunity in the 1960s, and was trained as an early-childhood education worker. At the completion of her training, she was hired as an early-childcare worker. She describes how she felt:

I was making a hundred dollars for the first time in my life, so I was just happy, you know? I really got involved—in welfare issues, rent strikes, food co-ops. It got me out of the house, out of my rut. I got to meet a lot of people and the kids got happier, because they were with me most of the time and they were active too. And then I started thinking about getting a divorce even though I had had a third child during this time and was pregnant again.

Gwen got her divorce and worked until federal funds were cut back from community-based programs in the early 1970s. Since she had never passed her high school equivalency test, she could not begin work on a college degree; without the higher degree, she was virtually unemployable in a more competitive job market. She describes the cyclical nature of jobs for community workers: "They build your hopes up to let you down. I don't want to go through this again. I've been trapped in every situation." She remarried and therefore has not had to go on welfare again, but she is extremely concerned about the future of her marriage, because she is not able to pull her weight financially. She feels she has not had the leverage in her marriage that she would have had if she had been helping to pay the bills and, furthermore, that her husband resents the fact that she's not bringing in a paycheck.[64]

Gwen Johnson is clearly a victim of the federal government's attempts to "regulate the poor." As Frances Fox Piven and Richard Cloward have pointed out,[65] during periods of social unrest and political disorder, services are expanded in order to pacify the poor, and during quiet periods, these services are retracted. During the 1960s Gwen was trained, but only enough to be able to get a job in times of human-service expansion and experimentation. Once this period ended she was nearly back to where she had started, except she now had higher expectations and perhaps the knowledge that she could work effectively in the larger society. But, as anyone who has been unemployed for any length of time knows, the feelings of competence and self-confidence that come from working effectively, particularly at a job you enjoy, vanish rapidly as the weeks of unemployment roll by.

What is the future likely to hold for women in the labor market?

According to the Bureau of Labor Statistics, civilian employment rose by 7.7 percent between January 1981 and September 1984, a gain of 7.5 million jobs.[66] But what kinds of jobs are these, and what jobs are there likely to be in the future?

Many of the new jobs are professional, technical, and managerial, but many others pay low wages and some are part time. Many are in suburban areas, not in urban areas where unemployment rates have often been the highest; some analysts suggest that companies are drawn to the suburbs because there is a large pool of white female workers whom "the employers see as more malleable and home-oriented than other workers, newer to the job market, less likely to be interested in unionization and more interested in working part time with minimum benefits."[67]

Moreover, the largest increases in the number of jobs have come in the service sector—hotels and motels, medical care, and legal and social services—areas in which women predominate and in which wages are notoriously low. Many experts predict that higher-paying blue-collar jobs will decline and be replaced by lower-paying jobs in the service sector, leading to the increasing feminization of the work force. Janet L. Norwood, head of the Bureau of Labor Statistics, pointed out to a congressional committee early in 1985, "We have a number of manufacturing industries in real trouble. They haven't gained a single job in the 26 months of recovery." Lumber, furniture, rubber, and plastics were among the industries she cited.[68] Other analysts suggest that women will face new problems caused by the use of computers and the export of jobs traditionally performed by women, such as those in the textile, shoe, clothing, and electronics industry. In clerical work, for example, according to Mary C. Murphree, a consultant to the Federal Woman's Bureau, many office jobs will be lost due to the use of computers, other jobs will require greater skills, and many of the new jobs created will be in "low-level" word- and data-processing work.[69]

Thierry J. Noyelle, a researcher in the Conservation of Human Resources at Columbia University, has stated that changes in the work force are producing

a stratum of managers, professionals, technicians, teachers, and other highly skilled employees living in a relatively well-protected and well-paying economic world, and a large strata of assembly workers, clericals, and service workers who find it increasingly difficult to make ends meet and to deal with the stress associated with unrewarding and somewhat insecure work.[70]

There is no question that some women will find work in the higher stratum, but it is equally sure that the vast majority will be working in the lower one, doing unrewarding work and finding it difficult to make ends meet.

The most positive trend for the future seems to be the concept of "comparable worth." Since most women continue to work in the low-paying "pink collar" ghetto and since "women's work" is valued so much less—and hence paid at such a lower rate than men's work—the concept of equal pay for equal work will not materially alter the low wages of female workers. The theory of "comparable worth," which calls for equal pay for jobs that are different but are comparable in nature, can, however, bring women's wages far more closely into line with men's wages.

In December 1983 the American Federation of State, County, and Municipal Employees (AFSCME) and the comparable worth movement won their biggest victory to date: A federal judge in the state of Washington found that the state practiced " 'direct, overt and institutionalized' " discrimination and ordered it to pay women workers nearly $1 billion in back pay and wage increases. He further directed the state to work out a system that would raise women workers' salaries approximately 31 percent. Comparable-worth cases are now proliferating. There have been similar suits within the electrical industry; within Michigan Bell; at the state level in Minnesota; at the city level in San Jose, California; and within the federal government itself. Some government jobs that have been found to be of comparable worth are registered nurses and vocational education teachers in Minnesota; typing pool supervisors and painters, also in Minnesota; licensed practical nurses and correctional officers in Washington state; and mental health technicians and automotive mechanics in Illinois. In each of these pairs, the salary for the typically "woman's" job was significantly less than the salary for the comparable "man's" job.[71] By mid-1985 several states, including New York, Iowa, South Dakota, Minnesota, and New Mexico, had allocated millions of dollars for pay equity, and twenty-two other states were studying the issue. In May 1985 the city of Los Angeles adopted a union contract that included $12 million in raises for pay equity over the next three years.[72]

The comparable worth solution to women's economic inequality suffered a severe setback in September 1985 when the Washington state ruling was overturned by a federal appeals court. The three-member panel of the court stated that federal laws banning sex discrimination in employment did not require an employer to provide equal pay for different jobs even if studies by the employer indicate the jobs have the same value. The union that originally brought the suit indicated that an appeal to the Supreme Court was likely.[73]

There is no question that the comparable worth doctrine could cost employers enormous sums of money; but whatever the costs, they may well be less than the cost of supplementary welfare, food stamps, Medicaid, and other social welfare measures that are now necessary to compensate for the low salaries women are currently earning. Moreover, women might finally earn some decent measure of what their work is actually worth—and feel a sense of self-respect at the same time.

4

WELFARE: HOW TO KEEP A GOOD WOMAN DOWN

The welfare system is absolutely demoralizing. They deliberately demoralize you. They give you a minimum standard of living—rent, food, phone bill. It is not really livable. And the way they deal with you is humiliating. I feel ashamed.

—*Elizabeth Cameron*
Former welfare worker,
current welfare recipient

It is ironic that *welfare* has become our euphemism for Aid to Families with Dependent Children. There are, of course, other means-tested programs that provide financial assistance to people in need, but usually when we speak of *welfare*, we mean AFDC. It is particularly ironic because AFDC has very little to do with *welfare* in the true meaning of the term.

According to the Shorter Oxford English Dictionary, "welfare" is "the state or condition of doing well or being well; good fortune, happiness, or well-being . . . ; prosperity." Good fortune? Happiness? Well-being? Prosperity? Not in the welfare system we have developed in the United States. If Elizabeth Cameron is right and the system is demoralizing, humiliating and unlivable, how did it get that way? Are we helping the women and children who make up the vast majority of AFDC recipients, or are we really punishing them for being poor?

Our current system of poor laws—for that is, of course, what the welfare system is—is rooted in our Colonial Poor Laws and before that in the English Poor Law of 1601, which established for the first time civil or governmental responsibility for relief for the poor. The breakdown of the medieval economy, the development of the factory system that gave rise to seasonal and cyclical unemployment, the increasing numbers of beggars and vagabonds during the sixteenth century, and the widespread food scarcity and social disorder of the end of that period combined to produce a law that affirmed the state's responsibility, according to historian Walter I. Trattner, "to supplement ordinary efforts to relieve want and suffering and to insure the maintenance of life."[1] The Poor Law directed the authorities to provide apprenticeship for needy children, work for the able-bodied, and to provide home relief or institutional relief for the incapacitated, helpless, or "worthy" poor.[2]

Conditions in the New World, however, differed dramatically from those in the Old. Since resources were abundant and the population sparse, labor was at a premium and unemployment was not a major social problem. Moreover, the colonists had greater opportunities for social mobility because the class structure was less rigid than it had been in England. Therefore, "The belief was engendered that no man need be poor, save for his own indolence and depravity."[3] At the same time, seventeenth-century Americans believed that "a well-ordered society was hierarchical" with "the great ones, high and eminent in power and dignity" at the top and "the poor and inferior" at the bottom. Each group had special privileges and responsibilities—"the poor to respect and show deference to those above them, the well-to-do to aid and care for those below them."[4]

While conditions in North America were favorable for many, others arrived in desperate need. The British Parliament authorized the practice of shipping to America groups that were considered undesirable in England—convicts, beggars, vagrants, political prisoners, the unemployed, and even orphans. Moreover, the trip across the Atlantic was long and debilitating: "Passengers were packed into tiny ships with filthy and foul-smelling quarters, lack of adequate food and drinking water, and exposure to disease; many never survived the wretched conditions of the voyage; those who did frequently reached shore ill or infirm."[5] In addition, conditions in the New World were harsh, and many were forced to live in poverty or near poverty. The colonies were soon faced with caring for the poor, the old, the disabled, and others who could not care for themselves.

In 1642 Plymouth Colony enacted its Poor Law, with Virginia following suit in 1646, Connecticut in 1673, Massachusetts in 1692, and the other colonies enacting similar legislation. The Colonial Poor Laws established the principle that the administration of aid was to be left to the lowest level of government—in New England, the town; in the South, the parish. Local authority over poor relief has remained part of the American system and has continued, in large part, to determine the nature of that system.

The Colonial Poor Laws had three major provisions: "outdoor relief," which provided financial aid for poor people in their own homes; indenture; and institutional care, which was provided mainly in almshouses and workhouses. "Outdoor relief," however, was not developed to any significant extent until the passage of the Social Security Act of 1935, which established the welfare system as we know it today. It is significant that the practice of helping people financially while enabling them to remain in their own homes was neglected, while the practice of removing people from their families and social milieus both through indenture and almshouses was widespread. This pattern continues today in the multimillion-dollar business of foster care, which removes children from their homes rather than provide adequate financial resources and supports that might keep many families together. The notion that a poor child is better off away from his/her family, who are presumed to be defective in one way or another, is one that took root during the colonial period; despite the efforts of reformers and social theorists, it has flourished ever since.

Apprenticeship was widely used as a way of dealing with poor, illegitimate, or orphaned children. In colonial times, the town had the authority to remove children from their families simply if they were not being taught a trade. By arranging an apprenticeship, local authorities ensured that the young person would continue to live with a family—albeit not his/her own—and that the town would be spared the necessity of providing financial support. Indenture, a system whereby one person could buy or contract the labor of another for a specific period of time, was another method of dealing with poor children. At the end of the specified time period, the indentured individual was technically free to leave.

The other major method of dealing with the poor, the almshouse, became more widespread after the Revolutionary War. The Protestant ethic, which emphasized "salvation through diligence, frugality, and virtue,"[6] led to the view that if an individual failed it was his/her own fault. "Poverty was a personal matter; only the individual could overcome it."[7] Moreover, while lip service was paid to the distinction between the "worthy" and the "unworthy" poor, "most people tended to regard all the needy with contempt."[8] Outdoor aid, it was felt, only perpetuated poverty. The mayor of Boston, Josiah Quincy, who chaired a state commission on public outdoor relief in 1821, expressed clearly the viewpoint of the early nineteenth century when he stated, "Of all the modes of providing for the poor, the most wasteful, the most expensive, and the most injurious to their morals and destructive to their industrious habits is that of supply in their own families."[9] It was felt that aid to families in their own homes both removed their fear of poverty and destroyed their will to work, thereby encouraging a life of idleness and dissolution. Emphasis was therefore placed on the use of institutions—almshouses and workhouses. Public assistance would provide almshouses for the "worthy" poor—orphans and young children whose parents could not care for them, the elderly, and the permanently disabled—and the "unworthy" poor, the able-bodied, were institutionalized in workhouses in which they worked for their keep. This was intended to ensure that they were not "getting something for nothing" and, at the same time, it was hoped they would learn the habit of hard work.

During the mid-nineteenth century, the county, rather than the town, was given administrative responsibility over public assistance; indoor relief, primarily almshouses, became the central response to poverty. In 1824, for example, Massachusetts had 83 almshouses; by 1840 there were 180; and by 1860 the number has risen to 219.[10] Little attention was paid, however, to conditions within these institutions:

> Into most were herded the old and the young, the sick and the well, the sane and the insane, the epileptic and the feeble-minded, the blind and the alcoholic, the juvenile delinquent and the hardened criminal, male and female, all thrown together in haphazard fashion. Nakedness and filth, hunger and vice, and other abuses such as beatings by cruel keepers, were not uncommon in the wretched places, vile catchalls for everyone in need defined by one reformer as "living tombs" and by another as "social cemeteries."[11]

As outrage developed around conditions in the almshouses, reformers sought to remove the children who had been herded into these institutions along with the adults. To this end, orphanages were established during the first half of the nineteenth century. The term *orphanage* was actually a misnomer since most of the children who were taken to them were not orphans at all but poor children whose families could not care for them. It was felt that more support could be mobilized for the children if they were labeled *orphans* than if they were simply termed *poor*.

Indenture persisted during this period but was eventually replaced in the latter half of the nineteenth century by the "free" foster home. Being placed in such a home was similar to indenture. The family was not paid for the upkeep of the child; the child was expected to work for the foster family and to remain there until adulthood. The major difference between indenture and the "free" foster home is that the child was technically "free" to leave. This system lasted well into the first half of the twentieth century and was eventually replaced by foster care as we know it today.[12] The "free" foster home arrangement, like indenture and apprenticeship before it and foster care today, focused on separating poor families and on removing children from what were often considered harmful home conditions; it paid little attention to the conditions of the place to which they were sent.

In the early 1900s social reformers began to be concerned about the widespread practice of removing children from their own homes.

A resolution highlighting this concern was produced by the first White House Conference on the Care of Dependent Children in 1909:

> Home life is the highest and finest product of civilization. It is a great molding force of mind and of character. Children should not be deprived of it except for urgent and compelling reasons. . . . Except in unusual circumstances, the home should not be broken up for reasons of poverty.[13]

Support was building for some kind of public aid to mothers and children, but there was also considerable concern that the money only go to "worthy" parents and that such aid not relieve fathers of their financial obligation to support their children. In 1912, Mary Richmond, a pioneer in the field of social work, stated, "So, far from being a forward step, 'funds for parents' is a backward one—public funds not to widows only, mark you, but . . . funds to the families of those who have deserted and are going to desert."[14] And Homer Falks, secretary of the New York State Charities Aid Association, also expressed concern that public relief might encourage "anti-social" behavior:

> . . . to pension desertion or illegitimacy would, undoubtedly, have the effect of a premium upon these crimes against society. . . . It is a great deal more difficult to determine the worthiness of such mothers than of the widow, and a great deal more dangerous for the State to attempt relief on any large scale.[15]

But because of the widespread support for aiding needy children and for reversing the policy of removing them from their own homes, in 1911 Illinois passed the first mothers' pension law, the Funds to Parents Act. Two years later, twenty states had passed similar legislation; ten years later forty states had done the same.[16]

In 1933 the Children's Bureau published a study that showed that, in 1931, 82 percent of those given aid were widows and that the overwhleming majority of recipients, 96 percent, were white.[17] This pattern arose largely through the local authorities' efforts to separate "worthy and deserving" mothers from those who weren't.

Widows, as Homer Falks pointed out, were thought to be the most legitimate recipients of funds, and other groups—such as women who were deserted by their husbands or divorced or separated, those whose husbands were imprisoned or disabled, or, most suspect of all, unmarried mothers—were eliminated whenever possible. In addition, the local administrative unit had the right to conduct an investigation into the character of the mother to see if she was "physically, mentally, and morally fit to rear her children."[18] The result was the weeding out of almost everyone except white widows.

Established by the Social Security Act of 1935, Aid to Dependent Children (ADC), as AFDC was originally termed, preserved many of the elements of the legislation that established widows' pensions. For fifteen years ADC provided funds only for dependent children; it was not until 1950 that Congress added a caretaker grant to provide for the mother's essential expenses and changed the name to Aid to Families with Dependent Children (AFDC).

ADC was administered at the state and local levels with grants from the federal government to aid in the financing. Local control, differences in local economies, and differences in ideologies across the country have been responsible for vast discrepancies in the amount of money provided from state to state. In December 1939, for example, Arkansas provided an average of $8.10 per month to families with dependent children, while Massachusetts provided $61.07.[19] Other characteristics of ADC and later of AFDC were the continued denial of aid to unemployed men, often called "man-in-the-house" rules, which forced men out of the home so that the women and children might receive aid; continued discrimination against black mothers and their children; continued discrimination against women who were seen as "unsuitable" mothers—usually a euphemism for unmarried mothers; keeping people off the rolls or terminating them for minor technical reasons; underbudgeting recipients; and periodically forcing recipients to work in menial jobs in return for their benefits.

Piven and Cloward claim that many of these practices, and in fact the very nature and structure of the U.S. welfare system, are fundamentally an effort to regulate "the political and economic behavior of the poor."[20] They state:

Historical evidence suggests that relief arrangements are initiated or expanded during the occasional outbreaks of civil disorder produced by mass unemployment, and are then abolished or contracted when political stability is restored. . . . Expansive relief policies are designed to mute civil disorder, and restrictive ones to reinforce work norms. In other words, relief policies are cyclical—liberal or restrictive depending on the problems of regulation in the larger society with which government must contend.[21]

The significant expansion of the welfare rolls during the 1960s is a clear example of the use of relief to quell civil disorder, while the restrictions placed on relief in the 1970s and, to a far greater extent, during the Reagan administration, ensures that there is a large labor force available for low-wage work.

Let us look briefly at the current system of Aid to Families with Dependent Children. First, a few facts:

- Four out of five AFDC families are headed by women;
- Sixty-eight percent of all AFDC recipients, a total of over 7 million people, are children;
- Half these children are eight years old or younger;
- Approximately 45 percent of the children on AFDC are eligible because their parents are divorced or separated;
- The size of AFDC families is decreasing—over 40 percent of families on AFDC have only one child;
- Forty-five percent of AFDC recipients are black;
- One out of every nine children in the United States depended on AFDC for all or part of 1984;
- One out of every four American children will depend on AFDC at some point in his/her life.[22]

Despite the 1961 reform that permitted states to extend aid to families having an unemployed father in the home, only twenty-six states have elected to use this option, and AFDC is still overwhelmingly a program for women and children.

To what extent does AFDC actually help families out of poverty? A study done in the early 1950s of over sixty-five hundred AFDC families in thirty-eight states, the District of Columbia, and Alaska found that income levels of AFDC families were too low to care for the children properly. A decade later, a similar study showed, "The income of many AFDC families is not adequate to provide even a minimum level of living. A vast majority can be considered living in dire poverty. . . ."[23] Most recently the Children's Defense Fund stated, "In most states, AFDC payments are intolerably low, failing to provide even a minimum level of decency."[24] In fact, only one state, Alaska, pays maximum benefits that are higher than the poverty threshold.[25] As the Children's Defense Fund has pointed out, the maximum payment for a child in Mississippi in 1983 was ninety-nine cents a day, or $30 a month; Alaska provided the highest amount in the nation, $5.96 per child per day. Supplemental Security Income, in contrast, provided an average monthly payment of $7.59 per day, or $231 a month, for a disabled individual. The states set the amount of the AFDC grant; the federal government sets the benefit levels of SSI.[26]

To look at one state in some depth, in 1982 a typical AFDC family in Massachusetts consisted of a mother and two children who were eligible for aid because their adjusted total income did not exceed $4,550 annually. The average AFDC parent in Massachusetts was thirty-one years old. Seventy percent of the recipients were white; 60 percent had at least one child under the age of seven, and 78 percent were single-parent families. Due largely to a significant increase in female-headed, single-parent families, the Massachusetts AFDC caseload expanded dramatically during the 1970s. In 1970, 77,000 Massachusetts families were receiving AFDC; in 1980 the number had grown to 124,000. The number had been projected to nearly 140,000 in 1983, but the federal cutbacks embodied in the 1981 Omnibus Budget Reconciliation Act caused a nearly 25 percent reduction in the caseload. By 1982 the number of families receiving AFDC in Massachusetts had been reduced to 92,000.[27]

While the number of families receiving AFDC was decreasing in 1982, approximately one in ten Massachusetts citizens, more than half a million people, lived below the poverty line. Although the vast majority, nine out of every eleven poor people, in the Commonwealth are white, during this period one out of every four blacks was officially poor and four out of every ten black families had incomes under $10,000. Moreover, half of all Hispanic families living in Massachusetts had incomes less than $10,000.[28] And yet the number of families receiving AFDC was being reduced. Four out of seven poor families were headed by women, and 94 percent of these families had children under eighteen years of age. Over one-third of the children living in Massachusetts were poor; more than sixty thousand of them were under the age of six.[29] And yet the number of families receiving AFDC was decreasing.

These reductions in AFDC caseloads, of course, mirror reductions all over the country. Since the Reagan administration took power, there have been, according to the Children's Defense Fund, "Two waves of devastating AFDC cuts, one in Fiscal Year 1982 and another in Fiscal Year 1983." First the Omnibus Budget Reconciliation Act of 1981 "slashed" $1 billion off the $7 billion AFDC budget. This, combined with the resulting billion-dollar loss in state matching funds, constituted a total loss of almost $2 billion in 1982. Furthermore, the Tax Equity and Fiscal Responsibility Act of 1982 cut an additional $85 million from the AFDC budget for the fiscal year 1983.[30]

In addition to the outright cuts in funds, the federal government enacted new provisions that the states had to accept to be eligible for federal funds, along with optional provisions that they could accept or reject. Among the mandatory provisions enacted for the 1982 fiscal year that resulted in millions of families losing their eligibility were: lowering the level of eligibility; changing the way eligibility is calculated for working parents so as to reduce the number who can receive AFDC; counting a stepparent's income in calculating eligibility, whether that income is available to the child or not; not allowing federal AFDC assistance to women pregnant with their first child until the sixth month of pregnancy (previously states could claim federal reimbursement from the time pregnancy was medicaly confirmed); and imposing stricter limitations on young people of ages eighteen to twenty-one receiving AFDC. The federal government also required states to calculate AFDC retrospectively—(if a family had a sudden drop in income, they would have to wait up to two months for the AFDC grant to reflect their increased need)—and required families to report on their income and any other relevant information on a monthly basis.[31]

Optional provisions of the 1981 act included: allowing the states to count the value of food stamps and housing subsidies in determining eligibility and benefit levels; allowing states to require recipients to "work off their AFDC grant for no pay in often meaningless, dead-end jobs," or, *Workfare*, which has also been called the new "workhouse without walls"; and allowing states to set up other types of work programs for AFDC recipients.[32]

The result of the mandatory and optional provisions enacted for the 1982 fiscal year alone was the loss of eligibility or the reduction of grants for an estimated 725,000 families, most of whom were working families, families with a stepparent in the home, or families with a dependent child over nineteen. In Ohio, for example, over 95,000 cases were either reduced or terminated out of an average monthly caseload of 204,000.[33]

The policies of the Reagan administration have resulted in a dramatic drop in the number of poor families receiving AFDC. In 1979, 88 percent of all poor families were receiving AFDC; by 1983, only 62.9 percent were AFDC recipients.[34] If we examine the number of poor children receiving AFDC, the discrepancy is even greater. After a high of 83.6 percent of poor children receiving AFDC in 1973, by 1983 only 53.3 percent were recipients. The percentage dropped gradually during the 1970s, but the most dramatic decrease occurred between 1979, when 71.8 percent of poor children were receiving AFDC, and 1983.[35] But not only have the numbers dropped precipitously, the amount AFDC provides relative to the poverty level has decreased significantly as well. In 1960 the maximum AFDC benefit of the median state provided 63 percent of the poverty threshold for a family of four; by January 1985 AFDC was only providing 43 percent of the poverty threshold.[36] What this means, of course, is that very few poor families are actualy helped out of poverty by AFDC. It has been estimated that only 4 percent of all families who were poor before they went on welfare moved out of poverty due to their AFDC grant in 1983.[37]

In twenty states, the loss of AFDC in recent years has also meant the loss of Medicaid; for many it has meant the loss of food stamps and housing assistance as well. Many families whose income was so low that they had been eligible for AFDC lost that supplementary aid and are now even less able to meet their basic needs. They are by any standard "truly needy," to use the Reagan catchword, and they are not being helped.

One Georgia mother of three, a fifty-one-year-old woman who earns $269 a month working part time as a cleaning woman at a church, lost her supplementary AFDC and with it her Medicaid benefits. She has serious health problems and her job provides no health insurance.[38] Many working mothers would have been better off after the cutbacks if they had stopped working and simply gone on welfare full time. The mandatory provisions for the 1982 fiscal year clearly provided disincentives for parents continuing to work. One Maine mother continued to work after her supplementary AFDC aid of $180 per month was discontinued. She and her child were then forced to live on $376 per month; after essential expenses she had $56 a month to buy food and to pay for clothing, laundry, transportation and medical costs. She stated:

> I am badly in need of dental work, my daughter needs new shoes but there is no money left for these things. And I know of women who are in situations worse than mine—who have more children than I do, who pay more rent, who are not able to stretch their food stamps and pennies as far as I can, whose children have their only real meal at noon at the day care center or the baby-sitter's.[39]

These stories of real deprivation—deprivation amid almost unbelievable abundance for some in the United States—are echoed across the country. Since our first poor laws were passed, there has been a wrenching ambivalence about this society's responsibility to the poor. On one hand, we profess belief that government has a moral obligation to care for poor people; on the other hand, we despise the poor and assume that adequate financial support will simply encourage their "slothful, deceitful ways."

Moreover, American antipathy toward the poor and toward programs that purport to serve the needs of the poor is fueled by remnants of the Protestant ethic holding that hard work, thrift, and material success in this world were signs that salvation in heaven was waiting in the next. This belief supports the notion that those who work hard are truly better people than those who do not and that the road to redemption is not just through hard work but, more specifically, through capitalism. Secretary of Labor John R. Block, in discussing the plight of farmers on the verge of bankruptcy and whether the Reagan administration would provide them with additional federal support or cut back existing support, stated the 1980s version of the Protestant ethic: "Dignity is when you make your money out of the marketplace."[40] Those who do not *earn* their income obviously are not supposed to feel a sense of dignity or be treated with dignity and respect.

Ambivalence toward the poor is acted out every day in welfare offices all over the country, both through the amount of money provided to AFDC recipients and through the attitudes of welfare workers, who often mirror the disdain and distrust felt by the wider society.

Joan is a thirty-five-year-old divorced mother who lives with her three-year-old son in Tucson, Arizona. She receives $180 per month from AFDC—(an annual income of $2,160)—plus $139 in food stamps each month. She says, "We get by, but it is because we mainly eat macaroni and cheese, beans and rice."

Gertrude Manning is a thirty-three-year-old Maine mother of four who looks at least twenty years older. With long, dark, straggly hair, several teeth missing on the bottom right side of her mouth, and lines that come only from worry, she looks like someone out of a 1930s Dorothea Lange photograph. "I had my first child before I was twenty. I am a grandmother because my daughter was pregnant before she was sixteen."

Mrs. Manning's husband was laid off from his job repairing machines in a cotton mill in June 1982 and was out of work for fourteen months. They had to manage during this time on unemployment compensation, for as long as it lasted, and on food stamps.

Since we are married, there is no way to get AFDC. What most people would have done is to tell them we were separated but I felt I shouldn't have to lie. I knew we needed help but we've made it this long without their help and we'll make it the rest of the way. The welfare worker asked, "Are they all his children?" Because if some of them were someone else's children they would be entitled to some help.

My husband and I, we hold each other up. We have never asked our families for help because my husband is too proud. In fact, when we have gotten occasional food orders from the city, he has gone down and worked them off at $3.35 per hour. You have to work for what you want; nobody gives you anything free.

Gertrude Manning clearly has more scruples than the welfare system, for the Maine practice of not giving aid to families with unemployed fathers present encourages either the breaking up of families or cheating the system. For people like Gertrude Manning who are not willing to do either, the system forces them and their children to live in abject poverty.

Elizabeth Cameron, once a welfare worker, today a welfare recipient, provides further insight into the welfare system. She has a serene, almost luminous look about her and speaks softly, in a mild manner, until she becomes excited about what she is saying; then her words come more rapidly, emphatically:

After I graduated from college I came to New York and went to work in a welfare office. They hired me off the street. I thought I was a wonderful caseworker at the time. I tried to help people and I didn't hassle them. I was kind-hearted. I had no qualifications, so when people had serious problems, I couldn't help. I either handed out the money or I didn't hand out the money.

But I didn't see people as real. I came from the sixties, when socializing between races was considered exotic, so that when I related to my clients who were Hispanic I didn't see their problems, their joys, and their sadnesses. I just saw them as very different. I really did not have any emotional involvement with these families. I didn't really understand them.

Elizabeth continues by talking about her current experiences as a welfare recipient:

The way they deal with me today is humiliating. They keep you waiting for hours and to two small hungry children three hours might as well be thirty. And then you have to bring them to the bathroom and it's filthy.

Elizabeth states with some bitterness that the welfare workers do not see her as a person with valuable time. In fact, "The outside world doesn't see what I do as valuable. I have a lot to do. I take care of my children, I have to go shopping, I have to go to La Leché League" [where she is a very active volunteer].

She talks about the problems of interacting with the welfare workers and how tight the budget is:

When I applied most recently, the welfare worker would not give me carfare. They are supposed to give you carfare for yourself and for a child if you must bring your child. They wouldn't give me the carfare for a nine-year-old. So for $1.50 what do you do? Do you pull out your big guns over $1.50? I had no cash. Every dollar is a quart of milk. My welfare worker said, "Don't nickel and dime me to death," but what was I do do?

She feels the welfare department is staffed by people who are "the world's rejects." They are "incompetent and feel so superior only because they work in that setting. They deliberately demoralize you."

"The welfare budget is not really livable," she states flatly. "If you don't cheat, you can't live on it. There is nothing extra. No real pleasures." She says again, with greater emphasis, "You can't live on welfare without outside help."

While the inadequacy of the money is a constant and real problem, Elizabeth feels that the hardest part is the humiliation; it is, of course, particularly painful for her since she used to sit on the other side of the desk: "Yes, I've been hungry at times but the worst thing is the treatment by the welfare office." Recently she spent the whole day there trying to get legal fees for her eviction notices; she chafed and raged at how she was treated and diminished. "I have to go to the very center where I worked and there are still people there who were there when I worked there. There is a burden of grief, shame and misery on me. I feel it in my chest."

As Richard Sennett and Jonathan Cobb have stated in their

analysis of the American working class, *The Hidden Injuries of Class*, "Dignity is as compelling a human need as food or sex, and yet here is a society which cast the mass of its people into limbo, never satisfying their hunger for dignity. . . ."[41] Sennett and Cobb are describing the plight of blue-collar workers who feel shamed and demeaned by their position in American society. They point out that these workers survive by keeping "a certain distance from the problems of class and class consciousness,"[42] by separating themselves from their feelings when they are interacting with the world of work, by becoming alienated from much of public life—in much the same way as the poor attempt to protect themselves from the not-so-hidden injuries of poverty. They try to deal with the welfare bureaucracies with resignation and deadened emotions. They leave "the real me" somewhere else when they must cope with the intrusive questions, the unspoken (and all-too-often spoken) criticisms, the disregard for their humanness. But not Sonia Morales. She never leaves her "self" behind. She's out there fighting, asserting her personhood all the time.

Sonia Morales, a small, wiry, Hispanic mother of two boys, talks quickly, nervously, gesturing for added emphasis. Sonia is on welfare in order to complete her education. An extremely intelligent, articulate woman from the Bronx, she wanted to go to college after she graduated from high school, but her mother "did not want to waste money on it." She took a year-long secretarial course instead and then worked for three years as a secretary at a supermarket. After she married and had two children, she took a course at a local community college and discovered "Damn it, I'm a smart woman!" Just arranging babysitting and getting to classes was an incredible hassle, she recalls. She had to take two buses to bring the children to their grandmother's every day, run to classes, run back to the grandmother's, and then get the children home. But she felt it was well worth it, and after completing two years, she went on to a four-year college. At the community college, she feels, she got her "self-esteem"; her experience at the four-year college made her "feel like a human being."

During this period Sonia and her husband separated; consequently, the only way for her to continue school was to go on welfare. She remembers the caseworker who handled her initial application: "That bitch! I hated her with all my life!" Sonia had "dressed decently" and walked into the welfare center "like a human being, like a person" but found that "the workers only want to treat you like a nonperson." When she sat down, the worker turned to her and said, "That's an expensive blouse you're wearing." Sonia asked what that had to do with her application; the worker replied, "Nothing." The worker denied her application "on technical loopholes." She applied again, three times in all, and was rejected each time until she hired a lawyer who threatened to bring the case up for appeal.

She pays for college through scholarships and cannot even tell her caseworker that she is attending because it is against regulations for AFDC to support students in four-year programs. AFDC only provides aid for students in two-year or vocational schools. Many recipients and critics of the system feel that this is one of the most blatant examples of the AFDC policy of trying to keep the poor poor.

Although Sonia usually attends classes dressed in jeans and a casual sweater, she always "puts on decent clothes" to go to the welfare department. "I don't care how sick or exhausted I am, I always wash and set my hair and go in there looking like a human being. I will not play the role of a welfare recipient!"

While Elizabeth and Sonia have been describing the inadequacy and indignity of AFDC in the North, many professionals and recipients feel that being a welfare recipient in the South is the most difficult, the most degrading. As a social worker in Atlanta stated, "The South is always the worst, and in the South there is the Upper South and the Lower South, and the Lower South is the very worst." In Southern Georgia, for example, one day a month is designated for pickup of food stamps; if you miss that day, that's it. You have lost out on food stamps for the entire month.

According to Dorothy Johnson, a handsome, vibrant, articulate black social worker who lives and works in Atlanta, the counties in Georgia that are responsible for administering AFDC are like "little nations" and the client population is "very fearful." She continues: "Welfare is a political football all over this country. There is a need to adjust the welfare rules and to reform welfare policies all over the United States."

Shirley Trussell, director of the DeKalb County Family and Children Services in Georgia, reports that there has been a dramatic increase over the past year or two in requests for emergency aid, both among the new poor and among the chronic poor. She feels this increase stems from Georgia's "trimming the rolls," both the AFDC and the food stamp rolls. County workers can, however, give emergency aid to a family, but only one time. When asked what a family did if it had received emergency aid once and was in dire need again, one worker replied dryly, "Pray a lot."

Dorothy Johnson continued by talking about the new poor:

They will use all of their resources rather than go to welfare. They're not going to take that ugliness, that humiliation. Georgia will not give welfare to a two-parent family. These people are treated so badly that they would rather sell dope and steal instead.

She raises the question of whether the system is at fault or the caseworkers, and while she grants there is a problem with insensitive workers, she feels a great deal of the problem is with the regulations.

There is a one-and-a-half-hour set of questions to ask before someone can get on welfare, and these kinds of questions would take the Virgin Mary to make people not feel badly.

There is an insensitivity to poorness. Workers here are still looking in the refrigerator and looking for men's shoes. The system is mean. But a good worker has to convert a mean system. Caseworkers sit there and treat you like dirt. Somehow they've got to be humane.

Georgia, moreover, is one of the states that is currently using Workfare. According to Sandra Robertson, director of the Georgia Citizens' Coalition on Hunger, there was a big move to institute Workfare, a program that forces welfare recipients to work off their AFDC grants in all of Georgia's 159 counties, but it is currently being used in only eight counties. Recipients on Workfare receive "no added income and do not even get enough to live on," Robertson states with feeling. "The average grant for a family of three is $202 per month." She feels that the recipient gets nothing out of Workfare:

> The possibility of on-the-job training is a pretense because one only gets the most menial jobs—cooking, washing dishes, custodial work. If people do not get some training, their skills are not marketable. Workfare is not moving women from point A to points B or C. Workfare is abusive and exploitive of poor people. There is very little difference between workfare and slavery!

Many poor people survive only because they have a network of family and friends they can rely on when their money runs out, their food stamps run out, when they don't have a place to stay. In her moving autobiography, *I Know Why the Caged Bird Sings*, Maya Angelou describes this system of mutual aid in the black community: "Although there was always generosity in the Negro neighborhood, it was indulged on pain of sacrifice. Whatever was given by Black people to other Blacks was most probably needed as desperately by the donor as by the receiver. A fact which made the giving or receiving a rich exchange."[43]

Anthropologist Carol Stack, in her excellent book *All Our Kin*, documents the strategies for survival among poor blacks in a Midwestern city during the late 1960s. Facing a welfare system that simply did not provide enough money to live on, the families that Stack lived with and observed used a variety of techniques to get by—swapping, sharing, trading—both within family groups and among friends who functioned as kin. They often helped each other even at the cost of getting ahead themselves. Perhaps Ruby Banks, a young mother who became a close friend of Stack's, says it best:

> I don't believe in putting myself on nobody, but I know I need help every day. . . . I don't believe in begging but I believe that people should help one another. I used to wish for lots of things like a living room suite, clothes, nice clothes, stylish clothes—I'm sick of wearing the same pieces. But I can't, I can't help myself because I have my children and I love them and I have my mother and all our kin. Sometimes I don't have a damn dime in my pocket, not a crying penny to get a box of paper diapers, milk, a loaf of bread. But you have to have help from everybody and

anybody, so don't turn no one down when they come round for help.[44]

Ruby is expressing the ironic truth of survival among many poor groups—the individual cannot survive without the help and support of the group and, at the same time, the obligation to the group may prevent that same individual from moving up and out.

Vilma Coombs, a twenty-eight-year-old Brooklyn mother of four, talks about the survival techniques of the women she knows:

Nobody on welfare makes it without help. Help from their mother, from their father, from brothers or sisters. Everybody has different survival skills. What's wrong if I sit with my neighbor's child while she goes to school and she pays me $15? But according to the Welfare Department that's fraud.

Vilma goes on to describe how moving into a somewhat better neighborhood can deprive women of the mutual aid and emotional support that enables them to get by. During a particularly difficult period in her own life, she had a good friend, a female friend. "She was my support and I was her support. If I didn't have bread, she had some bread. If we didn't have bread, we'd make bread together." Recently her friend moved away and so did she. "Now if I don't have bread, I have to make do. Now I don't have those kinds of neighbors and that kind of support."

Elizabeth Cameron in the Bronx talks about the importance, the necessity of this kind of mutual aid. She describes a woman in her building who is on welfare and has a "minimum amount to live on. Her life is so bleak. I saw her going down to the corner and coming back with one quart of milk and I knew that she must not have money for anything else to eat, so I sent her some food stamps in the mail."

If Elizabeth knows someone is particularly needy, she buys groceries and takes them to her. She feels that God provides for everyone and that these small gestures will be repaid in time.

I've learned if you really want to help someone you just have to do it. You don't say, "If you ever need something call me," and all that crap. People are not going to ask for help. You just must offer it when you know they need it. I know a lot of good people and they help each other. Women who are living in poverty need those kinds of assistance.

Elizabeth summed up her philosophy by saying, "Everything I give comes back." Or as Ruby Banks put it, "Everything that goes round comes round. . . ."[45]

Cheryl Stewart in Atlanta practices the same kind of mutual aid. She is a black woman in her early thirties, the mother of six children. She also has five sisters and two brothers, and according to her, they all practice "sharing and caring." Recently when two sisters did not have any housing they had to move in with her, and for a time, twenty-two people were living in three rooms. They shared food, clothes, money, everything. This was the only way to survive. Cheryl says that if they don't help one another, they are "going to lose it all."

One of the key issues AFDC raises is whether the welfare system as it is currently organized promotes chronic dependency. There are many who say that it does. There are those who claim that young women become pregnant in order to qualify for AFDC and then use that money to set up their own households. There are those who claim that the benefits provided by AFDC are so minimal that it is virtually impossible for a family ever to get ahead. There are those who claim that just being a welfare recipient is so stigmatizing and debilitating that recipients take on a sense of fatalism, of hopelessness and powerlessness that robs them of the ability to do something else with their lives. And there are also those who say that AFDC is a system of state paternalism that seeks to control poor women's lives as familial paternalism once did. This analysis suggests that the welfare system is the latest form of social control over women, in this case over single women with children, and that the inevitable result is dependency.

There is substantial evidence, however, that the issue of welfare-induced dependency has been exaggerated. The study conducted by the University of Michigan's Institute for Social Research cited in Chapter 1 found that in half of the cases in which welfare—defined as AFDC; Supplemental Security Income; "other welfare," such as state-administered General Assistance and food stamps—was utilized between 1969 and 1978, it was "used only to bridge a process of digging out following some major crisis—a divorce, a job loss, or perhaps the death of a spouse." The process generally ends, according to the researchers, with a "new foothold in security: a part- or full-time job or, for some female household heads, marriage or remarriage."[46] The remaining half of recipients appear to belong to two categories: one of recipients who are using welfare to supplement income from other sources, and another of recipients who are essentially completely dependent on the welfare system.

For example, between 1969 and 1978, 25.2 percent of all Americans received one of these forms of welfare at some time. Of these, 12.3 percent received some form of welfare in one or two of the ten years, 8.5 percent received some form of welfare in three to seven of the ten years, and 4.4 percent, who were termed "persistent" welfare recipients, received some form of welfare in eight or more of the ten years. Of this 4.4 percent, only 2 percent received benefits that amounted to over half of the family's income in eight or more of the ten years.[47] The researchers did find that the overwhelming majority—four-fifths—of those persistently dependent on welfare were living in female-headed families and were more likely to be black than white. Furthermore, on the issue of intergenerational welfare dependency, the study found that "most adult children from welfare families were not receiving welfare income themselves, and most of the adults who were receiving welfare income did not come from welfare households."[48]

What do these data mean for the welfare-dependency issue and for social policy in general? First, it seems to indicate that at least half of all welfare recipients do not become chronically dependent on the system but rather use it to get through a difficult period. Of the remaining group, the data indicate that a significant percentage use welfare to supplement inadequate income; if that is dependency, perhaps we need to raise wages.

The final group, the "persistent" welfare recipient—only 4.4 percent of all Americans, less than 20 percent of welfare recipients—indeed seem to be chronically dependent on the system. It must be stressed, however, that the stereotype of the chronically dependent welfare recipient seems to be based on the actual experiences of a small minority of recipients. This does not mean that the issue is not a real one or that it does not need to be addressed; but it is only through understanding exactly who needs welfare benefits, and for how long, that we can develop a truly humane social policy.

What is truly remarkable, of course, is that these families survive at all: That these women can still plan and hope and struggle for a sense of dignity after being humiliated and degraded by a welfare system that maintains them in absolute poverty is a testament to their courage, their strength, their perseverance. Moreover, the technique of mutual aid, of "sharing and caring," that some poor families, particularly black families, have developed enables them not only to survive economically but provides some of the social and emotional support they so desperately need.

Few would deny that our welfare system, particularly Aid to Families with Dependent Children, needs to be fundamentally restructured. Other societies have developed very different techniques to provide for their mothers and children and to protect family life. In the final two chapters of this book we will look at some of these alternatives and explore ways in which the United States might develop a system that could actually lead to the real meaning of *welfare*—"good fortune," "happiness," and "well-being."

5

BUT WHERE ARE
THE MEN?

somebody almost run off wit alla my stuff/& I was standin
there/lookin at myself/the whole time & it waznt a spirit took
my stuff/waz a man whose ego walked round like Rodan's
shadow/was a man faster n my innocence/waz a lover/i made
too much room for/almost run off wit alla my stuff/& I didnt
know i'd give it up so quik/& the one running wit it/dont
know he got it/& i'm shoutin this is mine/& he dont know
he got it/my stuff is the anonymous ripped off treasure of
the year.[1]

—*Ntozake Shange*

Over and over as I interviewed women in different parts of the
country I heard stories of men walking out on women. Sometimes
the couple was young and had been together a short time, other
times they were middle-aged and had been together for many
years; but almost always, the man was the one who walked out—
often with little or no warning—and the woman and children
were left to cope as best they could. From the women of Maine
to the Native American families of New Mexico, I met mothers
and children trying to make it on their own and trying to deal
with their pain and anger.

Men are not always the ones who walk out, of course. Sometimes the women leave; sometimes the split is mutual; and sometimes the man was never really there. But whether because of divorce, separation, or not marrying at all, the grouping that remains is mothers with their children, children with their mothers. And where are the men? Some have simply vanished, gone on to other things. Others have started new families. Some feel that they cannot live up to their roles as fathers because they cannot live up to their roles as breadwinners.

Barbara Ehrenreich, in her recent book *The Hearts of Men*, claims that over the past thirty years American men have been fleeing from commitment to the family. She points out that in the 1950s "adult masculinity was indistinguishable from the breadwinner role...."[2] Gradually, according to Ehrenreich, the prodding of cultural forces such as *Playboy*—which encouraged, as one sociologist has described it, the "fun morality"—and the health profession's warning that the stress that came from the role as breadwinner could well lead to coronary heart disease encouraged men to drift more and more toward a commitment to self, toward "doing one's own thing," and away from the confines and conflicts of wife, children, mortgage, and the pressures of new shoes for the first day of school. As Ehrenreich states, "The result of divorce, in an overwhelming number of cases, is that men become singles and women become single mothers."[3]

While there is little doubt that much of Ehrenreich's analysis is valid, it is not the whole story. In the first place, her analysis is valid not just for men but for much of American society as a whole. The shift toward concern with self, with individual needs and desires, with personal growth, toward narcissism, has been widespread and is a result, I believe, of fundamental societal developments over the course of the twentieth century—urbanization, the changing nature of work, and the development of a consumer society.

Urbanization has, as is well known, been a major factor in the fragmentation of primary groups. The pressures, variety, and opportunities of the city, together with the anonymity it provides, have made it increasingly possible for individuals to shake off their obligations to others, to walk away without fear of censure from the "group," for there is hardly any group left. If family members are scattered, if there is no defined community, if there are no elders to censure, why not simply walk away from upsetting and restrictive commitments?

While urbanization was disrupting networks of community and kin, specialization was becoming the primary mode of work in twentieth-century America. As French sociologist Emile Durkheim pointed out nearly a hundred years ago, when societies are small and everyone does much the same kind of work, a "collective consciousness" develops based on similar socialization and shared experiences and values. When, however, each person does just one small piece of an overall task, and this task has little relationship to what others are doing, individualism is fostered. Durkheim predicted that such a division of labor and the resulting growth of individualism would lead to a breakdown in commitment to social norms, the situation Ehrenreich seems to be describing.[4] Add to urbanization and an extreme division of labor the pressures of a consumer society—in which we are systematically taught to believe that we are what we wear, what we own, what we buy; an unrelenting pressure to acquire new goods in order to redefine ourselves continually—and a social milieu develops in which individualism and self-gratification are rewarded, and commitment to others is devalued. That commitment is particularly constraining if it seems to diminish one's own options, one's own pleasures, one's own "personal growth."

And, of course, men are not the only ones who have been affected by these profound changes in American society. Women, and specifically those in the women's movement, have been affected by the emphasis on individualism, by the increasing legitimacy of individual needs and aspirations, of individual happiness. If "We Shall Overcome" was the anthem of the 1960s, perhaps Madonna sings the anthem of the 1980s in her song "Material Girl."[5]

It is striking, however, that while many women are concerned with the quality of their lives, with their own development and careers, with their "material world," they remain, as Ehrenreich correctly points out, the primary caregivers for their children. While many men have abdicated their parental responsibilities, women for the most part have not.

Part of the explanation of women's special relationship to their children lies, clearly, in the special nature of the mothering role, with the bonding that takes place in utero and then during the first few weeks and months of an infant's life, and the ongoing intimate relationship women continue to have with children. But another part of the explanation of the male ability to avoid the responsibilities of fatherhood may well lie in the nature of the fathering role in our society. Is the role of father such that it produces a lack of genuine involvement with children, a lack of real connectedness? Are the majority of fathers simply expected to bring home a paycheck and occasionally to throw a baseball around—and is this kind of relationship just too tenuous to bind men to their children? With the increasing erosion of the patriarchal role, we must develop an equally meaningful way for men to relate to their children.

Profound class differences exist in the ways men relate to their families today. The models written up on the women's pages of leading newspapers—of men trying to take paternity leave, of "househusbands," of a recent best-seller in which a father lyrically describes the first year of his daughter's life—are those of relatively few, usually highly educated, upper-middle-class men. While a fair number of men near Columbia University or in Harvard Square or in Berkeley may lovingly carry their babies in Snugglies, it is hardly a common sight at the entrance to auto plants, in accounting firms, or among men who hang out on the streetcorners of urban ghettos. Clearly behavior that is encouraged and rewarded in one segment of the upper middle class is considered unacceptable in much of the rest of the country; until the perceptions and values and norms of the larger society change, we cannot rationally expect individual behavior to alter significantly.

The bottom line of the male flight from commitment, of many fathers' lack of involvement with their children and, above all, of economic factors usually beyond the individual's control, is that the majority of men who are not living with their wives and children are also not supporting them. The issue of child support has received considerable attention over the past few years because of the unprecedented increase in the number of female-headed families during the 1970s. The importance of child support to the economic well-being of mothers and children is underscored by women's low earning ability. According to a Working Paper published by the Wellesley College Center for Research on Women, women "with the sole custody of children experience the most severe decline in family income."[6] A spring 1982 Census Bureau survey found that over 8 million women are raising at least one child whose father is absent from the home. Of these 8 million women, only 5 million had been awarded child support by the courts. Of the women who were supposed to be receiving payments in 1981, 47 percent received the full amount, 37 percent received less than half of what they were supposed to receive, and 28 percent received no payments at all.[7] Ironically, the women most likely to receive court-ordered child support are "educated, employed, divorced women" rather than separated, never married, minority women.[8] The average annual child-support payment in 1981 was $2,180 for white women, $2,070 for Hispanic women, and $1,640 for black women.[9]

Why don't men pay child support more regularly? Some men withhold payment in reaction to the bitterness of a divorce, some as a way of protesting what they feel is an unfair financial settlement, and some because they want to use their money to recapture the sense of being single, of being free.

Betty Levinson, a New York lawyer who devotes approximately one-third of her practice to matrimonial law, feels that in most divorce cases she sees there is simply not enough money to support two households. These families, mostly middle and upper middle class, are "premised on plastic." Often these couples cannot afford to separate; both husbands and wives must learn to "trim their expectations in planning for their lives after divorce."

On the issue of nonsupport Levinson feels that many men would rather pay for a lawyer than support their children. She suggests that one scenario is: "Now that it's over I can't deal with you anymore. You represent a failure for me and therefore I don't want to deal with the kids either because I associate the kids with the failed marriage and with you." Another scenario is that the man has remarried and is supporting his new wife and her children who, in turn, are not being supported by their father. Part of the message such a man gives to his former wife is, "When you took custody you took responsibility." The fathers who say this, according to Levinson, are frequently men who do not see their kids very often, because they live in another state or for some other reason.

The third scenario involves the father who sees his kids, but mainly for Sunday visits. According to Betty Levinson, "It's incredible the kind of money these fathers will spend on these weekly visits—theater, ski trips, and so forth—but they resist giving more in the way of child support. Often the father's feeling is, 'Yes, I understand that the child needs this now, but I have to think of my future.' The ultimate responsibility for the children," she states flatly, "is with the mother. No matter what happens, the mother takes care of the children."

Researchers and activists, both those who work for more stringent child-support legislation and spokespersons on behalf of men's groups, agree that the payment of child support is often tied to the altered parent–child relationship. Researchers have found that after divorce fathers often experience a loss of identity, a loss of status within the family, and a "particularly poignant sense of loss associated with the altered father–child relationship. The divorced father is no longer part of the day-to-day life of the child, but is abruptly relegated to a visitor status. . . . Many fathers cope by distancing themselves from the parent–child relationship."[10] What better way to do this than by withholding financial support?

James A. Cook, president of the National Congress for Men, a four-year-old coordinating group of 125 men's rights organizations with ten thousand members, also ties the problem of economic support to fathers' lack of access to their children. He asks, "Can we levy responsibility on these fathers without an equivalent right, the right of access to the child?"[11] John A. Rossler of the Equal Rights for Fathers of New York State agrees: "Many men have had to beg for access to their children. The system of divorce in America often results in the removing of all fathering functions save for one, the monetary obligation. A man is more than a wallet to his kids."[12] Rossler and other representatives of men's groups strongly endorse custody reform: "Whether you call it joint custody, shared custody, liberal visitation or co-parenting, we are talking about actively involving the noncustodial parent in all areas of his child's upbringing."[13]

Betty Levinson, on the other hand, feels that joint custody is a very "trendy" issue; it is thought to be "the thing to do." She claims that men are made to feel that if they do not demand joint custody that they are not the fathers they should be. But it is, she points out, a very difficult arrangement. The husband and wife must cooperate extremely well for it to work. She goes on to state emphatically:

> Joint custody becomes an economic bludgeon on the wife by the husband. Asking for joint custody or trying to take custody away from the mother is a surefire way to freak out the mother. And after they have freaked her out, the father and his lawyer will often say, "Okay, you take 75 percent of our financial agreement instead of 100 percent and I'll give you full custody." It has become a way of negotiating the money.

On August 16, 1984, a comprehensive bill to enforce payment of child support became federal law. Approved by unanimous roll-call votes in both houses of Congress, the new law requires child-support orders issued or modified after October 1, 1985, to permit the withholding of wages if a parent becomes delinquent in payments and enables states to " 'require that an absent parent give security, post a bond, or give some other guarantee' " to ensure final payment of child support in cases where there has been a pattern of delinquency.[14] This law is a significant victory for those groups that have been advocating more stringent regulations and collection methods to improve the rate of payment of child support.

But voluntary nonpayment of child support is clearly only one facet of the problem of the absent father. Many fathers provide little or no support—either in economic or emotional terms—to their children and to the children's mothers because they are unable to play the traditional fathering role, that of breadwinner. In January 1983 approximately 12 million people, over 10 percent of the American work force, were actively looking for jobs and were the officially designated unemployed. While that number has since fallen to 7.2 percent, this stark figure, the highest rate since the Great Depression, has stimulated additional studies on the physiological, psychological, and sociological aspects of unemployment.

First, it must be pointed out that federal unemployment statistics significantly minimize the problem of unemployment. Figures released by the Bureau of Labor Statistics do not include those who reluctantly move from full-time to part-time employment; those who take jobs well below their skill level; those who must move from one temporary, low-paying job to the next; and those who become "permanently discouraged" and stop looking for work altogether. Nor do the statistics, as one researcher has movingly written, "reflect the anxiety, depression, deprivation, lost opportunities, violence, insecurity, and anger people feel when their source of livelihood is severed and they lose control of a significant aspect of their environment."[15] As Paula Rayman, sociologist and director of the New England Unemployment Project, has written, "When an adult has work taken away, the focus of life's daily pattern is removed. Time and space, the sense of self, are radically altered, and what is left is a sense of impotency."[16]

The work of Johns Hopkins sociologist and epidemiologist Harvey Brenner demonstrates the dramatic effect unemployment has on the entire family's health and well-being. Brenner has found, for example, that admissions to psychiatric hospitals, deaths from cardiovascular and alcohol-related illnesses, homicide and suicide rates increase significantly during peiods of economic decline.[17] Other researchers have found that male unemployment is associated with high blood pressure, alcoholism, increased smoking, insomnia, anxiety, and higher levels of psychiatric symptoms among men. In addition, "The wives in unemployed families were significantly more depressed, anxious, phobic, and sensitive about their interpersonal relationships" than spouses in families in which there is no unemployment.[18] The longer the period of unemployment, the greater the stress on the family and on family cohesion. In a study of the unemployed in Hartford, Rayman and Ramsey Liem found three times as much marital separation among the unemployed group as among the control group.[19]

Clinical observations of unemployed people who go to social agencies for counseling indicate that they are coping with feelings of loss, anger, and guilt—a "sense of losing a part of the self." Observers have likened these feelings to feelings of bereavement. Studies find that people anticipating or experiencing unemployment "suffer loss of self-esteem, loss of personal identity, worry and uncertainty about the future, loss of a sense of purpose, and depression."[20] With these reactions to unemployment, is it any wonder that family stability is being undermined?

While there has been a limited economic recovery since the height of the 1982–1983 recession, many workers' incomes have declined sharply since the late 1970s. For example, the average income of workers laid off by the United States Steel Corporation's South Works in Chicago has fallen in the last five years by 50 percent. Over two thousand workers were laid off from 1979 to 1981, and another thirty-three hundred were laid off from 1981 to 1983. Many of these workers have had long periods of unemployment; 46 percent remained unemployed as of October 1984. The laid-off workers, whose annual household income averaged $22,000 in 1979, had a median household income in 1983 of approximately $12,500. According to one worker, "To go from earning $20,000-plus to being at an employer's mercy for $3.35 an hour is devastating."[21] Moreover, unskilled workers and black and Hispanic male workers have extremely limited opportunities for work and suffer from the highest unemployment rates. In a 1983 study of the New York City job market, it was found that the decline in manufacturing and the expansion of the service sector have led to a decrease in job opportunities in the city for workers with few skills and limited education. Of all adults, black and Hispanic men twenty-five to thirty-four years old "generally do the worst in the job market": They experience extended periods of unemployment, withdraw from the labor force because they become "discouraged," and have a high rate of involuntary part-time work. Moreover, among blacks and Hispanics, the length of unemployment for men is twice what it is for women: for black men, twenty-seven weeks; for black women, twelve weeks; for Hispanic men, twenty-two weeks; for Hispanic women, nine weeks.[22]

Nationally, unemployment among blacks is officially twice the rate for whites, but the statistics tell only part of the story. Researchers at the Center for the Study of Social Policy claim that the true figure is that 4 million out of 9 million working-age black men—46 percent—are jobless. For white men the comparable figure is 22 percent.[23] Unemployment of this magnitude must have a dramatic impact on family stability and therefore be a major cause of the feminization of poverty. In 1960, according to this method of calculation, approximately three-quarters of all black men were employed; today only 54 percent are employed. Since 1960 the number of black families headed by women has more than tripled.[24] There is little question that the unemployment of black men has had a direct impact on the rise of black female-headed families.

Furthermore, unemployment is only one of many severe problems black men must face. The National Urban League recently released a report stating that black men must deal with a "singular series of pressures from birth through adulthood." The report stated, "The gantlet that black men run takes its toll at every age." In addition to the problems of educational and employment discrimination, Dr. James McGhee, the league's research director, cited higher mortality rates, greater likelihood of being arrested, and the rising incidence of self-destructive behavior such as drug and alcohol abuse. Black men have the highest death rates from accidents and violence of all groups, and their suicide rate has risen far more sharply in recent years than that of white men.[25] In addition, homicide is the leading cause of death for black males ages fifteen to forty-four. Black men represent only 5 percent of the U.S. population but represent 44 percent of its homicide victims.[26] Many studies suggest that there is a direct correlation between feelings of frustration, powerlessness, and hopelessness and high rates of violence. According to sociologist and researcher on black families Andrew Billingsley, because of racial discrimination, many black men are distant from "any meaningful engagement with the economy, education and the social system."[27]

Elliot Liebow, in what has become a classic study of streetcorner black men in Washington, DC, points out the close connection between a man's work and his relationships with family and friends: "The way in which the man makes a living and the kind of living he makes have important consequences for how the man sees himself and is seen by others; and these, in turn, importantly shape his relationships with family members, lovers, friends and neighbors."[28] Liebow points out that the unskilled black man has little chance of obtaining a permanent job that would pay enough to support a family. He eventually becomes resigned to being unable to play the traditional father role, and rather than being faced with his own failure day after day, year after year, he often walks away.

Ironically, the children with whom these men are closest are not those they have fathered and therefore have an obligation to support; but rather the children of the women they are currently seeing, who have been fathered by someone else. With someone else's children, whatever the men can give in the way of financial or emotional support is more than they need to give, and it therefore represents a positive gesture rather than yet another failure.[29]

What is saddest about these dismal facts is how American ideology, which is apparently accepted by the majority of Americans and has been legitimized by the Reagan administration, blames the poor, rather than racism and the economic system, for their plight. While some of these issues were briefly addressed during the 1960s, the War on Poverty was woefully inadequate to reverse the damage done, particularly to blacks, in our society; and no sooner did it get started than Vietnam, inflation, and the Nixon administration had begun to subvert it. As Michael Harrington has so aptly stated, "The savior that never was became the scapegoat that is."[30]

American policymakers have an uncanny ability to obfuscate and compartmentalize social problems—to recognize on the one hand that the United States has an unacceptably high level of unemployment, particularly among specific groups, and to recognize that we also have an incredibly high number of female-headed families, particularly within the same groups; but to avoid the cause-and-effect relationship between the two phenomena. This unwillingness to recognize the obvious correlation between the lack of economic opportunities for millions of American men—a lack of opportunity that will consign them, in all likelihood, for their entire lifetimes to the bottom of the class structure—and their lack of commitment to and steady participation in family life, is a shocking denial of the obvious impact of social and economic factors on the well-being of the family group.

As Eleanor Holmes Norton, former chairperson of the Equal Employment Opportunity Commission and currently a professor at the Georgetown University Law Center, has stated:

This permanent, generational joblessness is at the core of the meaning of the American ghetto. The resulting, powerful aberration transforms life in poor black communities and forces everything else to adapt to it. The female-headed household is only one consequence. The underground economy, the drug culture, epidemic crimes and even a highly unusual disparity between the actual number of men and women—all owe their existence to the cumulative effect of chronic joblessness among men.[31]

This avoidance has several advantages for those who seek to maintain the status quo in the United States: It discourages those at the bottom from developing a viable political and economic analysis of the American system, instead promoting a blame-the-victim mentality; a false consciousness of individual unworthiness, of self-blame; a belief that if only the individual worked harder, tried harder, he would "make it" and be the success every American thinks he should be. Not only does the unemployed male blame himself for not getting and keeping a decent job, thereby being unable to provide for his family in the way he would like, but the woman may also blame him. As one woman in *Tally's Corner* says with a bitter smile, "I used to lean on Richard. Like when I was having the baby, I leaned on him but he wasn't there and I fell down. . . . Now, I don't lean on him anymore. I pretend I lean, but I'm not leaning."[32] Or the woman blames herself for not choosing her man more wisely, for not holding the family together despite the odds, for being either too assertive or not assertive enough. And yet virtually no one blames an economic system that deprives millions of workers of jobs and then somehow indicates it is their fault.

Sandra Wittaker, a black woman from California who is raising her two children alone puts it this way:

Black men are able to cope far less than black women. They are feared more by society and therefore have far fewer opportunities. All the men I have known, my brothers, my father, my male friends, my husband, have not made it in society. Many of them take to drinking and dope—some kind of escape. Black males are suffering far more than females.

My son has had three role models and none of them were any

good. He has not had a mature man to model himself on. . . . He has nightmares. He's afraid of being a failure and he's already opted out. By the time he was four, my son did not even want to be black. It is terrible to watch your child and know that he is going to be hurt constantly.

If there is a group that has been hit even harder than blacks, it is Native Americans. Unemployment among the 1 million American Indians is said to range between 45 and 55 percent, but it reaches 80 percent in some areas and in some seasons.[33]

Among the Pueblo Indians who live approximately sixty miles southwest of Albuquerque, New Mexico, for example, the unemployment rate is 70 percent. After the nearby uranium mines were closed in 1981–1982, there were no other jobs available. According to Jean Eller, a young physician who worked at the Acoma Canoncita Laguna Indian Health Hospital in Acoma, New Mexico, people now just "hang around." There is nothing for them to do. And the young people are torn between their desire to find a job in a nearby town or city and pressure from their elders to return to the reservation. The elders are afraid the young people will lose touch with their culture if they move off the reservation, but there are few opportunities there, either.

Tied to the unemployment rate, Dr. Eller believes, is an enormous problem with alcohol and a suicide rate that is the highest of any ethnic group in the country. Alcohol is mainly a male problem; some of the younger women drink, but the older women usually do not. According to Dr. Eller, there are three bars, run by non-Indians, near the reservation. One bar half a mile from the reservation serves "all the beer you can drink" free on Monday nights. These bars serve thirteen-year-olds, fourteen-year-olds and never check their ID's. "Many people hate these places and would like to blow them up!" Dr. Eller states quietly but angrily. She feels the significant amount of wife abuse that exists on these reservations is directly related to the amount of drinking, particularly on the weekends.

According to other medical personnel who work in the area, women are the backbone of the Indian family. Many feel that men have fallen apart more than women and are in a "cycle of destruction." The rates of alcoholism, wife abuse, child neglect, homicide, and suicide are at least three to four times the national rate.

There is also a high rate of teenage pregnancy, particularly among girls fifteen and under. The men rarely support their children, and some women move up and out of the reservation; many are, in fact, ostracized by their communities for doing so. The infant is then often cared for by the grandmother and brought up with the grandmother's own children as siblings. Indian women are clearly not first-class citizens even within Indian culture but they have very little recourse since the tribal councils are largely run by men.

The reservation in Acoma is in the middle of incredibly beautiful terrain. As you approach Acoma, the earth varies from beige to darker shades of brown, sometimes flat, sometimes hilly, with stark red clay rock formations that look almost like amphitheaters. Acoma is famous for handsome pottery, much of it black, white, and clay-reddish brown; several of the potters from this reservation sell to private collectors, some to museums. Mt. Taylor, snowcapped even in late spring, can be seen in the distance. Amid this truly splendid scenery, the reservation seems unbearably barren and depressed. During the day there is hardly a man to be seen. There are only women, children, and dogs—scrawny, hungry-looking dogs who roam near the houses.

Lena Ross is a heavyset woman with a weathered face and dark hair pulled back at the nape of her neck. She has moved within the past few days to a modern adobe-colored house in a settlement of new homes, most of which are still empty. The house has several bedrooms furnished with beds and colorful quilts and blankets, a kitchen with the latest in modern appliances, and a large, empty living room.

Ten of Lena Ross's thirteen children and her two grandchildren live with her. She has no husband. "I take care of the children myself," she tells me. She receives AFDC for the children who are still in school, and social security for the grandchildren. While we talk, her one-and-a-half-year-old grandson sits on his grandmother's lap. He is a lively boy with long, dark hair and beautiful dark eyes. He is wearing a good-looking blue-and-white-striped shirt and is playing with a small car. Through the living room window is a picture-postcard view of Mt. Taylor.

While some of these families' material needs are being met, there is an overriding sense of hopelessness, of being caught in a net not of their own making, and from which they cannot get free. For they know, as a CBS news report stated succinctly, "Their destiny is in the hands of strangers."[34] The juxtaposition of the new, modern house and this immovable hopelessness is profoundly disturbing.

Mary Sanchez is a thirty-six-year-old mother of five. Her oldest child is seventeen, her youngest ten. Her seventeen-year-old sister is also living with her; she finished only the eighth grade and has two children, one four and one ten months old. In addition, Mary's oldest daughter has a ten-month-old who also lives there, and one of her brothers lives with her as well. In all, eleven people live in a small wooden house off of a small dirt road; Mary's parents live next door.

Mary and most of the children are on welfare and receive food stamps. The two youngest, the ten-month-old babies, are not on welfare because the welfare worker said she wanted to force the fathers to pay for their upkeep. Mary told the worker to forget it.

Both of the men who fathered her children are dead. The first died of natural causes, but the second, the father of four of her children, died while hitchhiking with another man and two women. "They all must have been drunk," she says simply, "and weaving down the street. A gas truck was coming along and swerved to avoid hitting them. The truck turned over and exploded and all four were burned to death. When relatives went to claim the body, they couldn't tell who it was."

The entire time we talked, a soap opera was on in the background, an intricate melodrama of well-dressed upper-middle-class Anglos lulling these women and their children through the day. The women do not seem despairing but rather fatalistic. When I asked if it was hard for them to manage, they said they managed. When I asked what could be done to make things better, they couldn't think of a thing. It feels as though it takes everything they've got just to get from day to day.

6

DAY CARE: DO WE REALLY CARE?

Child development advocates stress that what the nation saves by skimping on child care today may seriously harm many individuals and later cost the society much in remedial health, education, penal, welfare, and manpower training bills. . . . The early childhood years comprise one-tenth of humans' lives, and the dignity, respect, and well-being with which persons can live during those years should be of concern to all.[1]

—*Pamela Roby*

Day care is one of those murky issues on which many Americans do not really know where they stand. Are we for it or against it? Is it good for children or harmful to them? Will it facilitate their social and intellectual development or undermine their emotional well-being? Is it perhaps somewhat "un-American" for a mother to leave her child during the first few years of life? That is what the Russians, the Chinese, and the Swedes do; is that what we want to do? Why do we seem so very ambivalent about this important topic?

Although one child-care specialist has recently stated, "Day care has become as American as apple pie and baseball,"[2] the facts do not confirm her optimistic statement. Not only have funds for day care been cut back over the past four years but, perhaps even more importantly, the rhetoric of the Reagan administration and its allies has undermined public perception of the need for day care by nostalgically recalling and mythologizing another era—perhaps the 1950s, more likely the 1920s—and longingly trying to recapture it.

In this image of small-town America, we are led to believe that father went to work every morning and returned home every evening to hugs and shouts of joy, that mother had hot cocoa and homemade cookies ready for well-behaved children returning from school, and that in case of an emergency grandmother was down the block, only too glad to help out when needed. Children set up lemonade stands on tree-lined streets, large families gathered for Thanksgiving dinner, and friends of long standing were available to provide mutual aid and support in times of hardship—perhaps a scene out of a Jimmy Stewart movie, with everything working out just fine in the end. There is little evidence that this Norman Rockwell image of America ever existed except, possibly, for a limited number of middle- and upper-middle-class families; it surely is not the reality of today. But this image, this rhetoric, has been used by an administration that has tried, and succeeded to a remarkable extent, in removing supports from families under the guise that they will be encouraged to return to an idyllic Never-Never Land.

Other voices, from other viewpoints, also attack day care. Recent allegations of sexual abuse of children by workers in day-care centers in California and New York have shocked parents, professionals, and the public. These incidents highlight a critical problem that has existed in American society for many years: The flagrant disregard for the well-being of children resulting in the absence of a responsible, coherent child-care policy.

First let it be said that thousands of child-care workers across the United States are providing excellent, loving, imaginative care for children, often under extremely difficult circumstances. Reports of various forms of abuse of children in day-care centers are, however, not new. Each time such a report surfaces, it is greeted with headlines, shocked pronouncements by politicians, and sanctimonious editorials, all of which are forgotten as soon as the headlines fade.

Marion Blum, educational director of the Wellesley College Child Study Center, has recently written a powerful critique of day care. She points out that in our extraordinarily materialistic society, children are viewed as things, as commodities around which others can make a profit. She rightly condemns such equipment as cage-like cribs, harnesses and leashes that treat children as though they were animals rather than humans in order to minimize the number of caretakers and to maximize profits.[3] She points out that because of the high turnover of preschool teachers, and the fact that teachers work shifts that may not coincide with the children's hours at the center, children must relate to a variety of adults during their day-care experience. She points out that eight hours or more is a long time for a three- or four-year-old to be away from home and to be required, for the most part, to behave according to preset schedules.[4] She and others have pointed out the difficulties for overworked caregivers trying to maintain proper sanitation, particularly in younger age groups in which the children may not be toilet trained. She points out the higher rates of colds, flu, diarrhea, and even hepatitis A in children who attend day-care centers.[5]

Finally, Blum notes that day care has involved a "transfer of roles from one group of exploited women—mothers—to another group of exploited women—day-care staff."[6] Day-care workers are among the lowest paid adult wage earners in our society, with little or no opportunity for advancement, little or no prestige, and very little in the way of benefits. According to the Children's Defense Fund, "Two out of three center-based caregivers earn below poverty level wages and 87 percent of family day-care workers earn below the minimum wage."[7] The status of preschool teachers clearly indicates the lack of value we place on women and children in our society.

Why is day care so inadequate in the United States? Why is it so exploitive of children, of day-care workers, of the parents themselves who often have no other choice? Is it because day care is seen as "nonproductive" in a society so geared to materialism and productivity? Is it because it serves the needs of two groups—women and children—who are particularly powerless? Is it because in a system not committed to full employment, decision-makers really do not want women in the labor force possibly taking jobs away from men? Is it because many, particularly people in positions of power, want to maintain the patriarchal family, and day care is seen as a force undermining that power relationship? A brief look at the history of day care in the United States may provide some insights into some of these issues.

Part of the hostility, or at best ambivalence, toward day care in this country arises from the fact that it has always been perceived as a service for the poor. Day care began in the United States in 1854 with the establishment of the Nursery for Children of Poor Women in New York City. This and other early day nurseries, as they were called, were modeled after the French crèche, a form of care for the children of working mothers founded in Paris in 1844. The crèche, a response to the increased number of French women working in factories, was also used to improve the health of infants and children and to lower the infant mortality rate. Mothers breastfed their infants in the crèches and were taught methods of hygienic child care. In 1862 crèches received official recognition, and regulations were issued that had to be met in order for the crèches to receive government subsidy.[8]

Day nurseries in the United States received no such official recognition. Most were sponsored by churches, settlement houses, or voluntary social agencies. Their goals were "to prevent child neglect during a mother's working hours and to eliminate the need to place children of destitute parents in institutions. They served an underprivileged group, handicapped by family problems."[9]

The nursery school, on the other hand, evolved out of a middle-class concern that children be given an early childhood educational experience. The first cooperative nursery school in the United States was organized in 1915 by a group of University of Chicago faculty wives in order "to offer an opportunity for wholesome play for their children [and] to give the mothers certain hours of leisure from child care. . . ."[10] A far cry from the goals of the day nurseries— no one talked about hours of leisure for poor women!

Nursery schools, influenced by educational pioneers such as Maria Montessori and models such as Robert Owen's infant school in Scotland, were to have an impact on the development of day care; but the two streams remained fundamentally separate. In fact, according to one observer, "In general . . . the day nursery was regarded with a kind of contempt by nursery school people, and the relationship between the two institutions was not always smooth."[11]

Day care grew rapidly during the depression of the 1930s when nursery schools were financed by the Federal Emergency Relief Administration and then by the Works Progress Administration (WPA). In 1933 President Roosevelt authorized the establishment of nursery schools to care for "children of needy, unemployed families or neglected or underprivileged homes where preschool age children will benefit from the program offered."[12] All personnel, including teachers, nurses, cooks, clerical workers, and janitors, were to come from relief rolls. By 1937 the centers were serving forty thousand children; this effort is still considered by professionals to have provided excellent care, including health care and nutrition, as well as education.[13]

But day care really expanded during World War II, when women now essential to the war effort entered the labor force in large numbers. While the U.S. War Manpower Commission stated in 1942 that "the first responsibility of women, in war as in peace, is to give suitable care in their own homes to their children," the Community Facilities Act (the Lanham Act) passed in June of the same year provided the federal resources necessary to establish day care for the children of working mothers. During this period the federal government spent $51,922,977, matched by $26,008,839 from the states, to fund 3,102 centers that cared for 600,000 children. Though this effort was a significant one, it has been estimated that these centers only served approximately 40 percent of the children in need.[14]

World War II was also a time for innovation in day care. The Kaiser Shipbuilding Corporation in Portland, Oregon, for example, opened two centers at the entrance to each shipyard. The Kaiser centers, which were open twelve months a year, twenty-four hours a day, attempted to meet the mothers' needs as well as care for their children. The services provided included shopping for the mothers, mending clothing, caring for children with minor illnesses, and providing "carry-out dinners at low cost to parents who worked long hours."[15] But at the end of the war, when the shipyards closed, the centers closed with them. What this experience indicates, of course, is that when the United States as a society makes day care a priority, it can provide high quality, imaginative services that provide for the needs of children and their parents.

Following the war, when women were encouraged to leave their jobs and to return home so that returning veterans could move into existing jobs, the "Lanham centers" were closed in every state but California, where due to the availability of state funds they remained open.[16] In the late 1940s and 1950s, a period noted for its conservatism, particularly its political conservatism, women were encouraged to remain at home and to devote themselves to their children and to homemaking. Moreover, women across the country found themselves increasingly isolated and confined to homogeneous communities by the postwar migration to the suburbs. Hand-in-hand with their geographical isolation was the confinement to home and to the role of mother that stemmed from the wave of popular psychology loosely based on Freudian thinking. Mothers were cautioned that their toddlers would be forever maimed emotionally if they were not toilet trained just right, if separation anxiety got out of hand, or if sibling rivalry was not handled with appropriate sensitivity. The newest version of the domestic code, or the role of supermom, as it was now called, was in its heyday!

Nevertheless, the number of working mothers continued to rise. In 1940, 1.5 million mothers were in the labor force; by 1950, there were 4.6 million. By 1959, approximately 7 million mothers were working outside of the home, and there were day-care facilities available for only 2.4 percent of their children.[17] The message was clear: when American society needed women in the labor force, it provided day care for their children; when it wanted women to remain at home, day care was virtually eliminated.

The 1960s was a decade of significantly increased federal funds for preschool care but "in a pattern calculated to reinforce an already segregated system of services—public day care for the poor, private nursery schools or child-care centers for the affluent, and potluck for those families who fell in neither category."[18] The 1960s—a time of economic prosperity that encouraged women to seek jobs in the labor force; a time of heightened concern about the poor that led to the War on Poverty; a time of political activism centering on civil rights, women's rights, welfare rights, and, of course, the Vietnam war—was also a time of increased concern about day care. In a series of amendments to Title V of the Social Security Act in 1962, day care was defined for the first time as a public child-welfare service. The goal of day care was "to provide adequately for the care and protection of children whose parents are, for part of the day, working or seeking work, or otherwise absent from the home or unable for other reasons to provide parental supervision."[19] Placing day care in a child-welfare context assured that it would be perceived primarily as a service for the poor and near poor, as well as for families with special problems, such as child abuse and neglect. According to one observer:

> In statements about day care standards emanating from the Child Welfare League of America and from the U.S. Children's Bureau, the working mother was lumped together with a variety of pathological conditions and defined as a problem. In those statements day care was never discussed as a service for normal children from normal homes.[20]

In 1967, in an effort to reduce public assistance rolls, day care was further tied to welfare by amendments to the Social Security Act that linked it to the Work Incentive Now (WIN) program. Day care was expanded to include children of the working poor and "became virtually embedded in public assistance."[21]

Project Head Start, developed at the same time, was a multidisciplinary program created to give children from "disadvantaged" backgrounds a comprehensive program of education, medical care, and social services; it utilized many aspects of educational philosophy that had previously benefited children in nursery schools. It also incorporated the strategies that were developed during the 1960s which encouraged people's involvement in their own services. Community representatives and parents became actively involved in day care for the first time; and while many of the Head Start programs were models of what many professionals thought preschool care should be, Head Start further stigmatized day care as a program for the poor, the near poor, the disadvantaged, those with "problems."

Limiting day care to those disadvantaged groups, while the middle and upper middle classes are able to purchase care for their children, places the working-class parent in an almost intolerable bind. The working-class mother often can neither qualify for day care nor afford to place her child in a private setting. Since the two-parent working-class family is often just surviving economically, usually because of the wife's income, what are they to do about child care if there is no relative available? One option that some are driven to is deceiving the day-care center, a solution that takes a great toll on the parents, on the center and, ultimately, on the child.

Maria Perez is a small, slim woman in her late thirties who came to this country from Colombia when she was twenty-one. She works in the mornings as a floor secretary in a large teaching hospital in the Bronx. The hospital is within a few blocks of her home and near the day-care center attended by her two younger children. Her husband is a commercial artist in the catalogue department of a large department store and, for a time, worked a second job. Working two jobs meant that her husband left the house at seven o'clock in the morning and did not return until twelve or one in the morning. According to his wife, "He never saw his children except on weekends." The oldest child has just completed first grade at a local parochial school.

Mrs. Perez has struggled long and hard to get where she is now. She had graduated from high school in Bogotá with a degree in literature and philosophy, but because she knew practically no one and knew no English at all when she arrived in this country, she took a job in a factory sewing by hand and later as a bus girl in a Horn and Hardart cafeteria. After learning typing at night school, she worked for a taxi company for five years. When she became pregnant with her first child, she stopped working and did not plan to return to work until her youngest child entered first grade. But her husband was laid off his second job and could not find another; at this time, when her youngest child was eighteen months old, she felt she had to go back to work. She went first to Manpower, a private training program, to study Speedwriting and to brush up on her typing and her English. She describes what happened next:

When I got finished with the Manpower program I tried to get my children into a day care center so that I could go to work. My counselor at Manpower and I—we tried four or five day care centers but my income was too high. You know it's terrible the way the society has things set up so that if you make a little money you can't get into programs. You have to be on welfare or you have to be separated in order to get into a day care center, and my counselor, he told me that what I had to do was I had to say that I was separated. I had to put my husband out of my life and I had to tell them that he only gave me sixty dollars a week. He only gave me twenty or thirty dollars more than that a week, really.

So he called up the day care center for me and told them that I was separated and what my husband gave me. I couldn't do it myself because I was shaking too much.

If Maria Perez had told the day-care center her true income, she would have had to pay $50 per week per child and then, according to her, ''I would be paying much more than I was making. It would be impossible. We need for my husband to work and for me to work in order to live a decent life.''

Ultimately, the head of the day-care center discovered that Mr. and Mrs. Perez were not separated. Maria Perez felt humiliated and had to take her children out of the center since she could no longer afford to keep them there. She feels extremely critical of people who go on welfare when perhaps they could work, and she resents the fact that they qualify for day care when she, who is working so hard, does not.

You know, there should be free day care centers just as there are free schools for older children. If you go to high school nobody asks if you're married or single or how much you earn. It's free and it's for everybody. There should be day care from three or four years on for everybody even if you're not on welfare.[22]

When Richard Nixon vetoed the 1971 Comprehensive Child Care Act, the number of employed mothers in the United States exceeded 12 million. One-third of all mothers with preschool children—4.5 million women—were in the labor force, leaving some

6 million children in need of care. Less than 10 percent, or approximately 625,000 children, were being cared for in licensed centers in 1970.[23] In summer 1970 the National Council of Jewish Women began a study of day care in the United States. Council members in all parts of the country visited 431 licensed and unlicensed centers that cared for approximately 24,000 children.[24] They interviewed day-care workers, working and nonworking mothers, but above all they observed the conditions under which children were spending their days. Their findings are particularly revealing, for they indicate both how good and how bad day care can be in this country.

Using standardized materials prepared by Mary Dublin Keyserling, former director of the Woman's Bureau, an agency within the U.S. Department of Labor mandated by Congress to deal with issues involving women's employment, the interviewers visited profitmaking centers, nonprofit centers, and family day care (day care for up to six children by a caretaker in her own home), and found that only 1 percent of the proprietary or profitmaking centers were "superior," 15 percent "good," 35 percent "essentially custodial" or "fair," and nearly half were considered "poor."[25] Among the nonprofit centers—which included Head Start projects, centers operated by churches, voluntary community agencies, community action groups, and other nonprofit auspices—9 percent were rated "superior," 28 percent were "good," 51 percent "fair," and 11 percent were considered "poor."[26] Perhaps a few illustrations will indicate the enormous variation among the centers and the appalling conditions in many of them. The study reported on three of the worst proprietary centers:

If ever there was a way to close a day care center, this one should be the first to go. The proprietor is not interested in child care but only in making a profit. She wants to get out of the business and will sell to anyone who will buy it. Back in a dark room, a baby was strapped in an infant's seat inside a crib and was crying pitifully.

They were kept in "cages"—cribs of double-decker cardboard—in one room with open gas heaters.

This is an abominable center [caring for 40 to 50 children, some of them infants]. Couldn't be much worse. One worker washed every child's face with a cloth dipped in a bucket of water one-tenth full. No decent toys. The center was run by high school girls without any adults present. The children were not allowed to talk. . . . Rat holes were apparent.[27]

An example from the other end of the scale was a nonprofit center under Head Start auspices located in a city in the Pacific Northwest. The center was staffed by a director, a college graduate who was professionally trained in early childhood education, four full-time workers, a part-time aide, and four volunteers. "There were thus fewer than five children to each adult. The services of a nutritionist, cook, nurse, and social worker were shared with a public school to which the center was related." The observer reported that there was "a good playground as well as good indoor and outdoor space and equipment" and that there was an "excellent educational program."[28]

Council members also visited family day-care homes. It was estimated in the early 1970s that "as many as 2 million children may be receiving care in homes other than their own while their mothers are away at work." Fewer than 5 percent were estimated to be licensed or supervised. The council's study found that 6 percent of the homes they observed were giving "superior" care, 29 percent "good" care; 51 percent were custodial in nature, providing "fair" care; and 14 percent were providing "poor" care.[29] In one Midwestern city:

This interviewer can still recall quite vividly one particular home she visited where she counted a total of eleven children—five infants and six other small children from about one to four years old of both sexes and almost naked, running and screaming in the four-room house. The strong urine smell, the stale odor of uneaten food everywhere, and the bugs crawling around made one nauseous. There was one very obese, sullen, unpleasant woman in charge. . . .[30]

And in a Northern city, the study found:

Mrs.—— has great understanding . . . love and warmth. . . . Very clean home, adequate to the needs of the children. Takes children out for play, to parks, local excursions. She shows tremendous interest in children. . . . Mrs. —— shows great imagination in handling the children in her care. She explained to us how important it is to give these children the feeling that they are wanted and loved.[31]

This study was completed over a decade ago, but there is no reason to believe that conditions have changed significantly since then—if anything, they are likely to have deteriorated. One of the most shocking findings of this study and of others similar to it is the lack of societal monitoring of these centers. Many of the family day-care homes that were found most objectionable in the council's study were being supported financially by local welfare departments. Welfare departments were, in many cases, paying for a child's care in a home that was not licensed and, furthermore, was not fit to provide such care. There is no doubt that welfare departments and day-care accrediting departments do not have the resources to visit, to observe, and to evaluate each and every setting providing care for more than one child. They could, however, have these resources and, moreover, they could put some of the very people whom they are now supporting through an inadequate, stigmatizing welfare system to work to protect the physical, emotional, and intellectual well-being of our children. Our societal ambivalence toward day care, toward working mothers, and possibly even toward children, permits this abdication of responsibility. It is, of course, the children and, in the long run, all of us who suffer.

Many who learn of the deplorable conditions in some U.S. day-care facilities blame the parents. "How can a mother leave her child in a place like that?" is a common response. Parents must, I believe, bear some of the responsibility for the environment in which their children are cared for when they cannot care for them themselves. Parents must learn what conditions are necessary for their children's healthy development and then demand those conditions. But what are parents to do when adequate care does not exist? What are they to do when adequate care exists but they cannot afford it? Perhaps in an era in which the extended family is rarely a viable, functioning institution—even in the black community, where there is a long tradition of grandmothers caring for grandchildren, the grandmothers today are often in the labor force and unable to help the young working mother; at a time when the traditional nuclear family is frequently not a viable, functioning unit, either; in an era in which communities offer few if any supports, the society must accept the role of monitoring services for children and other dependent groups. Just as we expect the Department of Public Health to monitor conditions in restaurants and health facilities, just as we expect the Board of Education to monitor what goes on in our schools, don't we have the right to expect comparable agencies to monitor the conditions in day-care facilities?

As of March 1984, according to the Children's Defense Fund, almost half of all mothers with children under three and almost 52 percent of mothers with children under six were in the labor force. More than 9 million children under six have working mothers, and 67 percent of these mothers work full time.[32] There is grossly insufficient day care for these children; it is estimated, for example, that 7 million children ages thirteen and under may be spending part of each day without adult supervision.[33]

During the first three years of the Reagan administration, federal programs that supported child care were cut dramatically. Title XX, the largest program providing federal support for child care, was cut 21 percent; the Public Service Employment Program of the Comprehensive Employment and Training Act (CETA), which helped to provide staff for child-care centers, was abolished. As a result, thirty-two states provided care to fewer poor children in 1983 than in 1981, and thirty-three states cut child-care spending. In 1981 Illinois served 28,100 children; in 1983, 18,000. In 1981 Delaware served 2,039 children; in 1983, 995.[34] One estimate is that the Reagan administration's budget cuts in the first three years resulted in eliminating child care for at least 150,000 children.[35] The group most severely hurt by these cutbacks are poor families headed by women. According to the Children's Defense Fund, "Most of the families using Title XX are headed by single women who need to work out of economic necessity."[36]

Yet another group hurt by the budget cuts is the working poor. Since 1980 ten states have tightened their requirements, and consequently fewer children of low-income working families are eligible for child care. Nineteen states have either increased their fees for child care or imposed new ones. The working poor have also been hurt by being eliminated from AFDC, thereby entirely losing their eligibility for publicly funded day care.[37]

But it is not only quantity that has been cut; quality has been affected as well. According to the Children's Defense Fund's analysis of the president's fiscal-year 1985 budget, "In the past three years, 24 states have reduced funds for training child care workers, 33 have lowered the standards for Title XX child care programs, and 32 have cut back on the number of child care staff."[38]

While eleven states increased their child-care expenditures between 1983 and 1984, in most cases the gains were not sufficient to make up for the cuts made in 1981. Consequently, many parts of the country report a serious gap between the need and the availability of child care. For example, New Mexico is serving approximately 3,700 children but estimates that more than 50,000 need child care; Georgia's Title XX–funded program serves approximately 8,200 children and has a waiting list of 5,000 for its funded centers; in Los Angeles County, California, there is no licensed child care available for the 135,000 children who need such programs.[39]

President Reagan has, however, continued to claim that his administration supports women's aspirations, including those of working women. As evidence of this support, the administration points to the recent increase in the federal income-tax credit for taxpayers who require child care in order to work or look for work. While this is an important development for many working parents, it clearly does not benefit the poor and the near poor who are most desperate for help with child care.

Perhaps the most significant development over the past few years has been the emergence of employer-supported child care. According to the Conference Board, a nonprofit business research organization, more than 1,800 companies are providing some form of child-care assistance to workers.[40] Child-care support by employers takes many forms. It includes providing or participating in the provision of direct services. The Conference Board study estimates that some 120 companies and 400 hospitals and public agencies sponsor day-care centers.[41] The range includes in-house facilities, such as that provided by Wang Laboratories in Massachusetts; facilities run by profitmaking chains, such as the Campbell's Soup operation, which is run by Kindercare; facilities run by nonprofit organizations, such as the employee-run center of Merck Pharmaceuticals. Some companies join together to form a consortium to run a center; others sponsor family day-care arrangements.

A second form of employer participation in their employees' child-care concerns is the provision of information and referral services, either offered on the work premises or through an existing community agency. Yet another form of involvement is employer-financed subsidy. The establishment of a Dependent Care Assistance Plan was made possible by the Economic Recovery Tax Act of 1981, making child care a nontaxable benefit for employees. The fourth mechanism whereby employers help their employees with child care is through more flexible working hours—flextime, job sharing, part-time work, or home work, also called "flexiplace."[42]

Is employer participation in child care the wave of the future? It has been estimated that, by 1990, 64 percent of all families will have working mothers and that these families will include 10.4 million children under six. Will private industries increasingly feel it is in their best interests to help families solve their personal problems, particularly the problems of child care? For more businesses to move into this area, they must see it as profitable in some way. As Dana Friedman has stated, "The fact that children are our nation's greatest resource is not the most convincing argument for bottom-line oriented business managers."[43]

There is no doubt that employer involvement in child care is a positive development; it has, for example, undoubtedly legitimized day care in the eyes of many who may have felt doubt or even antipathy. But there are problems with relying on employers to be major providers of child care. One major difficulty is that the current wave of employer-sponsored activity is generally voluntary. Most firms or unions or institutions that move into the area of day care do it because they need to recruit and retain skilled employees, because they feel their employees will, in the long run, have more stable work histories if some of their family problems are solved, or because they feel it is good public relations. As Friedman points out, industries that cater to the family market, such as Gerber Foods and Stride Rite children's shoes, feel a greater commitment to family issues.[44] But what of other working people in the country? Most of the companies that offer child-care options are nonunionized. Child-care benefits are, therefore, often not a right won through negotiation and guaranteed through a contract but rather a result of enlightened self-interest on the part of industry. But what happens when the industry's self-interest changes— if its profit margin shrinks and executives feel such services can be eliminated?

Which segment of the population is most likely to benefit from industry involvement in child care? Will this be yet another way of separating services for the poor from services for working people, many of whom are middle class? Corporate child-care programs are usually found in high-technology companies, insurance companies, banks and hospitals. Are we moving simultaneously toward improved child care for the fortunate few and reduced, often inferior care for the poor, the unemployed, and those workers unfortunate enough to work for companies that are either unenlightened or not making sufficient profit to consider breaking new ground in the area of child care? In addition, many of the companies now offering child-care services offer them as part of a "cafeteria" plan, whereby the worker must choose one benefit over another. Should a parent have to choose dental coverage over child care or vice versa?

Child care is still a two-class system in the United States. Those with adequate income can generally purchase first-rate care for their preschool children; those without adequate income are left at the mercy of the political and economic forces that determine social policy. While the poor, the near poor, and the working class sometimes have access to good care, more often than not they are faced with long waiting lists, inadequate teacher–child ratios, and a rapid turnover of caregivers.

Statistics from the National Center of Education show that 53 percent of children ages three to four whose families had incomes of $25,000 and above attended a preschool program in 1982, while less than 29 percent of children whose families had incomes below $25,000 were in preschool. In addition, approximately half of the three-year-olds and 72 percent of the four-year-olds whose mothers were college graduates were in such programs in 1982.[45] For child care, as for other human services, affordability and accessibility have become key issues.

That we still have extremely limited access to child care in the 1980s, twenty years after the War on Poverty and the initiation of Head Start, is particularly shameful since a study has recently been released indicating that a first-rate preschool experience may be of particular value to disadvantaged children. Conducted in Michigan by the High/Scope Educational Research Foundation, it found that poor black children with low IQs who received preschool education from the age of three "have grown up with markedly greater success in school and in their personal lives than a comparable group without early childhood education. . . ."[46] Following the children from age three through age nineteen, the researchers found that they had better work histories, completed more years of schooling, were involved in less crime, and had fewer teenage pregnancies than a comparable group that did not have early childhood education. Sixty-seven percent of the preschool education group had graduated from high school by the age of nineteen, compared to 49 percent of the control group.[47]

While the preschool education was not inexpensive—the cost adjusted for inflation at 1981 prices was $4,818 per child per year—the long-term savings to the educational system and to society were far greater.[48] But the financial savings is the least important aspect of this project. As Fred Hechinger has stated, "Neglect at an early age has been shown to mean wasted lives, with mounting costs to individuals and society, and the creation of a permanent underclass."[49]

There is little doubt that the absence of a high-quality, coherent, comprehensive day-care policy is a key factor in the perpetuation of poverty among women and children. Without access to affordable day care, women with young children are frequently unable to enter the labor force. Without adequate day care, how can a mother receiving AFDC hope to acquire skills or get a job in order to get off welfare? If we as a society are serious about economic equity for women, about stemming the feminization of poverty, and about giving every child a fair chance educationally, emotionally, and economically, one of our first priorities must be accessible, affordable, high-quality day care.

7

THE IMPACT OF POVERTY ON HEALTH AND WELL-BEING

> I'm crying 'cause they took away my future.
> —*Fernall Hoover,*
> *age eighteen*

Maria Perez, the Colombian mother of three mentioned in the previous chapter, talks about her fourth child:

> I had another child, too, a little girl. She died. I would have had two boys and two girls—four children. She died when she was one year old. She had ear infections and then a high fever and went into the hospital one day and died the next. Three or four days before, I brought her to the doctor and told him that she wasn't well and that she wasn't eating, and he said, "Oh, that's all right, just give her rice and beans." He gave her some injections and sent us home. Maybe he could have done something for her then.[1]

Elinor Thomas is a small, slim, black woman who was nearly forty when I interviewed her. She lives in a four-room apartment in a city-owned housing project in the Bronx with her husband, a clerk in a New York City post office, and her two sons, ages fourteen and eight.

Elinor's parents separated when she was six months old; her mother supported seven children by doing domestic work, baby-sitting, and occasionally resorting to welfare. Elinor describes her mother as a "perfectionist" and her mother's house as "immaculate."

> We had everything that was essential—we really had not only the necessities but we had the luxuries, too, because, even though Mother did have a hard time with the energy and the strength she had she just didn't leave anything out. . . . And then you don't forget on Sunday to go to church to praise God and you thank God for what strength you have and how He made you able to do these things for six days a week.[2]

When their middle child, Michael, was two, the Thomases discovered he had sickle cell disease. Sickle cell anemia is an inherited blood disorder caused by a defect in hemoglobin. Found mainly in Africa and in Mediterranean countries, the disease now afflicts one in every four hundred to six hundred black children in the United States. Approximately 2.5 million black Americans—one in ten—carry the sickle cell trait, caused by the abnormal gene. If both parents are carriers and a child receives the imperfect gene from both, he or she acquires the disease. There is no known cure.[3]

When Michael first became ill, the doctors could not discover what was wrong with him. While he was being treated for pneumonia, his mother noticed that his fingers were swollen and painful. She showed them to the doctor, a blood sample was taken, and it was discovered that Michael had sickle cell disease. Elinor describes what happened next:

> So then they asked all of us in the family to come in and have the tests. They found at first that my husband did not have the trait, little John [her older son] had nothing, and I was a sickle cell trait. I was a sickle cell trait—which I never knew in my life. . . . In less than a month the first crisis came on and he was in the hospital. And then it just kept going. But actually it only

lasted about sixteen months. I found out when he was exactly two and a half and he died two months before his fourth birthday.

Elinor continues by describing an incident that took place during one of Michael's hospitalizations:

In all the time Michael was sick, only one thing really hurt my feelings. There's one doctor, she was a female doctor. Michael was upstairs in the hospital on the ward and I had to go down to the hematology clinic to get the results of our blood tests, and that particular doctor, she really hurt my feelings very bad. She made me feel less than a—than anything. She made me feel so small. She said it's impossible for Michael to have sickle cell disease and I'm a trait and my husband is not a trait. So, I says, "Well, that's it." So she asked me, "Is Michael your husband's child?" And I mean she really hurt me, you know. I jumped back, like that, and I got hot all over. I says, "Of course he is." And I says, "But that is my only—that's my husband, you know!" I mean like she really embarrassed me; she made me feel so bad.

Now it's all right to ask some questions, to ask somebody a question like that, but then she gets up from her desk and she walks around and she closes the door and she says to me, "Come on, you can tell me the truth. I will never mention it and I won't put it down on the records." I said, "I told you the truth." And at that minute tears started coming out of my eyes. So she still insisted that it was impossible. But then the thing that really got to me is that I told her when I first went into her office that Michael was upstairs and he's going through his first crisis, and my husband was upstairs with him, so she says to me, "Well, when you go upstairs you don't have to mention it to your husband."

When I took that elevator and went upstairs, I was overflowing on the inside. I was burning up hot. And the moment I walked on to the ward and saw my husband, I broke out crying and I just ran and fell in his arms. And he got all upset. He said, "What happened, what happened?" And I just cried and I told my husband, "She is trying to tell me that you're not Michael's father." And then I had to turn around and get myself together and plead 'cause he was ready to go downstairs and blast, you know, all over. Of all the things that happened I think that's the worst part of it.[4]

Elinor Thomas and her family were victims not only of an illness that only afflicts blacks—one that many feel has received comparatively inadequate research funding because of that—but they were also the victims of an insensitive medical-care system as well. It is extremely unlikely that that physician would have asked the same questions in the same way if Elinor had been a white, upper-middle-class mother whose dying child's diagnosis did not quite seem to concur with the facts. And would Maria Perez's physician have told the wife of a corporate executive or a suburban professional woman to "just give her rice and beans" and then have sent them home? It is clear that class, race, and gender have a direct effect on the health and well-being of all Americans and on the health care we receive.

If you're poor, you're more likely to be sick, less likely to receive adequate medical care, and more likely to die at an early age. The effects of poverty on health and general well-being are clearcut and profound. Rather than attempting to catalogue the many ways low income affects health status, I will focus in this chapter on a few of the key issues for poor women and children: reproduction, mental illness, hunger, lead poisoning, and finally, how the child welfare system "takes away the future" of so many poor young people.

First, it must be stated that lower economic status is associated with higher rates of chronic illnesses, such as heart disease;[5] arthritis and diabetes;[6] hypertension and lung, stomach, and esophageal cancer, and mental illness.[7] With this higher prevalence of illness, low-income people are found in surveys to have more days of restricted activity and of disability than do higher-income people.[8]

Not only do low-income people have poorer health status than other groups in our society by essentially every measurement; but when use of health services is compared to need for services, low-income groups have the lowest rate. While there is no doubt that the poor's access to medical services has significantly improved since the introduction of Medicaid, nonetheless, according to E. Richard Brown,

these benefits have not been sufficient to remove all inequities. Poor children make fewer visits to physicians than children from non-poor families. The poor of all ages receive less dental and preventive medical care than the non-poor. When people's health status is taken into account, the use of health services is still related to income; those better off receive more care than poorer persons in comparable states of health.[9]

In addition, the Reagan administration's cutbacks in health funding have adversely affected the health care of women and children. Because of cuts in AFDC, many of the families eligible for Medicaid lost that coverage. Many states made additional cuts in both the eligibility for and the range of Medicaid services in order to save money. According to the Children's Defense Fund,

> Federal cuts in the Maternal and Child Health Block Grant have led 47 states to cut back on services offered in maternal and child health clinics or to reduce the number of people eligible for care. Some 725,000 people, 64 percent of whom are children and women of childbearing age, have lost services at community health centers. . . .[10]

These budget cuts have also led to a nationwide decrease in the number of pregnant women, particularly nonwhite women, receiving prenatal care. In New York State in 1982, 21.3 percent of nonwhite pregnant women received late or no prenatal care—twice the national average for white women.[11]

To turn specifically to the health status of women, it is clear that women live significantly longer than men. In 1982, for example, life expectancy for all American women was 78.2 years and for men was 70.9 years. But when these data are analyzed by race, other significant differences emerge. Life expectancy for white females was 78.8 years and for white males, 71.5 years; for black women, it was 73.5 and for black men a shockingly low 64.9.[12] While women live longer than men, they report more physical and mental illness than men, have more days of disability, and utilize physicians and hospital services more frequently. Some of the physical problems faced by women, particularly poor women, are exacerbated by limited access to health care or by access primarily to impersonal, dehumanizing settings such as emergency rooms and Medicaid mills, in which care is episodic and fragmented and the patient is often little more than a faceless object.

Many special problems for poor women are related to reproduction. In the area of contraception, numerous studies have documented the experimentation on women, particularly poor, Third-World women, in the development of the birth-control pill. The original study of oral contraceptives performed in Puerto Rico in the 1950s used doses of estrogen considered dangerous by U.S. standards.[13] Third-World women in the United States have been frequent subjects of questionable experiments. In a 1970 experiment to test the pill, seventy-six Mexican-American women were, without their consent, given placebos (inactive substances) rather than active contraceptives. According to health activist and pediatrician, Helen Rodriguez-Trias,

> Ten became pregnant! Doctors did not even censure the investigators; on the contrary, the paper presenting the results of the experiment was well received. When questioned on methodology, the investigator replied, "If you think you can explain a placebo test to women like these, you have never met Mrs. Gomez from the West Side."[14]

Depo-Provera, an injectable, long-acting contraceptive, has long been a source of controversy. Developed by the Upjohn Company, experiments have shown that it causes cancer in test animals, is a suspected carcinogen in humans, and may cause birth defects. In 1974 a Food and Drug Administration advisory committee recommended limited approval of the contraceptive for certain groups such as the mentally retarded. Over the past decade it has been widely used on American women to prevent miscarriage during pregnancy and even more widely promoted for contraceptive use on Third-World women.[15] An estimated 11 million women in a total of eighty countries have been injected.[16] Widespread contraceptive use of Depo-Provera has centered in nonwhite, low-income groups in the United States as well. Arguing against even limited approval, one authority stated,

> It is my conclusion that there is no group of women for whom the risks are outweighed by the benefits of choosing Depo-Provera as a contraceptive. I see many reasons why limited use and limited

marketing won't work . . . including racial and class bias. The two places in our society where this drug was used most is Grady Memorial Hospital in Atlanta, which primarily services Black women, and Los Angeles County USC, which is primarily Hispanic.[17]

The National Women's Health Network has brought a suit against the Upjohn Comany on behalf of the women who have been injured by the drug.

In October 1984 an advisory board to the Food and Drug Administration recommended that Depro-Provera not be approved for general marketing in the United States. After noting that the drug appeared to cause cancer in monkeys and dogs, the board stated that such data "cannot be dismissed as irrelevant to the human without conclusive evidence to the contrary."[18]

The Dalkon shield, an intrauterine device widely in use in the early 1970s, has been found to have a pregnancy rate far higher than the one advertised by its maker, the A. H. Robins Company and to cause a high rate of pelvic inflammatory disease (PID), a common cause of infertility. While the shield was withdrawn from the domestic market in 1974, it was not until 1980 that Robins sent out a letter recommending removal of the shield from women in whom it had been inserted. During the fall of 1984 Robins mounted a more aggressive campaign urging women to have the device removed and offering to pay for such removal. Dalkon shields are still, however, available to millions of women in other countries. As with Depo-Provera, the National Women's Health Network has filed a class-action suit against A. H. Robins company, but this time on behalf of women worldwide. They are requesting that the court order an international recall of the shield.[19]

In spite of the Supreme Court's 1973 landmark decision, Roe v. Wade, abortion continues to be a major political and health issue, particularly for poor women. Since passage by Congress of the Hyde Amendment in 1977, states have been permitted to deny Medicaid payments for abortions. Currently, only fourteen states and the District of Columbia still provide Medicaid reimbursement for abortions. A study by the U.S. Centers for Disease Control found that an estimated five thousand to twenty-three thousand low-income women were forced to resort to self-induced or illegal "back-alley" abortions from 1975 to 1979. Seventeen deaths from illegal abortions occurred in those years. According to the same study, as a result of the Medicaid cutoff, an estimated 18 to 35 percent of poor pregnant women had to carry their unwanted pregnancies to term. In addition to the lack of funds, lack of medical resources in many parts of the country is a crucial problem for women wishing to have an abortion, particularly for poor women. According to the Alan Guttmacher Institute, in 1980, "fifty-one percent of the women in Indiana, 57 percent in Louisiana, 85 percent in the Dakotas, to take just a few examples, lived in counties that had no abortion facility. . . ."[20]

In a letter on behalf of the Planned Parenthood Federation of America, Dr. Walter A. Ruch writes:

> I will never forget the 16-year-old girl I attended in the Emergency Room of Memphis City Hospital. . . .
> The young woman was unconscious, almost chalk-white. Her brown hair was tangled and her pajamas were soaked from a burning fever. The friend who brought her said she had attempted an abortion the week before, using a knitting needle.
> We were unable to arrest the advanced infection.[21]

This incident took place in 1964, but Dr. Ruch is writing about it in 1984 because the limitations on publicly funded abortions and the drastic cuts in federal funding for family-planning clinics since the Reagan administration came into office are causing hardships for some women not unlike the dark days before Roe v. Wade. In Minnesota, for example, a 42 percent cut in federal family planning funds in 1982 forced the Minnesota Planned Parenthood to close forty-three family-planning outreach offices in rural communities and to terminate all family life education services, including those in schools. In Utah, in 1984 all federal funding for family planning for Planned Parenthood was cut off. According to Dr. Ruch, "Poor women can no longer obtain free or subsidized birth control services at Planned Parenthood clinics. Teenage sex education and family planning assistance have been virtually eliminated"; and in Tennessee, "A 24 percent cut in family planning funds for 1983 threatens to severely reduce birth control services and family planning education for poor women and teenagers.''[22]

Federal funds for all family planning were cut drastically, from $182.4 million in 1981 to $124 million in 1982. Funding remained essentially at the same level, $125 million in 1983, and then rose modestly to $140 million in 1984.[23] Clearly these budget cuts affect low-income women far more than middle- and upper-income women since the latter group can simply go to a private doctor for their contraception. Furthermore, as of June 1985, antiabortion legislation has been introduced in thirty-eight states; these bills seek to limit still further all women's access to abortion.

The Reagan administration, not content with imposing its views on family planning and abortion on American women, is also attempting to impose them on women all over the world, particularly those in Third-World countries. In a statement before the United Nations International Conference on Population in Mexico City in August 1984, James L. Buckley, head of the U.S. delegation declared, ''The United States does not consider abortion an acceptable element of family planning programs.'' He further clarified the American position by stating that the United States would not permit its contributions to other nations to be used for abortion, that it would ''no longer contribute to separate non-governmental organizations which perform or actively promote abortion as a method of family planning in other nations,'' and that before the United States contributed to the United Nations Fund for Population Activities, it would first require that the UNFPA not be engaged in or support abortion. Buckley called instead for development of a free-market economy as the ''natural mechanism for slowing population growth.''[24] In December 1984, the Reagan administration indeed cut off the entire U.S. contribution for the International Planned Parenthood Federation; the federation had not been and did not plan to use U.S. funds to advocate or perform abortions, but it had committed the unpardonable sin of using a small part of the monies contributed by other nations (1 percent of its total budget) for these purposes. Critics pointed out that the curtailment of funds would lead to increased numbers of unwanted pregnancies around the world and therefore, in many areas, to an increased number of abortions.

The Reagan administration has particularly targeted contraception for teenagers and in 1983 attempted to impose a so-called squeal rule, requiring all facilities receiving funds under Title X of the Public Health Service Act to "notify the parents of unemancipated minors within 10 working days that prescriptions for birth control have been dispensed to their children."[25] After protests from numerous groups and a challenge that resulted in a federal appeals court striking down the rule, the Reagan administration withdrew the regulation.[26] But many family-planning workers feel that the publicity surrounding the possible imposition of the "squeal rule" made many teenagers fearful of going to clinics for birth control.

Yet another area that has been particularly difficult for poor women is that of sterilization abuse. In the early 1970s reports began to surface of forced sterilization of women on welfare and women receiving care in publicly funded hospitals. In 1973 a suit was brought against the Department of Health, Education, and Welfare on behalf of two allegedly retarded black girls in Alabama, ages twelve and fourteen, who had been sterilized without their knowledge or consent in a federally funded program. The publicity given this case by the media and by civil rights and civil liberties activists generated such outrage that guidelines were established in 1974 to curb sterilization abuse. These regulations, however, according to Helen Rodriguez-Trias, "were largely ineffective and unknown or ignored by providers of sterilization services. . . ."[27]

According to Rodriguez-Trias, the number of sterilizations, particularly of nonwhite, low-income women, rose rapidly during the 1970s. Reports became more frequent of Mexican women being sterilized at the Los Angeles County Hospital without proper informed consent and of rising sterilization rates in New York City hospitals serving primarily black and Hispanic communities. In response to these reports, the Committee to End Sterilization Abuse (CESA) was organized. It is particularly significant that the immediate stimulus for the organization of CESA was the showing of the film *Blood of the Condor*, which exposed the support of the sterilization of Bolivian Quechua Indians by a program funded by the U.S. Agency for International Development (USAID). The connections between health care and the infringement of rights of poor women of color in the Third World, as well as poor women of color in the United States, have been clear and compelling.

In order to enable women to exercise greater control over their bodies and their lives, CESA, together with a variety of grassroots and professional groups, developed sterilization guidelines that would ensure that women would have as complete an understanding as possible of their birth-control options and would be free to make decisions unpressured by professionals who might not share their priorities. In 1978, spurred on by legislation enacted in New York City, HEW promulgated new, more stringent guidelines including a thirty-day waiting period, full explanation of birth-control alternatives and materials offered in the language best understood by the woman as well as more effective procedures for enforcement of the guidelines on sterilization abuse.[28]

The struggle against sterilization abuse was significant for several reasons: First, because of what was accomplished, the development and acceptance of effective guidelines; and, second, because of the process of developing and advocating for the guidelines. This was an issue on which low-income and middle-income women, professionals and lay people worked together, often with conflict and sometimes with misunderstanding but always with a common goal. And it was an issue on which the connection between the experiences of Third-World women and poor, nonwhite women in the United States was clear, and it helped to point the way to reforms in our own country.

Mental health is another area in which women seem particularly at risk. Many studies have indicated that all three groups—poor people, nonwhites, and females—do, indeed, have higher rates of mental illness than others in the society. Poor people have a higher rate of schizophrenic disorders and mental hospital admissions.[29] Women have a higher rate of institutionalization than men,[30] and nonwhites have a higher admission rate to state and county mental hospitals than whites.[31] In comparing the primary diagnoses of persons admitted to outpatient services in the United States in 1975, men had a significantly higher rate of alcoholic disorders, drug disorders, and childhood disorders, while women had a significantly higher rate of depressive disorders, neuroses, "transient situational disorders of adolescent, adult and late life" and "social maladjustments." Female rates for depressive disorders and social maladjustments were over twice the male rate in 1975. Moreover nonwhite women had a significantly higher rate of depressive disorders, schizophrenia, transient situational disorders, and social maladjustment than white women.[32]

What is the meaning of these data? Does the stress at having a low income in an affluent society, of being female in a male-dominated society, of being nonwhite in a racist society lead to a higher incidence of mental illness? Does this "triple jeopardy" place women, particularly poor, nonwhite women at greater risk of mental illness in our society? Or are women, perhaps more in tune with their feelings than men, more willing to recognize their emotional problems and to seek help for them?

Walter Gove and Jeanette Tudor, who have done some of the key work that seems to indicate that women suffer from higher rates of mental illness than men, claim that this discrepancy is due to women's role in society:

> There are ample grounds for assuming that women find their position in society to be more frustrating and less rewarding than do men. . . . [We] postulate that because of the difficulties associated with the feminine role in modern Western societies, more women than men become mentally ill.[33]

The work of Gove and Tudor has, however, been criticized on both methodological and substantive grounds. Their critics claim that they focused on diagnostic categories, specifically on neuroses and functional psychoses, in which the rates for females are high, excluding other diagnostic categories such as personality disorders and alcoholic psychosis, in which the rates for males exceed those for females.

Yet another possible explanation is that women who do not behave in expected, acceptable ways are labeled mentally ill far more often than men who behave in deviant ways. According to sociologist Edwin Schur,

> The general tendency to treat women as being emotionally disturbed is always present in the background as a ground for dismissing what a woman says or does and as an implicit "threat"

should she seriously step out of line. Notwithstanding well-intended professional justifications, the use of mental illness labels is always to an extent discrediting and stigmatizing. It is one thing to be deemed merely ".angry," another to be seen as "mentally ill," and another still to be defined as a "mental patient."[34]

Schur goes on to suggest that psychiatric diagnosis, largely developed by men, is yet another method of social control, a way of keeping women in line.

The perception of troubled women as "mentally ill" often leads to aggressive treatment for women of all classes but particularly for poor women who have least control over their medical care. Cora Jackson, a bright, verbal woman in her early fifties, raised her three daughters "on welfare" and then took a course to become a licensed practical nurse. She describes what happened next:

While I was studying to become an LPN I went to a lot of doctors because I was unhappy and upset about my life. I feel the doctors pigeonholed me as a divorced, unhappy woman and therefore prescribed Valium for me. I became addicted to Valium and became so depressed that they gave me shock treatments. I was so zonked out from the Valium and then from the shock treatments that I was completely unable to solve my problems and couldn't even pass my LPN course. It was then that I became so depressed and irrational that I tried to overdose.

The overprescribing of tranquilizers, particularly Valium, has been thoroughly documented. In 1979, for example,

160 million prescriptions were written for tranquilizers, over 60 million for Valium alone. Sixty to 80 percent of these drugs were prescribed for women. While the "pill for every ill" ideology of the pharmaceutical industry reaps high profits, Valium addiction is widespread and Valium abuse has been cited as the most common drug problem seen in hospital emergency rooms.[35]

Julia Soto, Director of Patient Services at a health center in Tucson, talked about the women treated at the center and their problems with Valium:

We see so many women with emotional upheavals and the answer is not in a Valium bottle. Almost all of the women I see are so depressed and many of them try to find their answer in tranquilizers. The solutions, instead, are helping the women to get jobs, helping them to find decent housing, helping them to exercise their rights, maybe even helping them to form groups to talk about their problems; but not to take Valium!

Many women's problems derive from socially conditioned expectations that they will be nurturers, wives, and mothers. A Maine mother of four whose husband had walked out one day suffered with depression and migraine headaches. An Arizona woman who suffered multiple losses and today is barely surviving economically perhaps phrased her feelings most poignantly, "I'm not depressed," she said in a flat voice. "I'd just as soon be dead."

Joan Miller, a twenty-nine-year-old, heavyset woman from Maine with a cheerful manner and a lively seven-year-old daughter, spoke of her marriage to one man who drank and battered her and her subsequent unhappy relationship with another man. After numerous arguments and separations during which she started to drink heavily because "I had no one to talk to and so many things to worry me," they split up—on their first anniversary.

I went into a real depression. I gained a lot of weight—47 pounds during the pregnancy. And I felt so guilty, guilty about how I was treating my daughter, making her help me, putting a lot of responsibility on her.

It seems like I was down in the pits for a long time and I had an awful guilt trip. My biggest problem was guilt. I would think that it was all my fault.

Depression and guilt—these women said over and over again that they felt it was their responsibility to make their relationships with men work and to care for their children; if something went wrong with either facet of their lives, they did not get angry, they became depressed and guilty—guilty because they were not fulfilling their role as they had been taught it should be fulfilled, guilty about their own inadequacies.

Economic expectations may be equally strong. Perhaps some

indication of how not making it in this society can erode a woman's confidence and sense of well-being is exemplified by the story of Marilyn Curry, a woman who is living well above the poverty line, who is struggling to stay there, and who feels like a failure. Marilyn is a twenty-nine-year-old black woman who works in an affluent college community in California. She speaks softly, carefully:

> I graduated from high school in 1972 in a small town in Southern California. I graduated from college in 1977. I started in Nursing and ended up in Health Sciences because of an administration foul-up. When I discussed the foul-up with the Dean, she told me, "Most blacks don't do too well in the sciences; why don't you try something else?"

She had her first child one year after she finished college and married seven months later; she then worked at a medical center, and nine months after the birth of her first child, she became pregnant again. After the birth of her second child, she stayed out of the work force for two-and-a-half years.

Marilyn's husband graduated from the same state college with a degree in sociology and then worked for some time as the director of admissions for a small private college. He had hoped eventually to become a college president but was brought sharply back to reality when the college closed. He then spent a year looking for a job and now is a "materials planner" for a local private company. A "materials planner," Marilyn explained, "makes sure all the parts are there." He started out at $5.25 an hour and now makes approximately $1,400 a month. He sees no other future for himself at the moment; he's depressed and she's depressed and they can "feel it in the relationship."

Marilyn currently works in a volunteer agency doing rent mediation, but feels she is being underutilized and wonders if it is because she's black. She got herself a college degree because that was supposed to be the path to success, but now she is "just making it." She and her husband cannot afford to buy a house in the community in which they live, a community she calls "an expensive ghetto." Making the point that poverty is relative, she says that they cannot even afford to buy her in-laws' house and that, therefore, in some very real sense, they are poor. She had never thought her life would be like this.

> I had always thought I would be a professional person who would have my home in order, my work in order, my kids in good schools and that we would live in a nice area where the kids could go to the park. In my community with marijuana as free as it is in the street, with people hanging out in the park and with glass in the sandbox my kids will never go to the park unsupervised.

She has done everything she was supposed to do in order to make it, and now she looks at her children and wonders how to guide them. And she is starting to wonder how much is her fault: "Maybe I just can't cut it." She recently told her husband that she wants to take an IQ test because she is afraid she is not very smart. While she is aware that some of her problems may be due to conditions beyond her personal control, at heart she blames herself, going as far as questioning her own intelligence. Her anger is turned inward and eventually may turn against her husband as well.

Yet another critical health problem that has beset the poor and near poor, and now has also begun to reach into the working class and even the middle class, is hunger. While the Reagan administration has questioned the extent of hunger in the United States, recent studies indicate that hunger has increased dramatically, especially during the recession of 1982–1983. In March 1985, a physicians' task force called hunger in America "a national health epidemic." The task force went on to state that the "problem of hunger in the United States is now more widespread and serious than at any time in the last ten to fifteen years."[36] After traveling to every part of the country, the group estimated that "up to 20,000,000 citizens may be hungry at least some period of time each month"[37] and that these people include the poor and the near poor—those who receive food stamps and those who do not, the young and the old, those who live in cities and those who live in rural areas.

Ruth Sterling, director of Northwest Second Harvest in Seattle, asserted that many people in need of food could be classified as the new poor: "We're getting a whole lot of people who don't know how to be poor. I mean people who have never had to cook beans from a dry state." And yet, while hunger in the United States seemed to be at the highest level since the Great Depression, with the United States Conference of Mayors declaring in summer 1983 that "hunger had become 'the most prevalent and the most insidious' problem facing the nation's cities," many antipoverty groups felt that the cutbacks in federal spending on nutrition programs were at least partially responsible for the increase in people seeking food at soup kitchens.[38]

Early in 1983 a study was initiated to investigate the extent and nature of hunger and malnutrition in New York State. Four hundred forty-six individuals were interviewed at a variety of sites: senior citizens' centers, emergency food programs, government offices such as income-maintenance and food-stamp offices, health centers and community sites. Seventy-four percent of people interviewed at all locations except the emergency feeding centers were women; at the feeding sites, 70 percent were men.[39]

When the respondents were asked, "Are you ever hungry and unable to obtain food?" almost 30 percent said yes; at the emergency feeding sites, 46 percent answered yes. In response to the question, "Do your children eat and sometimes you're unable to?" over one-third responded affirmatively, 70 percent at the emergency feeding sites. And when asked, "Do your children ever go to bed hungry?" nearly 20 percent responded yes, nearly one-third in the emergency feeding sites.[40]

Some of the most common reasons given for "food stress" were situations over which the individual had little control, such as recent loss of a job, expiration of unemployment compensation, or desertion by a spouse; not receiving food stamps even though eligible for them; or running out of government assistance (AFDC, food stamps, or social security) before the next installment was due to arrive.

The following are some of the experiences documented by Hunger Watch:

One twenty-six-year-old woman with two young children, who stated that her children sometimes go to bed hungry, said, "I was a cashier but I lost my job in December, 1983. It got bad when my unemployment ran out in May. . . . I haven't even been able to afford milk so Crystal [who is ten months old] has been drinking juice for a week."[41]

One woman said her children went hungry last year when her benefits were cut off after not responding to the government's request for a face-to-face interview. She said mail boxes in her apartment building are regularly vandalized and she never got the notice for an interview.[42]

A forty-five-year-old physically disabled widow had been approved for SSI but had not yet received a check. She has lost thirty-seven pounds since her husband died in 1980 and is now relying on canned foods from a Bronx food pantry to sustain her. Such food, she knows, is high in sodium and wrong for her high blood pressure.[43]

A twenty-six-year old woman with two children under five said that sometimes she's hungry and can't obtain food, but that her children eat even when she's unable to. "We have food only until Thursday and no check comes until Monday. When bills pile up, we have to cut back on how much food we buy. It may sound silly but a few months ago, I had to eat those instant potatoes for about a week just so I could feel filled up." She said her food stamps and welfare don't last the entire month.[44]

The report concluded:

This study suggests that many people are trapped in a hunger crisis in New York State and that population groups not previously hungry now lack adequate food. . . . In sum, it seems clear that the repeated public reports of increasing hunger in the United States cannot be dismissed as aberrations. Adequate responses to this urgent problem are needed.[45]

In New York City, a study by the East Harlem Interfaith Welfare Committee found that food emergencies in East Harlem, Brooklyn, and the Bronx rose significantly between 1980 and 1984. Many of the households reported that they literally had to beg, borrow or steal in order to obtain food.[46]

Ironically, while the number of hungry increased, government stocks of surplus dairy products rose to record levels. Officials of the Department of Agriculture acknowledged during summer 1983 that the government was holding 473 million pounds of butter, 1.3 billion pounds of nonfat dry milk, and 876 million pounds of cheese. Although these stockpiles were increasing significantly, government distribution of cheese was reduced because "it was adversely affecting sales in the commercial market."[47]

Those hit hardest by the cutbacks in food stamps have been women and children. The number of women who head food-stamp households is greater than the number of households headed by men; according to the Reagan administration, the typical food-stamp family of four consists of a mother and three children. In addition, four child nutrition programs—the School Lunch, School Breakfast, Child Care Food and Summer food programs were cut by $5 billion, 29 percent, over fiscal years 1982–1985. The Reagan administration has repeatedly attempted to cut the Special Supplemental Food Program for Women, Infants, and Children (WIC), but these efforts have been blocked by Congress. According to the Children's Defense Fund, "The program is still underfunded and reaches only about three million people, or one-third of those who are eligible. Several hundred counties have no WIC program at all, and many other counties maintain waiting lists and have to turn away eligible mothers and children. . . ."[48]

Furthermore, cuts in other programs—housing subsidies, energy assistance, Medicaid—invariably mean that families have less to spend on food. Food is what people scrimp and save on. You pay your rent because you'll be evicted; you pay for your heat or they discontinue it; you pay for medical care or you might not get any; what's left is for food.

In 1983 the U.S. Department of Agriculture conducted a series of workshops in various cities to educate food-stamp recipients about how to shop and eat nutritionally on food stamps. The menus planned could be purchased for $58 per week, the maximum food-stamp allotment for a family of four. The menus included economical foods such as dry beans, peas, and grains that had to be cooked from scratch and fewer expensive foods such as meat, fish, poultry, and cheese. A number of nutritionists interviewed by the food editor of the *New York Times*, including two who work with the Department of Agriculture, said that the menus and recipes were "not meant to promote long-term good health but to prove that a family of four could get enough to eat for $58." Another nutritionist, based with a Washington public-interest group, criticized the diet for not contributing to the prevention of disease. "This is not a diet I would want to recommend to anyone who wanted to lessen chances of cancer, heart disease, diabetes, or high blood pressure. It is a real disservice to low-income people."[49]

The menus were also criticized because, according to the Department of Agriculture, their preparation would take two-and-a-half hours a day, exclusive of shopping time. Clearly, such an investment of time would be unrealistic for a mother who works outside the home. It was also pointed out that the $58 a week meal plan would not provide enough food if there was a man or a teenager in the family.[50]

And, of course, whatever damage hunger or malnutrition may do to adults, the potential for permanent harm to children is far greater. The mother's nutritional status, both before and during pregnancy, has a direct effect on the size and weight of newborns. Low birth weight is directly correlated with both infant mortality and illness and is therefore of crucial importance.

According to a Canadian researcher, studies have shown that "infants born in poverty have higher mortality rates because of the lower birth weight, and that age, race, and socioeconomics were important only insofar as they were related to birth weight."[51] Others have demonstrated that the nutritional status of the mother even affects the brain size of newborns: "The larger brain size in newborns of mothers who were best nourished raises the possibility that fetal brain growth may reach its full genetic potential only under such circumstances of full nutrition."[52]

Perhaps the importance of health status in general and nutrition in specific can best be summarized as follows:

A scientific assessment . . . of the detrimental effect of poverty on health, nutritional status, physical and mental development and the intellectual potential of children, shows that poverty begets poverty. From this cycle of defeat it is obvious that disadvantaged mothers give birth to disadvantaged children of low birth weight who, in turn, give birth to disadvantaged children and thus the cycle is perpetuated.[53]

After birth the child's ongoing need for adequate nutrition, including total caloric intake, calcium, protein, iron, and other nutrients, has been well documented. So have serious problems in children's nutritional status, particularly that of poor children.

In 1983, for example, the Massachusetts Department of Public Health determined that "between 10,000 and 17,500 poor children in Massachusetts are stunted, due largely to chronic malnutrition. Nearly one in five low-income children . . . was either stunted, anemic or abnormally underweight."[54] Studies conducted by Cook County Hospital in Chicago between summer 1981 and summer 1983 found a 24 percent increase in the number of children admitted for diarrhea, dehydration, or failure to thrive. Thirty percent of all children coming to the hospital's emergency room were found to have abnormally low growth, and half of these children suffered from inadequate diets.[55]

Other recent research indicates that nearly 35 percent of all babies in the United States are iron deficient, making iron deficiency the most prevalent nutritional disorder in the U.S. Untreated iron deficiency, particularly during the first eighteen months of life, can produce anemia, can affect behavioral development, and cause a shorter attention span.[56]

Cuts in benefits in the food-stamp program, as well as the decreased resources available to the increasing numbers of people in need of them, have clearly affected children's well-being. The Massachusetts study that found up to 17,500 stunted children also found that 32 percent of low-income children who were eligible for food stamps were not receiving them.[57]

A country's infant mortality rate is one of the clearest indications of the overall health and well-being of its citizens. Many researchers and health activists have criticized the United States for its infant mortality rate, which is excessively high for an affluent, industrialized society. In 1980, for example, while the U.S. infant mortality rate was 12.5 deaths per 1,000 live births, fifteen other countries reported lower rates, the lowest being Sweden with a rate of 6.7, Japan with a rate of 7.4, and Finland with a rate of 7.7.[58]

In 1982 infant mortality in the United States dropped to its lowest rate ever—11.5 infant deaths per 1,000 live births.[59] This welcome decline notwithstanding, the gap between black and white infant mortality rates is widening; the black infant mortality rate was 86 percent higher than the white rate in 1978[60] and essentially twice as high in 1982. While the white infant mortality rate declined by 4 percent in 1982, the black rate rose 2 percent.[61] In fact, according to the U.S. Public Health Service, eleven states reported increases in their infant mortality rates in 1982; they were Vermont, Massachusetts, North Carolina, South Carolina, Alabama, Mississippi, Nebraska, Idaho, New Mexico, Utah, and Nevada.[62]

Many experts feel that these increases and the continued or widening racial discrepancy are directly related to the 1982 rise in unemployment and the budget cuts in health, social programs, and nutrition since the early 1980s. In any case, it is, of course, poor children and black children who are dying. An administration that is so concerned about the well-being of the fetus seems strangely unconcerned about infants' well-being after birth.

Despite the reform efforts of the 1960s and early 1970s to extend medical care to underserved populations, today "almost 9 million American children have no known regular source of health care; 18 million have never seen a dentist."[63] As the number of poor children grew in the early 1980s, cuts in Medicaid resulted in over 1.5 million newly poor children not having Medicaid coverage. Moreover, 700,000 poor children who previously had Medicaid lost those benefits in 1982.[64] It is estimated that fewer than half of all poor preschool children are immunized against preventable diseases, and the Childhood Immunizations Program has consistently been underfunded over the past several years.[65] During the first half of 1984, for example, the incidence of measles in the United States increased sharply. The National Centers for Disease Control reported a 60 percent increase in the number of cases from the first six months of 1983 to the first six months of 1984. Since the vaccine is thought to be 95 percent effective, the increase was undoubtedly due to the number of children who remained unvaccinated.[66]

Lead poisoning is perhaps the quintessential illness of poor children. In 1981 the U.S. Department of Health and Human Services found that more than half a million young children had been contaminated by too much lead. It was further found that 12.2 percent of all black children ages six months to five years had elevated blood lead levels, compared to 2 percent of white children.

The figure is 18.6 percent for inner-city black children![67] As is well known, high lead levels are caused by ingesting pieces of lead-based paint, which peels off walls in old, dilapidated housing, and by the fumes from leaded gasoline, particularly in inner-city areas that are ringed by busy highways on which millions of cars expel their fumes daily. The recent proposal by the Environmental Protection Agency to reduce the lead content of gasoline drastically by 1986 is an effort to lower blood lead levels in the U.S. population.[68]

Once lead enters a child's bloodstream, it is distributed to various organs of the body and may then cause the child to suffer from anemia, learning disabilities, behavioral difficulties, mental retardation, kidney problems, or speech, visual and hearing impairment; it may even lead to death. Lead poisoning is an illness primarily of poor children—one that is preventable. If lead poisoning is not eliminated, it will cost this nation more—in human terms, in moral terms, and in financial terms—than prevention could possibly cost, and far more than we can afford to pay.

This chapter has focused on the direct health consequences for millions of women and children living with severely limited economic means. Many of the health problems faced by these women and their children result from the lack of options that accompany poverty and near poverty. The federal limits on abortions, the dehumanized care at many facilities the poor are forced to use, even the high admission rate to mental hospitals, affect women in need who have no other place to go.

But examination of these issues has only skimmed the surface. What of the poor, often nonwhite children who are relegated to foster care and spend years of their childhood in "temporary" foster homes or group homes, never to be reunited with their parents or placed with a permanent, loving family? What of the poor children who make up the vast majority of "juvenile delinquents," who are sent to group homes or institutions where they learn how to be real criminals, receiving little in the way of treatment or even kindness? What of the hundreds of thousands of poor children who are placed in adult jails each year, sometimes without having committed any offense at all, where they may be exploited by other prisoners? What of the poor children who live in abysmal housing? What of the homeless women and children who, if they are lucky, live in crowded, unsanitary welfare hotels, several to a room, with no refrigeration and only a hot plate for cooking? What of the poor children who attend substandard schools and come out functionally illiterate? What of the poor teenagers who have virtually no hope of a steady job and must look ahead to a life of hustling or welfare or worse?

These are the realities of living in poverty for millions of American children. This reality is unavoidably shaping these young people's understanding of how American society views them, their importance, their worth; and this knowledge must inevitably be helping to formulate their own image of themselves.

Perhaps Fernall Hoover says it best. Fernall grew up in the West End of Boston. He had a history of bitter—some would say, vicious—and occasionally violent arguments with his mother; at the age of fifteen, he was sentenced to three to five years in jail for breaking and entering and carrying a gun. During his two-and-a-half years in jail, Fernall was placed in solitary confinement three separate times, the first when he was sixteen. When he was interviewed by psychologist and writer Thomas Cottle, he described the experience of solitary confinement:

First thing I realized, man, I didn't know the time. Room had no windows so I could never tell. . . . First I thought, I can dig it, they bring me my food, I'll make out, you know what I'm saying? But after a while they got you talking to yourself. I'd be standing in there yelling loud as I could, "Tell me the time. *Tell me the time.*" Ain't no one going to answer you. You know that, but it don't stop you. You just keep on yelling *"Tell me the time.* Is it the day or the night?"

Pretty soon, man, I figure I'm going crazy. . . . Then I start talking to myself, "You ain't going crazy, man. You're doing all right. You're going to be all right. Believe me, you're going to be all right. Just hang in there. . . ."

So I start to imagine the future, man, and there's nothing there. I can't see nothing, man. It's like a cell, all dark and nothing there, nowhere to go, nothing to see. . . . So I'm crying in there, man, like I was this little boy or something. I'm really crying. I ain't shitting you. I'm crying 'cause I ain't got no future. . . . I'm crying 'cause they took away my future.[69]

8

THE SPECIAL PLIGHT
OF OLDER WOMEN

The problems of old age in America are largely the problems
of women.[1]

> —Robert N. Butler, M.D.
> Former Director
> National Institute on
> Aging

They sit on park benches in the Bronx warming themselves in the
midday sun. They walk slowly, almost apologetically, through the
supermarket, choosing an apple or two and day-old bread, counting out the nickels, dimes, and pennies to pay an impatient cashier.
They are lined up in wheelchairs when the television cameras visit
their nursing home for the annual Christmas party. They are the
fastest growing segment of the U.S. population—women over sixty-
five—and nearly one out of every five lives in poverty.[2]

According to the 1980 census more than 25 million Americans,
11.3 percent of the total population, are age sixty-five and over.[3]
Because of the shorter lifespan of men, women significantly out-
number men in this age group; there are only sixty-eight males
for every hundred females. By the year 2000, according to current
projections, this ratio will be further reduced to sixty-five men for

every hundred women.[4] Moreover, the number of elderly people aged seventy-five and older, often termed the "old-old," is growing rapidly. This group now comprises 38 percent of the elderly population and is expected to grow to 45 percent by the year 2000. It is estimated that two-thirds of those seventy-five and over will be women.[5] By the year 2050, according to Robert Butler, a sixty-five-year-old woman can expect to live to age 85.7.[6]

The "graying of America" is no empty slogan. It is a description of our future. The census projections have enormous implications for our society—for health care, for social services, for housing, for recreation, for our productive capacity—but that is only part of the picture. The other part is that a large percentage of this rapidly growing group of older people can expect to live in poverty—many in abject poverty, many more in near poverty.

Elderly women today have a far higher rate of poverty than do elderly men. In 1984, according to the Census Bureau, 8.7 percent of men and 15.0 percent of all women age sixty-five and over had incomes below the poverty line. During the same year 13.1 percent of white women, 22.1 percent of women of Spanish origin, and an incredible 35.6 percent of black women lived in poverty.[7] Those hardest hit are single women—women who never married, women who are widowed, separated, or divorced. It is estimated that almost 90 percent of today's elderly poor women are single.[8]

Part of the reason that women are poor in far greater numbers than men is that they survive so much longer than men do, but they also experience far higher *rates* of poverty than do men. A recent study has found that almost half of the older women in America have annual incomes of less than $5,000; fewer than one in five men have incomes that low.[9] In 1984 the median income for women sixty-five and over was $6,020, while the median income for men was $10,450.[10] Older women's incomes were on the average 58 percent of the incomes of older men, a figure strikingly similar to the 64 percent working women earn compared to the earnings of working men. This similarity is not surprising since the causes of older women's poverty are, in great measure, rooted in the expectations, roles, and work experiences of women throughout their life cycle.

Women, for the most part, work in low-paying, dead-end jobs

that are mainly in the secondary labor market. Furthermore, many women work episodically and/or part-time, combining their jobs out of the home with their work inside the home. The combination of low-paying jobs, episodic work participation, and part-time work invariably means that the older woman has little in the way of savings, was probably not covered by a private pension plan, and will receive a low level of income from social security.

Moreover, the woman who wishes to find employment after age forty is often faced with discrimination because of her age, as well as her gender. There is considerable evidence that women over forty lose out on jobs both to men and to younger women. The limited job market for midlife and older women also translates into real economic loss as aging progresses. Employed women over forty-five earn even less relative to men than younger women do. But it is the woman entering the job market for the first time or reentering after an absence of many years who has the hardest time finding appropriate work.[11]

Age discrimination exists, of course, for men, too. A senior male employee may be "terminated" so that the company can hire a younger man at a significantly lower salary; older workers may be blocked for promotion or let go so that the amount companies pay out for pension plans is minimized; and the middle-aged man who loses his job may well have an extremely difficult time finding another.

But entry-level age discrimination is a problem particular to women. Women are told regularly that they do not have enough experience, or that they have too much, or that they do not have the right experience. The result is that older women, compared to older men, have higher rates of unemployment and longer durations of joblessness. Women's unemployment has exceeded men's every year from 1950 to the present; moreover, according to the U.S. Department of Labor, women make up the majority of "discouraged" workers who are not even counted in the unemployment statistics.[12]

Not only a woman's work history has a direct impact on her future financial status; her marital experience also has a significant impact as well. Most women are economically dependent in marriage; in exchange for childrearing and domestic services, the woman receives economic support. But, as one observer has noted,

> Divorce severs the redistribution of income from the family bread-winner to dependent wives and children. Divorce terminates women's access (through the spouse) to resources and status available to men. . . . Men leave the marriage with their earning ability and social status intact while women lose their primary income source and encounter a gender discriminatory wage mar-ket.[13]

In fact, following divorce the woman's standard of living generally declines while the man's standard of living rises.

No-fault divorce, originally seen as a major reform of an anachronistic, hypocritical set of laws that varied markedly from state to state, is now being viewed far less favorably by those concerned with women's issues. The first no-fault statute was enacted in California in 1970. In many states the only ground necessary for divorce today is the statement of either party that the marriage is "irretrievably broken." The divorce will be granted even if the spouse is in opposition. Prior to no-fault, if the spouse objected to the divorce, he or she at least had leverage with which to bargain for a more adequate financial settlement. Now, according to a Gray Paper published by the Older Women's League, "The no-fault divorce acts have too often proved disastrous to older women."[14]

For the older woman, often without job skills, experience in the labor market, or any real assets in her own name, divorce often means more than a sharp drop in income; for some it means outright poverty. As a woman from Indiana put it: "I feel physically I've worked harder than most men I know—but what do I have to show for it? . . . I was the homemaker—the Little League Mom, Church, Roommother at school, etc. I also helped my husband pour concrete, side a house, etc. I have nothing."[15]

If there are children, the father may or, as we have seen, may well not pay child support. While the notion of alimony, or spousal support, as it is sometimes called, has lost favor among many men and women, women's childrearing and homemaking roles combined with the segregated labor market place women, particularly older women, in a most vulnerable position financially.

One of the direct results of women's work patterns is that the majority of working women are not covered by private pension plans. In 1979 about half of all wage and salary workers, approximately 30 million people, were covered by retirement plans.[16] According to the 1980 White House Miniconference on Older Women, private pensions are available, however, to only approximately 20 percent of retiring women workers.[17] Other studies indicate that while 50 percent of employed men were covered by pension plans in 1979, only 31 percent of women were covered, and that the average private pension received by a man was $4,152 a year compared to an average of $3,427 for a woman.[18] Until the recent passage of the Retirement Equity Act of 1984, women were frequently denied pension benefits they might have accrued or that their husbands might have accrued.

Under legislation sponsored in the House of Representatives by Geraldine A. Ferraro, former Congresswoman from Queens, New York, and the 1984 Democratic vice-presidential nominee, workers will be allowed to participate in pension plans at the age of twenty-one instead of twenty-five; pension plans must count the years of service from the time a person turns eighteen instead of twenty-two, as under previous legislation; employees who have worked fewer than five years may take up to five years off without losing pension credit for earlier service; and pension plans may not be permitted to count a one-year maternity or paternity leave as a break in service.[19] This legislation clearly attempts to enable women who do not fit the standard work pattern to receive retirement benefits in a more equitable fashion.

The new law also addresses the many problems women had been having vis-à-vis their husbands' pension plans. According to the Pension Rights Center, a 1978 Department of Labor study showed that approximately ten thousand widows lost their pension benefits each year because their husbands died before the retirement age set by the pension funds, usually age fifty-five, and without signing over their benefits. The 1984 legislation requires payment of benefits to the spouse of a worker who had become fully vested or who had worked the required number of years even if the worker dies before the age of fifty-five. The legislation further requires written permission of the spouse before a worker can waive benefits for a husband or wife. Many pension plans offer workers a choice between higher monthly retirement payments if the survivor option is not taken or lower monthly payments if the survivor is covered.[20] The spouse will now have a voice in that decision; and since women generally survive men, the decision becomes a critical one for them.

Ideally, income for the elderly should mean the combination of savings, private pension funds, and social security. For elderly women, however, social security is often the only source of income. Over 90 percent of all elderly women receive social security.[21] For 73 percent of nonmarried women, social security makes up 50 percent or more of their income; within that group, for 34 percent of nonmarried women, it makes up 90 percent or more of their income.[22]

In 1982, according to economist and sociologist Charlotte Muller, "The median Social Security benefit for non-married women was $2,830."[23] Social security benefits—tied to income—vary widely depending upon the individual's gender, work history, and marital status. Benefit levels are higher for men than for women; for individuals who are part of a two-worker couple than for those who are not; for white couples than for black couples; for white women than for black women. Benefit levels are least favorable for widows and, particularly, for divorced women.[24] It is clear that the same groups—divorced women, black women, widows, and women who never married—are at risk over and over again.

In addition to social security, the needy elderly, along with the needy blind and disabled, are covered by the Supplemental Security Income Program (SSI), which was enacted in 1972 and put into effect in 1974. While social security is based on coverage obtained through employment and is not based on need, SSI is a cash assistance, means-tested, welfare program. Approximately three-quarters of aged SSI recipients are women. As Charlotte Muller has stated, "SSI holds it recipients to a minimal standard of living."[25] As of February 1984, the maximum monthly federal SSI benefit was $314 for an individual and $472 for a couple. About two-thirds of the SSI recipients received less than the maximum amount because they had other income.[26] Only half the states supplement the federal payment and even then many people are forced to live below the poverty line.

Health, of course, is a major area of concern for older people. Since 1965 a large part of the health expenses of the elderly has been borne by Medicare. While it was meant to remove the severe burden of the cost of medical care from older people—those most likely to need care and least able to pay for it—in fact Medicare today only pays for 44 percent of the health care costs of the elderly.[27] It has been estimated that older women spend one-third of their median income on medical costs.

While programs for the elderly, including Medicare, were not affected as severely by budget cuts during the first Reagan administration as programs for children, young adults and the unemployed, reductions in other areas such as nutrition assistance, low-income energy assistance, Medicaid, and housing assistance, as well as the elimination of the CETA program, have adversely affected older people.[28]

In a telephone survey of the elderly poor of Chicago, it was found that, from 1981 to 1984, 20 percent of this group did not seek help with medical problems even though they thought they needed medical care; 17 percent were turned away from pharmacies even though they had Medicaid cards; 29 percent cut down on medication and prescriptions; 15 percent did not have adequate winter clothing; 22 percent had trouble with their utilities; and 40 percent had cut down on food.[29]

The issue of dietary deficiency is a particularly important one among the elderly. It has been estimated, for example, that "approximately one-third to one-half of the health problems experienced by this group are believed to be directly or indirectly related to nutrition."[30] It is clear that the impact of the Reagan cutbacks on older Americans has been and will continue to be severe.

In addition to the direct burden of their own health expenses, older women must, if they are married, be concerned with ways of coping with a spouse's need for medical care and with ways of paying for that care. Since wives generally outlive their husbands, this is primarily a woman's problem. Not only do wives often care for their husbands at home as long as possible but they are often then required to find a way of obtaining long-term care for them.

While the emotional costs of institutionalizing a spouse may be devastating, the financial costs may be equally debilitating. As one researcher has noted:

> This individual, who is usually a woman, is forced to divide one income into two parts: one portion for the payment of nursing home costs and the second for her own living expenses. This not only keeps the community-based spouse from maintaining her maximum level of functional independence, but it also increases the likelihood of her entering a nursing home.[31]

If the couple's finances simply cannot be stretched to cover long-term care, the spouse may be forced to "spend down" until Medicaid eligibility is achieved, thereby impoverishing herself. But, of course, it is not only a spouse's illness that can force an elderly person to "spend down" to the level of poverty; the individual's own illness can require the same strategy in order to be eligible for long-term care. These women, victims of their own or their husband's illness, become yet another group of the new poor, people who have lived most of their lives as part of the middle class and suddenly find themselves among the poor or the near-poor.

The elderly new poor are to be found in many communities, even in affluent ones, often struggling to remain in an area with which they are familiar; in which they have some friends, some roots. In Palo Alto, California, even the senior center looks affluent. An old firehouse, it is a white, two-story building with handsome wrought-iron decoration and huge, exotic plants inside the front door. According to Kathleen McConnell, a young social worker who works at the center, many of the women she sees were originally in the middle and upper middle classes. "They are people caught by the times, by a spouse that died and by escalating costs." Many are widows, some moved here during their retirement years, and now that their husbands have died, they can no longer afford the rents. Others, according to McConnell, "have a house, have clothes left over from when they had much more money, and may even have a car, but they have no real cash to manage day to day.

Some are looking for subsidized housing; there is a waiting list of two to three years. Many spend their money on rent instead of food and some must spend their money down to the level of public assistance." But above all, she feels, "These women don't want to admit that they are needy. They look as though everything is o.k. but this image, which is good for their self-esteem, makes it very hard for them to ask for help."

Yet another problem, according to McConnell, is home care. Many of the women she sees are frail enough to need home care in order to be able to remain in their own homes. Home care in northern California costs, on the average, $8 per hour and many agencies have a four-hour minimum. While most women do not have the extra cash to be able to pay for this service, there is also a large group whose income is not low enough for them to qualify for Medi-Cal, the California version of Medicaid. "They make do," McConnell says, "with a combination of neighbors, friends, and relatives—a patchwork. But they often continue to decline and eventually end up in a nursing home where the state has to pay." The society's reluctance, once again, to provide intermediate, preventive supports at moderate cost results in that same society eventually paying for long-term care at a far higher financial cost and at an equally high social and psychological cost to the individual. Professionals who work with the elderly—nurses, physicians, social workers, and community workers—generally agree that an elderly person who is placed in an impersonal, long-term care facility is likely to deteriorate much more rapidly than the older person who remains in his/her own environment, among familiar people and objects. The uprooting of the elderly from their environment is often a harsh, cruel act that could be prevented by earlier, less expensive, and less drastic intervention.

As one social worker who works with the elderly has pointed out:

Some sense of power—some degree of control over one's destiny—is critical to the integrity of the human personality. The new resident, by virtue of age status, pauper status, patient status, and his losses and impairments, already has experienced an erosion of his sense of autonomy or self-direction. The institution actively participates in reducing the resident to total lack of power. The fact that most often it is the place of last resort, in itself gives power to institutional management and staff. After all, where will the old person go if he does not like institutional life?[32]

And yet there are those for whom some kind of institution is the only answer; then the problem may not be how to keep them out, but how to get them into an appropriate setting. The aged black, the poor, and the hard-to-care-for are clearly discriminated against and often very difficult to place.[33] A New York City group recently completed a survey of state records and found that white patients were accepted at better nursing homes, while blacks and Hispanics were relegated to poorer ones. According to the survey, of the 153 public, voluntary, and proprietary nursing homes in New York City, "All-white or virtually all-white populations were found at 54, many of which were said to offer the finest care available." The president of the group, Friends and Relatives of the Institutional Aged, stated, "Black and Hispanic aged find their final days are spent in a final segregation created by the nursing homes with the acquiescence of hospital-discharge planners and the state."[34] Many nursing homes are operated under religious auspices and are, of course, permitted to restrict admission to patients of their faith; they are not, however, permitted by law, if they admit patients of other religions, to exclude people because of their racial or ethnic background.

Potential nursing home patients are not only discriminated against on the basis of race; they are also discriminated against according to income. The nursing home industry is increasingly going after "private pay patients" rather than Medicaid patients because, as a senior vice-president of one of the leading nursing home companies has stated, that is where "the big money is."[35]

The shortage of nursing home beds, particularly for Medicaid patients, is expected to become critical by the end of this century; and not only are such homes not being built but the newest strategy is for companies to move into developing retirement communities for the affluent that guarantee "priority access" to a nearby nursing home. The deputy director of the health care statistics division in the U.S. Department of Health and Human Services has suggested that we might be moving toward a situation where "The wealthy have beds and the poor stand in line."[36]

Wherever they spend their final years, the overwhelming reality about old people in our society, particularly old women, is that they are extraneous. With American families increasingly fragmented, there is little room for the older woman within the family unit. With women of all ages working in increasing numbers, there is no one at home to care for the elderly who are often ill and cannot be left alone for long periods of time. And with rapidly changing notions about child care, many young mothers are unwilling to entrust their preschool children to the "out of date" ways of the grandmother. There are, therefore, few roles the older woman is permitted to play within the fast-paced, individual-centered family of the 1980s.

Often, after a lifetime of caring for others, elderly women are ultimately left to live in isolation. For old women are survivors in the true sense of the word. Most often they have outlived their spouses and their friends and have lost much of what made them valued in American society: their youth, their reproductive potential, their earning potential. The older woman is often devalued and ignored and is, in addition, frequently dependent on others, often strangers, for her day-to-day sustenance.

Our avoidance of the old, our reluctance to integrate them into our lives, to let them perform meaningful tasks, and to make adequate provisions for their well-being stems, in part, from our feelings about death. In avoiding the problems of old age, we attempt to avoid our old age; in turning our backs on the sick and dying, we attempt to turn our backs on our own inevitable deterioration and death. As Ernest Becker has stated with such force and clarity, "The idea of death, the fear of it, haunts the human animal like nothing else; it is a mainspring of human activity—activity designed largely to avoid the fatality of death, to overcome it by denying in some way that it is the final destiny for man."[37]

Some may be lucky enough to have a daughter or a daughter-in-law to help them—again, of course, it is women doing the caring—but these younger women are increasingly torn among their responsibilities toward their own families, their responsibilities toward the older person, and these days, a job as well. As many experts in geriatrics have pointed out, the current emphasis on alternatives to institutional care place the burden of care in the community on unpaid relatives or on low-paid health workers. Again, women are being placed in a caring role and are being exploited for fulfilling that role.

It is, of course, possible to develop alternatives to institutionalization. One such alternative is Miracle Square, a residence for elderly and disabled people in Tucson, Arizona. Established in 1982, Miracle Square is a pilot project financed partly by the residents themselves, partly through the U.S. Department of Housing and Urban Development (HUD), and partly by the local county government. It is home for nineteen residents, sixteen of whom are over sixty.

A converted motel, Miracle Square provides individual rooms for each resident and a communal area where the residents can socialize. According to Peggy McDonald, the warm, lively, gray-haired director, the goal is to provide "freedom and independence" for low-income people who do not really need to be in nursing homes but who may need a degree of caretaking. The residents are encouraged to do all they can for themselves and have their own stoves and refrigerators, but most of them also have a hot lunch provided by Meals on Wheels.

Virginia Dixon lives at Miracle Square. She is a young-looking, part-Cherokee, part-black, seventy-three-year-old mother, grandmother, and great-grandmother. Pictures of her handsome family line the walls of her comfortably furnished room. For twenty-five years she did domestic work and hairdressing in order to support herself and her daughter; her husband has been dead for forty years. Having spent her entire working life in the secondary labor market, Ms. Dixon's total income in 1983 from both social security and SSI was $302 a month, or $3,624 for the year. The poverty line for a single person in 1983 was $5,061. After paying $126.29 for rent at Miracle Square, Ms. Dixon has approximately $175 per month left for all her needs.

Virginia Dixon worked until her severe diabetes required her to be hospitalized. After discharge from the hospital, she was placed in a nursing home, where she remained for eight years. When I met her, she had been at Miracle Square for six months and said,

"I am happy. I think young and I go out often—as often as I can—just about every other day. Some people go on and on about 'I'm aging and I'm dying,' but I don't like to do that or to listen to it because it's a real stress on me. It bores me."

Edith Foster, a heavy, fifty-four-year-old woman who looks many years older, also lives at Miracle Square. She is missing all her front teeth and has large elastic bandages on both knees. She lies on her bed while we talk. Foster was married to a contractor who was killed in an automobile accident twelve years before when a truck went through a stop sign. She herself had been in a severe automobile accident several years ago. "I ran into a car and I was a pedestrian," she says with a giggle. Her name had run in the obituary column of the local newspaper, but she survived. She had been in nursing homes for five years prior to coming to Miracle Square a year and a half ago.

Although she seems quite severely disabled, she manages to go shopping three times a week, goes to church every Sunday, and helps another, more handicapped resident with her food preparation and with shopping. In response to my commenting about all she does for her friend, she said simply, "It makes me feel not quite such a burden."

For those older people who are relatively healthy and can live on their own, participation in community activities can make life worthwhile. Maria Ortiz, a small, extremely active sixty-seven-year-old woman, lives in the small community of Espagnola, New Mexico. She was married for over thirty-five years to a man who, among other jobs, was a uranium miner and a sheepherder. She raised three children and now has eighteen grandchildren and six great-grandchildren. Ortiz receives $228 per month from social security and $106 per month from SSI for a total annual income of $4,008. She also receives $25 worth of food stamps monthly. Out of this income she must pay all of her expenses, her rent, her food, her electricity, and her other bills.

Before Ortiz started working as a foster grandparent in the Family Learning Center in Espagnola, she suffered from severe rheumatoid arthritis, particularly severe pain in her knees. She had been in and out of the hospital and could barely walk. After she started working with the children, she found herself walking to work in the morning and home in the evening "with so much joy" that her physical problems completely went away.

Every day for four hours, she works with the children, primarily in Spanish because she and the teachers are concerned that the Spanish language and customs are fading among the Hispanic children of Espagnola. Having helped to organize the Foster Grandparent Council, she is a current member and a trainer for new foster grandparents. Maria Ortiz spoke with vigor and excitement. Her work at the center seemed to be of central importance to this vital older woman.

Ortiz's feelings of well-being that stem from her role in the community are echoed by older people all over the country. In rural North Carolina, Eva Salber, a community health physician, interviewed older people about their lives. Social supports, interconnections with others in the community, both family and friends, were found to be extremely important factors in the well-being of these older men and women.

Lillian Adams, age seventy-one, is described as a "natural helper" and "highly respected" in her community. A schoolteacher for forty-four years, she is currently active in several volunteer organizations, visits elderly shut-ins, brings friends to town for food stamps, and is generally helpful in a variety of ways. She talks about her life:

It doesn't take so much to make me happy like it does a lot of folk. If I can know that I can see people and people can come to see me, and I have something decent to wear and something to eat, and I can help people, that's about all it takes to make me happy. I do more for people now than I did when I was younger, like cooking things for people, carrying them, sharing vegetables with those who can't help themselves.[38]

Polly Williams, age seventy-five, talks about what's important to her in her day-to-day activities:

I'm not lonely. I pass the day doing a little housework, neighbors coming in, and I do a lot of visiting. . . .
The people here in the community, neighbors, we check on

each other. This one can look over at that house and she can tell what's going on over there; if the shades are not up by a certain time she goes to see why. . . . Long as anybody is well and happy I pay no attention to them, but if they need my help I am there if I can get there. This woman, the second house from here, was called up to Charlotte, her sister was sick. I go over and see if everything is all right and water her flowers, and when her water went off I called her brother and let him come to see why. I check on all the people that I know in the village, if I see anything wrong. I don't have time to go to the new senior center, I'm too busy.[39]

9

WHAT IS TO BE DONE? LESSONS FROM SWEDEN

> Today's social policy system can be said to fulfill three different functions. In part it is a matter of *social investment in the future*. ... Another part has to do with *income supplementation*. ... Finally, social policy seeks to give *compensation* to the victims of unfortunate circumstances. ...
>
> Together, [they] indicate an unremitting effort to use social policy as a medium to create greater equality and increased security for the majority of the population.[1]
>
> —*Toward Equality*
> *The Alva Myrdal Report to the*
> *Swedish Social Democratic*
> *Party, 1971*

Many of us, in thinking about the social and economic problems of the United States in the 1980s, are caught up in the clichés, the unexamined assumptions, the negativism of the current era. We are all too aware of the retreat from a commitment to social justice that was widespread during the 1960s and early 1970s, and of the current concern with self and with personal success and happiness. Changing "the system" or even modifying or humanizing it seems more and more utopian. Even those who think of themselves as activists, as change agents committed to equity, may retreat into work and family rather than be constantly confronted by a world filled with sadness and danger, a world that makes us feel increasingly impotent. Perhaps this withdrawal is most vividly illustrated by the opening paragraph of one of those newsy Christmas letters that come in the mail each year—this one fittingly from 1984:

> This year we adopted a new attitude: leave all of the world's woes on the T.V. screen, like just another sci-fi program, and deal with our own home, family and environment as being the only real world.

But of course that is not the real world, much less the "only" real world. For some, a way out of the despondency and disengagement that seem to be increasingly ubiquitous in the United States is literally to go beyond our country and our problems and attempt to examine the solutions other societies have developed. The benefits of cross-cultural observation and analysis are readily apparent: the recognition that many societies develop radically different ways of meeting similar needs; the questioning of our own assumptions; and, perhaps most important, the rekindling of the hope that some problems may indeed be soluble, given enough time, thought and energy.

But there are dangers as well: becoming so enamored with another system that you would like to transplant it as is into your own society, and becoming so admiring of another system that you fall into despair when it flounders or fails. While we use cross-cultural comparisons to stimulate our thinking, to broaden our perspectives, to see the world and its problems in new ways, we must always keep in mind that every society's political and economic system has evolved out of its history; its geography; its ecology; and of the social, political, and economic forces indigenous to it. Policies or solutions or patterns that work for one country may simply not be effective when transplanted to another.

Each society must develop its own way, its own solutions that stem from its needs, its history, its values, its goals.

To become disheartened about the possibility of fundamental reform when solutions that have seemed so appealing fall into disrepute or simply fail is so far too easy. We have seen this happen repeatedly over the past fifty years. Those travelers to the Soviet Union in the 1920s and 1930s who thought they had seen a future that "worked" were soon to learn that that society was developing in ways very different from what they had imagined; many, in reaction, made a 180-degree turn away from the socialism they had hoped to see, to a total condemnation of reform based on collective principles.

We are in danger of seeing a similar reaction today to events in China. Many of us who studied human services in China in the early 1970s found what we believed to be an exciting and inspiring model of a society committed to equity—equity between men and women, between old and young, urban and rural, between those who worked with their minds and those who worked with their hands. The incredible advances in health status, in the overall well-being of the Chinese people, were an eloquent testimony to what could be done to turn a society around if one but had the will and, of course, the power.

But today we see much of what made these advances possible being dismantled: In the rural areas the commune structure that provided the political and economic base for collectivism and for health and other human services has been replaced by the "responsibility system" which emphasizes individual and familial effort and undermines the orientation toward prevention and public health that made China, for a short time, a model to be emulated by countries all over the world. In both urban and rural areas in many spheres of life cooperation is being replaced by competition, lay participation in the administration of human services by professional control, and, above all, motivation by ideology or, in the Chinese idiom, "Serving the People," being replaced by the promise of individual economic advancement. Moreover, in recent years Western visitors have learned the extent of the oppression that many groups suffered during the Cultural Revolution. The "model" is unraveling in many places.

But cross-cultural comparisons can tell us much that is useful and, indeed, hopeful. Cross-cultural comparisons tell us that the only two industrial countries in the world that do not have a near-universal system of national health insurance are the United States and South Africa. Cross-cultural comparisons tell us that virtually all the European countries provide family or children's allowances for the entire population. Cross-cultural comparisons tell us that seventy-five countries, including many developing countries and every industrialized country except the United States, provide some form of statutory maternity leave and cash benefits to replace wages during that leave.[2] Cross-cultural comparisons tell us that countries as poor as China, as small as Israel, and as powerful as the Soviet Union have made substantial commitments to day care, often providing first-rate, imaginative services that both care for preschool children and enable their mothers to become part of the labor force.

Rather than examine the family policies of a broad range of countries, however, I think it would be more useful to review the policies of one in some detail. Sweden has become, during the past half-century, the prototype of the social welfare state. Both for those who applauded its efforts to secure the good life for its people and for those who deplore these efforts, Sweden has become the symbol, the model of a democratic state attempting to minimize inequality and to provide services that will make life more livable in the twentieth century. Perhaps more than any other nonsocialist country, Sweden has recognized the hardships, the displacement, the cost to the family in social and emotional terms of technological development and urbanization, and has attempted to assume significant societal responsibility for the well-being of its citizens. In addition, for the past twenty years Sweden has had a commitment to equality between men and women and has tried, through education, through the provision of services, and through close cooperation among the various sectors of society to bring such equality closer to reality. Sweden's family policy must therefore be seen as an outgrowth of its dual commitment to social welfare and to sexual equality.

Before examining Swedish family policy in some detail, it must be stated that Sweden is a small country approximately the size of California, with a relatively homogeneous population of 8.3 million inhabitants; immigrants, primarily from southern European countries and other Nordic countries, comprise approximately 10 percent of the population and are among the lowest-paid workers. Sweden is one of the richest countries in the world, with a per capita gross domestic product second only to Switzerland's.[3] Contrary to common misperceptions in the United States, the vast majority of all Swedish companies, 85 percent of those with more than fifty employees, are privately owned.[4] Economic development was rapid during the postwar period, particularly during the 1960s, but has slowed markedly since 1975; this slowdown has had, and continues to have, serious impact on social welfare policy. It must also be noted that one party, the Social Democrats, have been in power for nearly all of the last fifty years, a continuity of leadership rare among Western democracies.

Until well into the second half of the nineteenth century, Sweden remained an agrarian society in which "The male head of the family reigned supreme."[5] In fact, a law passed in 1734 declared that a woman, whether married or not, must be in the care of a guardian: "A wife's guardian was her husband, an unmarried woman's guardian was her father or brother."[6] In 1872 the law was modified so that an unmarried woman came of age at twenty-five, but a married woman remained permanently under the guardianship of her husband. A new Marriage Code in 1921 established, finally, women's equal status with men, both legally and economically.

During Sweden's long agrarian period men and women did very different kinds of work—as, in fact, they did in most societies. In the south of Sweden, women did the cooking, the weaving, and other household chores and cared for domestic animals. In the north, where men had to spend much of their time hunting, making long journeys to market, and in forestry, women were responsible for caring for the livestock and cultivating the land. Men's work and women's work were usually rigidly separated even though "women's work" was essential in maintaining the family. This differentiation between men's work and women's work remains today, despite the Swedish government's efforts to minimize the dual labor market.

During the period of industrialization in the second half of the nineteenth century, the population grew rapidly, and there was widespread unemployment that triggered a wave of emigration to the United States. At the same time, large numbers of unmarried women lived in the cities, and their availability as cheap labor helped to open up such new fields as teaching, medical work, and employment in the post office and in municipal administration. By the early 1930s the worldwide depression had reached Sweden, and rising unemployment prompted demands there, as in the United States, that "women who were married to men earning a 'reasonable income' should be forced to leave their jobs."[7] These demands were, however, rejected by the government; instead, in 1933 an economic policy was initiated that provided for large-scale public works projects and called for full employment.

During the economic crisis the Swedish birth rate dropped sharply. As a response to this decline, Sweden developed a family policy that would encourage couples to have more children and would enhance the well-being of the family unit. This family policy has been greatly expanded and continues today. Starting in the mid-1930s, Sweden also developed a social-welfare policy that would provide greater economic security for all, encourage equality between the sexes, and provide for the health and well-being of children.

During the 1960s Sweden embarked on a broad-based, intense sex-role debate. Not only were women's roles and women's need for equality discussed but men's roles were debated as well. Many Swedish policymakers had long felt that men as well as women suffered from rigid role differentiation. Not only did they feel that women's roles could not change unless men's roles were altered but that men would actively benefit from increased contact with children, increased ability to express their feelings, and participation in the domestic aspects of daily life. According to a political adviser to the Swedish Ministry of Labour:

We are also convinced that men themselves have everything to gain from greater equality between the sexes. Men have a higher suicide rate than women and are more often involved in violence and accidents. They are more commonly affected by heart attacks and other stress diseases associated with the welfare society.[8]

By 1968 equality between men and women became official policy in Sweden. According to Berit Rollén, under-secretary in the Ministry of Labour,

> We want to make it possible for everybody to find a paid job and to achieve economic independence. . . . Our aim is to apply this attitude to the whole of society, to working life but also to politics and family life. We want men and women to have the same responsibilities, rights, and obligations in society and in the home. And we realize that this will call for changes in the way in which society, workplaces, and the home are organized.[9]

The Swedes describe the family today as the "working family." Recognizing that the vast majority of women have always worked—albeit often in unpaid housework—Swedish society has attempted to develop conditions under which women and men will have equal opportunities in the labor market, in the home, and in the community.

According to Rollén, "The housewife represents a dying race. . . ."[10] In 1982, 77 percent of all women ages twenty to sixty-four in Sweden held paid jobs; moreover, paid employment is more common among younger women than among older women. This means that the highest employment participation rate is among mothers of preschool children. The typical pattern among women today is to work full-time until they have children and then to reduce their work to part-time. In 1982 nearly 47 percent of working women worked part-time, compared to only 7 percent of men.[11]

A dual labor market, one for men and another for women, still exists, however. Men essentially choose from among three hundred occupations; women from thirty. Furthermore, the jobs women hold tend, as in the United States, to be at the low end of the payscale. For example, 40 percent of all women in the Swedish labor force were hospital aides, sales clerks, office workers, or cleaning personnel. Of those employed in manufacturing, construction, and mining, 88 percent are men.[12] Women have moved into jobs in the public sector in significant numbers and, in fact, occupy approximately 30 percent of elective political positions, nationally, regionally, and locally.[13] Women have, however, made far less progress in the private sector, particularly at the executive level. One estimate is that only 10 percent of company directors are women and "barely 1 percent of the real decision-makers (managing directors and senior executives)."[14]

The wage gap between Swedish men and women has narrowed in recent years. Women in industry now earn, on the average, approximately 90 percent of what men earn. Most analysts ascribe the gains women have made in the labor market to four major factors: (1) the long period of economic prosperity during the 1950s and 1960s; (2) rapid expansion of the public sector, which has made job opportunities available to new entrants; (3) a system enacted in 1970 establishing separate taxation of husband and wife, each employed person being treated as an individual with his or her own income; and (4) a powerful trade union movement that has played a key role in promoting sexual equality. Between 80 and 90 percent of all workers in Sweden are unionized, and these unions have significant influence within Swedish society.[15]

Yet another facet of working life that has an impact on family life is the length of the work day. Parents of children under the age of eight may work a six-hour day, rather than the usual eight-hour day, with a proportionate reduction in pay. Swedish policymakers have long been concerned with individuals being able to adapt their work schedule to their personal needs. They recognize that people may wish to work longer hours before child-rearing, cut back on their work commitments during their child's early years, resume a full workload for much of their adult lives, and then, perhaps, diminish their number of working hours again as they get older. As Berit Rollén has stated, these innovations in the organization of working life

demand much greater flexibility in the organization of the individual workplace and the manner in which work is conducted there. This is an inevitable consequence of our wishing to give individuals greater liberty in planning their working life according to their own needs and preferences. It is also an inevitable consequence of a growing proportion of the population coming to be included in the labor force. When the whole of the adult population forms part of "the working family," working life can no longer be organized as if it only involved healthy young men with no family responsibility.[16]

One of the most significant changes in family structure in Sweden in recent years has been the growing proportion of babies born outside of marriage. In 1970, 18 percent of all newborns were born to unwed mothers; by 1980 that figure had risen to 40 percent.[17] With Swedish women working in such large numbers and with the large number of single-parent families—(many couples cohabit but do not marry, so it is extremely difficult to estimate with accuracy the actual number of households with only a single parent)—the Swedish government has put into place many measures that contribute to the basic well-being of the family unit and specifically to the well-being of the child.

There are, first of all, a variety of financial benefits for families. A children's allowance is paid for every child up to the age of sixteen, and up to age eighteen if the child is still attending school. The amount, 3,300 kronor per year (approximately $380), is paid for every child, regardless of the income level of the family. Since January 1, 1982, a special supplementary children's allowance of 4,950 kronor is paid for the third child, and 6,600 kronor for the fourth child and for each subsequent child.[18]

In addition to the children's allowance, which is universal, a means-tested housing allowance is available. There are two, one that is paid by the national government for each child and one that is funded jointly by the national and municipal governments, which is based on the amount of rent paid. In May 1983 approximately one out of every three households with children received a housing allowance.[19]

Sweden has dealt with the issue of child support very differently than the United States has. If the parents of a young child do not live together, the one who does not have custody is obliged to pay child support. If the parent who is obliged to pay does not or cannot pay the full amount agreed to, the national government will provide a "maintenance advance" to the child. The parent responsible for paying child support is required to repay the amount advanced, but in the meantime, the child will not have to suffer because of nonpayment. Moreover, if the amount of child support is clearly inadequate, the government will pay a "supplementary allowance"; the parent required to pay child support is not responsible for repaying this amount.[20]

Yet another way Sweden has attempted to provide for the well-being of the family is through parental insurance. This system, established in 1974 and financed through taxes and employers' contributions, enables either parent to remain at home for up to nine months at the time of the birth of a child, while drawing approximately 90 percent of his/her income. The nine months may be divided up between the parents in any way they see fit but must not be taken by both parents at the same time. The parents may take an additional three months' leave, bringing the total time to one year, but during these last three months they will only receive 37 kronor per day, which is less than most regular incomes.[21]

In addition to parental leave during the infant's first year of life, Swedish fathers are entitled a ten-day parents' allowance, at the time of the birth of the baby, to help care for the mother and the new baby or other children in the home; either parent may take up to sixty days' leave per year per child if the child or its regular caretaker is ill.[22] By these measures the Swedes have attempted to legitimize parenting even if it conflicts with the individual's role as a member of the labor force. By paying parents for caregiving during these necessary periods and by guaranteeing their jobs when they return from leave, the society is recognizing its responsibility to enable parents to care for their children without undue economic, professional or emotional stress.

One of the central goals of the institution of these parental rights was to encourage men as well as women to participate in child-rearing. In 1983, nearly ten years after the introduction of these programs, 25 to 30 percent of the fathers eligible for parental leave at the time of childbirth actually utilized it; the average period of time taken by this group ranged from ten days to one month. In a survey taken in 1981 it was found that approximately 76 percent of all new fathers exercised their right to be at home around the time of the delivery. Interestingly, and perhaps predictably, the younger the man, the more likely he was to take this leave. The entitlement that found the most favor with fathers was parental leave at the time a child is ill. In 1983 200,000 fathers, compared to 270,000 mothers, stayed at home to care for sick children; moreover, it was found that fathers stayed at home for the same amount of time as did the mothers.[23]

There has been considerable concern in Sweden that more men have not taken advantage of their rights to parental leave during the child's first year. A study done in 1981 found that "a clear majority of Swedish men approved of the . . . opportunities for paid days off" and that "quite a few of those who are not clearly positive toward these opportunities are not negative either, but instead are ambivalent. . . ."[24] A key factor in determining male attitudes was the man's perception of his workmates' opinion: "Those whose workmates would disapprove of taking time off from work for these purposes are also much more negative towards such leaves than those who perceive a positive attitude on the part of workmates."[25]

There was also differentiation on the basis of work site. Ninety-eight percent of those employed by the national government utilized their leave entitlement, while 84 percent of those employed by local governments and 74 percent employed by private companies took advantage of their right to parental leave. One analyst observed, "Men employed by private firms (and perhaps local government employees as well) probably believe, correctly or incorrectly, that their prospects for career advancement would suffer significantly if they took such leave."[26]

Sweden has developed a comprehensive system of maternal and child health that includes prenatal care and preparation and training (for both parents) for the delivery; advice on contraception, well-baby care, medical care of preschool children, medical care and treatment of chronically ill and disabled children; and training of parents on the care of preschool children. Health and medical services are provided through a health insurance system that is compulsory for everyone who lives and works in Sweden.[27] The system, both inpatient and outpatient, is primarily administered by local governments, the twenty-three county councils, and the three municipalities—Göteborg, Malmö, and the island of Gotland—that are not part of county council areas. As one analyst of the Swedish system has noted, "The equity principle is a basic principle of health services planning in Sweden. Everyone should be given equal care whenever possible, and it is the need for medical care, not the patient's financial resources, which should be the entrance ticket to the system."[28]

The combination of an extremely high standard of living and an accessible, affordable health care system has led to the Swedes having some of the best health statistics in the world: Their infant mortality rate, 6.8 per thousand live births in 1982,[29] is one of the lowest, and their life expectancy, 73.4 for men and 79.4 for women in 1982 is among the highest in the world.[30]

Despite these efforts, socioeconomic differences in health status persist in Sweden. According to Edgar Borgenhammar, professor of health services management at the Nordic School of Public Health, "Lower social classes have more chronic diseases, more limited vision and more difficulties in hearing, and also have more manifest psychiatric problems." He goes on to state that unemployment and a lower level of education are also associated with increased health problems and that immigrants "generally have worse health problems than the rest of the population."[31] Nonetheless, Sweden has made extraordinary efforts to make first-rate medical care available to the entire population.

In the area of family planning, since the abortion act became law on January 1, 1975, the woman herself is the one who decides if she is to have an abortion. Specifically, abortion is free until the end of the eighteenth week of pregnancy. Before the twelfth week the woman need only consult with a doctor; after the twelfth week she must also consult with a social worker but she may be refused an abortion only if "the operation involves a risk to her life and health."[32] An abortion before the end of the eighteenth week may not be refused without being reviewed by the National Board of Health and Welfare, and abortion must not be performed after the eighteenth week without approval of the Board of Health and Welfare. Since the end of the 1960s there have been no reported illegal abortions in Sweden.[33]

Since the new law was passed, the abortion rate in Sweden has remained relatively constant. Moreover, the teenage abortion rate—and the teenage pregnancy rate—which had been increasing markedly during the early 1970s has since decreased. The birth rate for women ages fifteen to nineteen, for example, has been cut in half, from 31.1 per thousand women in 1973 to 15 in 1981.[34] This dramatic decrease is at least partially due to education in the schools, from a very young age, about reproduction and sexuality, to widespread family planning education, and to widely available and largely free family planning services.

On January 1, 1976, a year after the abortion act became law, a new sterilization act went into effect. The act emphasizes the individual's right to choose this form of family planning and the voluntary nature of the procedure; it stipulates that only the woman herself may take the initiative for a sterilization procedure. Every sterilization must be preceded by an information session with a doctor or a social worker in which the nature and consequences of the procedure are thoroughly explained and alternative forms of birth control are described.[35]

During the 1970s the single most important family policy issue was child care. Since the Swedish government, and indeed most institutions within Swedish society, had made a serious commitment both to equality between men and women and to enhancing the well-being of the family unit, the expansion of child-care facilities was considered an urgent priority.

Child-care programs are a municipal responsibility in Sweden. Facilities are generally located in residential areas, near where the children live. Unlike the pattern in countries such as China, preschool facilities at the workplace are rare in Sweden.

There are several different kinds of facilities for young children. Day nurseries, generally open from 6:30 A.M. to 6:30 P.M., take children from six months to seven years. Because of the availability of parental leave until the child is one year old and because of waiting lists for available places, relatively few children as young as six months attend.

Part-time groups generally care for older preschoolers, children ages four to six. In 1975 a law was passed requiring all municipalities to provide a preschool place for all six-year-olds. These programs usually run three hours a day, five days a week, and are comparable to kindergarten in the United States.

Yet another alternative is the family day nursery. In this instance, the municipality hires a woman to care for up to four children in her home. These facilities are supervised by the municipality.

Recreation centers, also known as "leisure time centers," are available after school and during school vacations to care for school-age children, ages seven to twelve, whose parents are working or studying full time.[36]

While Sweden has strongly emphasized the provision of child-care facilities, as of 1980 existing centers had space for only 30 percent of the children from birth to age six. In spring 1980, 43 percent of all preschool children were cared for by a parent in the home; 17 percent were in a day nursery, and 13 percent in a family day nursery; 14 percent were being cared for through paid private child care, and 6 percent through unpaid, private caregivers, primarily relatives; 3 percent were in a part-time group; and 4 percent were at home with mothers who were caring for other children as well. According to a survey conducted in 1980 by the Swedish National Bureau of Statistics, 48 percent of those preschool children whose parents were "gainfully employed" or studying had places in the municipal child-care system.[37]

Although Swedish policymakers have recognized over the past ten to fifteen years the urgent need for additional preschool facilities, particularly with increasing numbers of young women entering the labor force, their commitment to day care of extraordinarily high quality has often meant an inability to move ahead in numbers of places as rapidly as many would have liked. Swedish day nurseries are surely among the best day-care facilities in the world. From the modern, relatively spacious and somewhat avant-garde centers in Stockholm, stocked with the most up-to-date equipment, to day nurseries such as the one in the suburbs of the small city of Västerås, located in a lovely old wooden house surrounded by trees and grass, which prides itself on the close relationships among children, parents, and staff, preschool facilities in Sweden are indeed enviable. They are, almost unfailingly, warm and welcoming, and decorated colorfully, ingeniously, sometimes with Scandinavian fabrics and always with stunning posters and the children's artwork. Close attention is paid not only to the children's physical environment but to their individual development, to their health and well-being, and to their social development.

The children are sometimes grouped by age, more often today into sibling groups ages two-and-one-half to seven. The notion is that, by mixing different ages, children can have the experience of playing different roles in the group, of helping one another and of being helped, of caring for others and being cared for. The caregivers include preschool teachers, who have been trained in a two-year course following upper secondary school, and children's nurses, who are trained through a two-year program within upper secondary school or through a special one-year program. The most common ratio is one adult for every four or five children, with the infant programs having even fewer children per adult.[38] Creative play is stressed, with children working both in small groups and singly if they prefer. The development of the individual and the child's ability to be part of the larger group are both felt to be essential learning experiences.

Special facilities are available for immigrant children ages five and six who speak a language other than Swedish in the home. These children have priority in obtaining places in preschool facilities and are offered training in their "home language." For at least four hours a week children may, on a voluntary basis, be taught by a teacher who speaks their native tongue; participate in unilingual part-time groups from the age of four; and join unilingual sibling groups at day nurseries or in a variety of other settings in which their original language is used.[39]

In 1981 the cost of preschool care was estimated at approximately 44,000 kronor ($5,000) per child. The central government paid at that time a subsidy of just over 21,000 kronor for each child in a fully qualified day nursery. The state subsidy for family day nurseries was 3,250 kronor per place, plus 35 percent of the municipality's gross expenses for the program. Parents' fees vary from municipality to municipality and are dependent upon income, but the average fee paid by parents was approximately 4,000 kronor ($460) in 1981. Part-time preschools are free for six-year-olds and for younger children needing special care. There is no fixed fee for after-school care; the amount is often linked to the day nursery fee but is set at perhaps 40 to 50 percent of that amount.[40]

In addition to benefits that stem from Sweden's family policy,

Swedish citizens are entitled to a comprehensive variety of other benefits under their social insurance system. These include health insurance, sickness benefits, old-age pension, disability pension, work-injury insurance, unemployment insurance, and a variety of special measures to help to care for the elderly. In addition, "social assistance" is available for those individuals who are still in need after receiving other benefits. It is worth noting that social assistance in Sweden, what we in the United States would call "welfare," accounts for only 1 percent of social-welfare expenditures and benefits at most 5 percent of the population. According to Sören Kindlund of the Swedish Ministry of Social Affairs, "Those receiving social assistance do not represent a significant proportion of the families with children. . . . Two thirds of the social assistance beneficiaries are childless adults."[41]

But, despite this extensive system of benefits, many problems remain. *Crisis* is the word most commonly used by the Swedes themselves these days: economic crisis, social crisis, welfare crisis. But why should the Swedes be talking of crises when, according to a report prepared by the Swedish Secretariat for Futures Studies,

> Sweden has experienced an unparalleled process of development over the past hundred years. It has been transformed from a poor agrarian society with blatant economic inequalities to an advanced industrial society with a well-developed system of social security and more egalitarian living conditions than past generations could have dreamed of.[42]

The term *crisis* is used because the Swedes are aware that "one child out of every nine in Sweden does not feel liked by anybody" and "one person out of every eight age eighty or over [often feels] very lonely."[43] They are concerned because the "number of persons age eighty-five and over will grow by 70 percent during the remaining years of this century."[44] They are concerned because "it is estimated that between one-third and half of all morbidity is connected with the abuse of alcohol."[45]

They are concerned because Sweden desperately needs additional day care. In 1976 the Swedish Parliament adopted a five-year program to construct 100,000 new day-nursery places.

Because of economic difficulties, only 55,000 places had been completed by 1980 and it is uncertain when the remainder will be completed.[46]

And perhaps, above all, they are concerned about "the financial problem of finding the resources to expand child care, care of the aged and medical care in an economy characterized by stagnant output, tax weariness and a growing budgetary deficit."[47] The importance, the necessity of societal involvement in the care and welfare of the population has long been acknowledged; but the Swedes are not sure they can afford to maintain the level of care necessary to provide for an aging population whose family structure is increasingly fragmented and whose community structure is increasingly undermined by geographical mobility and the onslaught of technology.

Moreover, many Swedes are currently questioning the role of the welfare state and arguing that it must be cut back. Factors such as the high rate of taxation, a sense that government is playing too great a role in people's lives, and a feeling of disillusionment with the ability of the state to solve all of society's problems are leading to a degree of dissatisfaction with policies that have been entrenched in Sweden for fifty years.

But, to return to the United States, what significance, if any, does the Swedish experience have for us? It teaches us, I believe, that a society—albeit a small, homogeneous one—can mobilize around a central issue and develop indigenous methods of bringing about fundamental change. It tells us that with sufficient consensus and leadership, the public, private, and nonprofit sectors can work together to address problems central to the well-being of the people. It shows that, despite these conditions, it is extremely difficult to bring about change, change in people's attitudes, and change in behavior; and that any group hoping to significantly alter long-standing patterns and relationships between those who have more and those who have less must be in it for the long haul. But it also tells us, finally, that with imagination, with careful thought and planning, and with a leadership that seeks to correct injustices and bring people together, society can be made more responsive to the needs of women, children, and families in particular.

10
A CALL FOR A U.S. FAMILY POLICY

> It is my strong view that the American people have been sold a set of *false* choices by our national leaders who tell us we must choose between jobs and peace; between filling potholes in our streets and cavities in our children's teeth; between day care for 5 million latchkey children and home care for millions of senior citizens; . . . between arms control and building the MX! There are other choices—fairer choices— that you and I must insist our political leaders make.[1]
>
> —*Marian Wright Edelman*
> *President, Children's*
> *Defense Fund*

We have examined the problems of the growing number of women and children in the United States who are living in poverty. This examination has not attempted to be definitive or exhaustive but, rather, has tried to highlight some of the key issues and underlying causes of the problem. What has become clear is that the causes are varied and complex and that the solutions therefore must be multifaceted.

Despite the glitter and glamour that preoccupy much of the media, the sense of optimism that we are told the American people feel and the real gains made by some women, many of the underlying causes of the feminization of poverty are, of course, rooted in American society. The fact that women are overwhelmingly the caretakers of children is a key determinant of their secondary economic status. Whether within the two-parent family unit or in a single-parent family, women, for the most part, provide the nurturing, the day-to-day care, the hands-on childrearing. Men may impregnate and walk away; women are there for the next twenty years. Moreover, it is not just the men who walk away; the society has walked away as well. The lack of prenatal care and well-baby care for all Americans; the lack of first-rate, accessible day care and after-school care; and the lack of an adequate child welfare system for those in dire need all indicate that American society has told its mothers and children that they will have to go it alone. If they are lucky enough to be affluent, they *may* put together a healthy, rewarding life for themselves; if not, that's the way it goes. Through our policies we are saying that this society will tolerate black children dying in the first year of life at twice the rate of white children; we are saying that it is acceptable for some mothers and children to while away their lives in rat- and roach-infested welfare hotels while others live in almost unbelievable luxury. We are tolerating the existence of two unequal societies, with the most vulnerable suffering the most severely. Above all, to those who don't make it, we are saying, "It's your own fault"; blaming the victim has become national policy. The Reagan administration's cutbacks have clearly indicated that this is a society increasingly based on the survival of the fittest, and while an unencumbered woman *might* be able to hold her own under these conditions, she surely cannot with a thirty-pound three-year-old strapped literally or metaphorically to her back.

As the emergence of the new poor, the recession of 1982–1983, and the large number of people adversely affected by the Reagan administration's budget cuts have demonstrated, millions of Americans are constantly at risk. Millions of women are a divorce away from destitution; millions of workers are a layoff away from poverty. An illness, an unexpected pregnancy, the death of the primary wage-earner, or the move of a company plant to a Third-World country can precipitate a family's fall into dire straits. What must be stressed is that many of these events are beyond the control of any given person and therefore cannot be handled by the individual alone. The United States must recognize, as have Sweden and so many other industrialized countries, that the society must provide a humane environment in which people can live, work, thrive, and raise their children. The old supports of family and community must be replaced by some societal supports.

The United States must develop a comprehensive set of policies that will both strengthen family life and protect the well-being of women and children. I am not going to try to map out the many reforms that are needed within American society generally; I am, rather, proposing a three-pronged family policy that, if implemented, would go far toward minimizing the number of women and children living in poverty, would begin to protect their health and well-being, and would faciliate family cohesion and mutual support. There will be those who say that we cannot afford such a program. To them I say we cannot afford to continue on our present course. We are an extraordinarily rich society; we simply must decide how we wish to spend our wealth, and whether or not we want to develop a national policy that will work toward eradicating the drastic extremes that are so injurious to a healthy democracy. There will also be those who say this program does not go nearly far enough—that *all* Americans must be protected against poverty; to them I say we have seen that women and children are particularly vulnerable to shifts in the economy, in family life, in social policy, and therefore should be singled out, at this time, for special action. Perhaps a policy that puts women and children first will lead eventually to a more humane society policy for all Americans.

The agenda I am proposing includes three major areas of reform: the arena of work; universal entitlements specifically connected to the lives of families, particularly those with young children; and the welfare system. This is a broader agenda than is usually considered under the rubric "family policy," but I believe it is extremely important to recognize that employment policy *is* family policy, welfare policy *is* family policy; and surely the amount of maternity leave, prenatal care, and day care a society provides constitutes this policy as well.

The humane environment we seek to create must, I believe,

support and strengthen both the two-parent family *and* women's place in society so that they, and their children, can lead healthy, rewarding, independent lives. We cannot get so caught up in "women's" issues that we lose sight of the fact that the overwhelming majority of American women and men clearly believe in marriage and in the two-parent family. While the divorce statistics are extraordinarily high, so are the statistics for marriage and remarriage. A given marriage might not work, but most people are looking for one that will. If we want to contribute to the stability of the family and diminish the incidence of family violence, divorce, and desertion, we must work toward the goal of full and fair employment. The opportunity to work at a job that offers some measure of dignity, security, and respect—with rewardable recompense—is a fundamental right of both women *and* men, as well as the foundation of a meaningful family policy.

More specifically, we must mount a multifaceted effort to solve some of the problems of women in the workplace. We must, first of all, begin to pay women who work in traditionally female jobs a living wage. It must be recognized, moreover, that women do not work primarily for "self-fulfillment" or for the "extras," but rather because they are supporting or helping to support themselves and their families. Ending the economic discrimination in "women's" jobs, possibly through some system of "comparable worth" or "pay equity," must be a central task of the 1980s. We must also build in dignity, a sense of autonomy, and pathways to promotion in traditionally female occupations, for this is where the vast majority of women work and will continue to work for the foreseeable future. No matter what the trendy magazines and women's pages tell us, most women will never carry a briefcase.

We must also move toward enabling women to enter maledominated occupations. In order to make significant changes in employment opportunities for women, collective action will be necessary, for it is clear that individuals, for the most part, cannot solve these problems alone. As the strike by clerical and technical workers at Yale University so vividly demonstrated, collective action can both raise the consciousness and feelings of worth of female workers and mobilize the leverage necessary to force employers to improve salaries, benefits, and working conditions.

Guaranteeing women respect and pay equity on the job will both enable them to be more independent and will strengthen the two-part family, for these goals are, of course, complementary. Sharing economic responsibilities does not weaken family life; it strengthens it. The traditional model of the male as the sole breadwinner not only places too much power in his hands; it also places too much pressure on his shoulders. As so many families have found, rigid role differentiation diminishes both men and women. More flexible participation in all spheres of life enriches the individuals, their children, and the society at large.

Enabling women to participate equally in work, moreover, will go far toward enabling them to lead independent lives if they should choose or are forced to do so. Many of the women I interviewed decried the continuing socialization of women to perceive themselves as dependent. Over and over they deplored the belief of so many women that they could not survive without a man, that society sees a woman without a man as incomplete, deficient, worthy of blame. But, in fact, under present conditions, women with children who have little education or skills do find it exceedingly difficult to survive on their own. Women's acceptance of these notions reflects the reality of most women's lives and then, of course, this acceptance then perpetuates that reality. While we must strive to alter the attitudes of both women *and* men, and particularly of young people who will soon be socializing yet another generation, what we must strive even harder to change is their reality. As long as women are kept in low-paying, dead-end jobs, making 64 percent of what men earn, they will be dependent. The quickest and, indeed, the only fundamental way to alter women's attitudes and life strategies is to enable them to become economically independent, to have rewarding jobs, to feel a sense of worth and self-respect.

If we want to discourage teenage women from becoming pregnant and having children before they are truly mature and able to care for them, alternative roles are needed. Family-planning information and services are, of course, essential. A recent study by the Alan Guttmacher Institute found that American teenagers become pregnant and give birth at significantly higher rates than do comparable groups in other industrialized countries. Moreover, the United States is the only developed country in which teenage pregnancy is increasing. The study indicates that widespread sex education and the greater availability and use of contraception are the central factors in the lower incidence of teenage pregnancy and birth in European countries.[2]

But equally essential in the prevention of teenage pregnancy is having other viable options. If a young woman's realistic choices are between working as a waitress, where her income is dependent on the generosity of the customer; or in a sweatshop in the garment industry; or behind the counter in a fast-food restaurant, who can blame her for choosing or just happening to have a baby? As Sarah Gold from the Bronx so aptly phrased it, "I had a baby to get off the D train." At least with a baby you have someone to hug! If we want our young people to postpone childbearing, we must offer them real alternatives, a life with other rewards, other ways of feeling good about themselves, other ways of finding meaning and hope. Until then young women who perceive no other opportunities will at least have the role and status that comes with motherhood, along with the gratification of being loved and needed and of loving someone in return.

It is not enough for those of us concerned about women's issues to speak out only on women and work. We must also recognize that a fundamental force in the destabilization of the American family is male unemployment. If we want men to be around to be active partners and fathers, we have to make sure they have the opportunity to work and to be rewarded appropriately. Within this broad goal we must focus on special groups within the society—black teenagers, black males, and Native American men. The negative impact of male unemployment on the well-being of the family has been clearly documented; what is needed now is action.

In viewing employment policy as one component of a broad family policy, we should seriously consider giving parents of young children the option of working part time. As we have noted, in Sweden parents of children under eight may work a six-hour rather than an eight-hour day, with a commensurate reduction in their pay. Such an option would enable parents to spend more time with their children and would reduce the number of hours children spend in day care. As sociologist Janet Poppendieck has pointed out, families with young children and full-time jobs live under great stress. Trying to make it all work often leads to anxiety, guilt, and the feeling of not doing a first-rate job anywhere. She points out that because of extended life expectancy many people will be working later in life than they have until now. She suggests that work be viewed in its entirety within the life-cycle and that during some periods, such as a child's early years, and perhaps during an individual's later years, part-time work may fit in more effectively with other needs and demands. The society would have to accept this option, of course, if parents are not going to be penalized— either overtly or covertly—for taking it.[3] Conflicts would exist, many institutions would resist such change; but it is a change worth exploring.

We might consider permitting parents of children under six to work three-quarter time for reduced pay. This option would have several advantages: There would then be more work to go around, so that we might move closer to our goal of full employment; we would be sending a clear signal to parents that caring for children is an important task, worthy of support by employers and poli-cymakers; and some pressure would be taken off day-care facilities. Moreover, people would be taking an active role in planning their own lives, not simply marching in lock step through them. In an era in which individuals too often feel they are programmed by factors beyond their control, having options in the central issues of work and family responsibilities could help to ease the stress, the ambivalence, and the role conflict that so many parents deal with on a day-to-day basis.

Beyond fundamental change in employment opportunity, Americans must rethink our special responsibility as a society to mothers and children. What is our societal responsibility toward the next generation and toward the women who nurture them? Despite our occasional bouts of nostalgia, it is clear that the 1980s are not the small-town America of the 1920s: A high divorce rate is a fact of American life, and when families break up or come upon hard times, there is no one to take up the slack. There is no grandmother nearby to babysit or to send over a casserole; chances are that she's living in another city or working to take care of herself in her old age. Families are fragmented, and each nuclear unit must focus on caring for itself.

If we indeed believe that the next generation is our collective future, we must guarantee all mothers and children basic services necessary to their well-being. All mothers share the vulnerability that comes with childbearing and childrearing. We have seen that middle- and upper-middle-class women are not immune from poverty when a man walks out, or when illness strikes, or when they get older. It is not simply those now poor who are at risk; millions of additional women are also in danger of falling into poverty. We must therefore recognize our commonalities, not focus on our differences, and join together to demand—for all of us— an investment in the future. It is to our society's ultimate benefit to protect the integrity of the family unit but the investment must be in *all* mothers and *all* children.

The development of programs for particular groups is sometimes necessary—the elderly, people with certain disabilities, and those who have undergone extreme oppression need special attention and specific services. But singling out groups has its negative side as well, for it often stigmatizes those individuals and pits one group against another. Day care for welfare recipients causes resentment in the working class; special subsidies to one group cause divisions between it and other possibly equally needy groups.

Moreover, if we once again call for programs only for the poor, the funds will not be forthcoming in the conservative decade of the 1980s. And if some such programs are developed at the national or local level, they are at risk of being cut or eliminated when it suits the political policymakers. We have repeatedly seen programs gutted when their short-term purpose has been served, when they have quieted restive populations as they did in the late 1960s and early 1970s, or when they no longer serve a national agenda as day care did during World War II.

It is only through universal entitlement that we will provide services of high quality. As long as services are provided for the poor alone, they will be inferior and constantly subject to cutbacks or elimination. Just as the passage of Medicaid institutionalized a two-class system of health care and just as the emphasis on day care for the poor and nursery schools for the affluent has given us a two-class system of preschool care, so will any future programs for the poor alone produce unstable, stigmatized services vulnerable to every shift in the political winds.

What *are* the fundamental supports that mothers and children need? The family policy I propose includes basic elements that are already available in most industrialized countries of the world. In the conservative, every-person-for-him/herself climate of the 1980s, this policy might be seen as utopian, as pie-in-the-sky, but it is not. It is a sensible, pragmatic agenda based on the principles of prevention, fairness, and concern for the well-being of all American children. It is also a policy that encourages good parenting, that states clearly that parenting is important, that the well-being of children is important, and that the society is willing to commit itself to strengthening family life.

First, the United States must have a federally mandated maternity and childcare leave policy. As Sheila Kamerman, Alfred J. Kahn, and Paul Kingston state in their excellent book, *Maternity Policies and Working Women*, "U.S. employment practices with regard to pregnancy and childbirth seem to reflect the most niggardly approach of any advanced industrialized country. . . ."[4] They point out that every industrialized country *except* the United States provides some statutory maternity leave or parental benefit.[5] The minimum paid leave among the more industrialized countries is twelve weeks. Fourteen weeks is rapidly becoming the minimum, and the most frequent pattern among European countries is five months.[6] As we have seen, leave for either parent can be as long as twelve months in Sweden. Most countries permit the woman to take some portion of leave before delivery, providing 90 to 100 percent of her wages. The benefit is tax-free except in Sweden and Canada and is universal, available to all women, regardless of income.[7]

Since October 1978 the United States' policy has been "to require that employers treat pregnancy and maternity the same as any other illness or disability, and that employers treat their women employees who become pregnant or give birth to a child just as they would treat a man who is temporarily disabled or ill."[8] In addition, federal and state employees are entitled to specific benefits. While this stipulation is a beginning, it surely does not approach being a coherent maternity leave policy available to all.

Viewing pregnancy and childbirth as just another form of disability has been seen as a mechanism to protect women from discrimination by the employer. But pregnancy and childbirth are not disabilities; they are usually perfectly normal occurrences in the life cycle that permit a society to repopulate itself. While the circumstances, timing, and number of children a woman has may be private decisions, the society as a whole is profoundly affected by each new individual and has a real stake in the well-being of the newborn. It is the absence of this recognition that separates the United States from so many other countries.

A policy for the United States might begin with paid maternity leave—a minimum of twelve weeks that the woman could take around the birth of the baby. It would be her decision, based on her physical condition, the nature of her work, and her own inclination, that would determine how much leave she would take and whether she would take part of it before delivery or all of it afterward.

Following this period, we should institute a national, universal childcare leave that should last for a minimum of six additional months. Either parent, including adoptive parents, should be entitled to take any part or all of the leave, provided that only one parent use it at a given time. In this way the father would have the opportunity to participate in childrearing from the start and might develop more of a commitment to his children than many fathers have today. Such a leave would enable the child to be nurtured during most of the first year of life by a parent and to develop the bonding that is so essential to future development. The program would require an insurance component, with employers and the government each contributing a certain percentage of the funds needed, so that the parent would be guaranteed a significant percentage of her/his salary during the leave. Such leave would, of course, be voluntary. The parent's job—or a comparable one—benefits, and health insurance would be guaranteed during this period.

Prenatal care should be available to all women at a cost they can afford. The Children's Defense Fund recently reported that only 79 percent of white women and 61 percent of black women begin prenatal care early in pregnancy. Among teenagers, only 58 percent of whites and 47 percent of black teenage mothers had prenatal care during the first trimester.[9] The health of the pregnant woman is too important—for her well-being, for the child's well-being, and for the future of the nation—to be left simply to chance or to the vagaries of the marketplace.

Every woman must be guaranteed first-rate, accessible health care, including family planning services, during pregnancy and in the postpartum period. Such care, of course, would be most effectively organized and promoted within a national health insurance system with universal entitlement and comprehensive coverage or within a national health service, but we cannot wait until the United States is ready to establish a health-care system for all of its people; women and children must be given priority.

The infant and small child must also be guaranteed accessible, affordable care, both well-baby care and care in times of illness. It is a national disgrace that almost 9 million American children have no regular source of health care and that less than half of all poor preschool children are fully immunized against preventable diseases. Adequate health care must be a right, not a privilege, for the entire population, but particularly for children, for whom regular health care is essential. Medicaid has clearly not been an adequate answer for the millions of mothers and children who do not have health insurance and cannot afford to pay for health care out of their own pocket. Significant numbers of poor children are not even eligible for Medicaid benefits. For example, 26 percent of poor children are not eligible for Medicaid in Washington, D.C., and as many as 80 percent of poor children are not eligible for Medicaid in Wyoming.[10] Again, first-rate, accessible, comprehensive maternal and child health services must be available in every part of the country—in rural areas and in the inner cities—not just in the affluent suburbs. It is the society's responsibility to make sure that these services are available; we can do no less.

Canada and many European countries contribute to the support of children through a system of children's or family allowances. Some of these originated, as did Sweden's children's allowance, as part of a broader pronatalist policy that was a response to a dramatic drop in the birth rate. These children's allowances do not amount to a great deal of money—Sweden provides approximately $380 per year per child, and the federal government of Canada provides even less; in 1982, 26.91 Canadian dollars per child per month. But a children's allowance for every child under the age of eighteen represents a commitment by the society to the well-being of that child, and to some families it can make a real difference. It would also help to subsidize those parents who choose to work reduced hours during the child's early years. If this money were taxable, it could be taxed back from affluent families, but the principle of universal entitlement, of avoiding yet another means-tested program, would be established.

The United States must also establish a national system of day care and after-school care, not for the poor alone but for all children in need. While the federal government would establish broad guidelines and contribute to funding, all other aspects of day-to-day administration, including licensing, hiring, inspection, and quality control must be left to the states, local governments, and community groups. In a heterogeneous society such as the United States, decentralization is crucial to the successful administration of a day care program. Parents have differing views of how a good day-care center should be run, and these views should be heard and incorporated, whenever possible, in the operation of the centers. Day care must be sensitive to cultural and geographical differences and to the local needs of parents and children; it should be of such high quality that it would serve families from all classes. Fees should be based on a sliding scale.

Without an adequate network of day-care facilities across the country, women are either bound to the home or are at the mercy of available child-care arrangements, no matter how inferior. It is a societal responsibility to ensure every child who needs such care a clean, nurturing, stimulating, and protected environment, whether in a group setting or in a family day-care setting. We must recognize the importance of day care to the well-being of the family unit, as well as to the health and future development of the child; we must recruit warm, knowledgeable caregivers, pay them a living wage, and provide them with an opportunity to advance in their profession. Only in this way will we be able to employ and retain first-rate people who want to make a commitment to early childhood education. There are plenty of caring men and women who want to work with children; we must show them that the society will value their efforts.

Finally, we must develop even stronger measures to ensure the payment of child support. While the 1984 child-support legislation represents an important initial step toward solving the problem of child support, it is just that—an initial step. Local law enforcement agencies must be far more aggressive than they have been in prosecuting fathers who are delinquent in their payments. In addition, the United States should consider Sweden's practice of guaranteeing child support if the parent does not pay, with the government—probably at the state level in America—assuming the task of recouping the money from the delinquent parent. This would diminish the use of child-support payments as a weapon in the domestic battle and would place the society firmly behind the child's right to such support. And once the states were involved in replacing unpaid child support, they would have a vested interest in ensuring that the pattern did not continue.

Thus, the heart of a new family policy for the United States would include paid maternity and childcare leave, maternal and child health care, children's allowances, a national system of day care administered locally for all families in need, and an aggressive child-support program. This model is no more than other industrialized societies have instituted, and several components are in place in many developing countries as well.

While many families' problems will be eased considerably by fundamental improvements in work opportunities and by the measures outlined above, a significant number of poor families will remain. Work is not the solution for all women, particularly for all women with preschool children. Some women will simply not have appropriate skills and/or education; others may wish to stay at home with their young children. And still others will need support for a period of time to tide them over during periods of crisis. The third component of a unified, three-pronged family policy must be welfare reform. I will not propose a detailed blueprint for the reform of the welfare system here; that must be done elsewhere, in far greater detail. I am, rather, proposing three basic changes that could fundamentally alter the nature of AFDC and its impact on women and children.

First, the application process and the determination of eligibility for Aid to Families with Dependent Children must be simplified. The present length of the application, the myriad of forms, proofs of residence, copies of utility bills, birth certificates, letters from landlords, and other assorted pieces of paper would intimidate a PhD candidate. The assumption of guilt until the applicant is proven innocent is unacceptable. The length of time between the initial application and the first check is often unacceptable, too. The process must be simplified and the application evaluated with minimum hostility and maximum speed and courtesy. When people are in need and asking for help is when they need the most support.

Second, the amount of grants must be raised dramatically. For one of the richest nations in the world to maintain millions of women and children far below the official poverty line is truly unconscionable. To force people to live in substandard housing; to skimp on food and, all too often, go hungry; and to live at a standard significantly lower than others in the society is to promote alienation, disease, and hopelessness. That is what our welfare system is doing—humiliating recipients, making them feel like outsiders, demeaned and degraded in front of their children and neighbors.

We must raise welfare payments at least to the poverty line. If $10,609 was the bare minimum for a family of four to survive in an urban area in 1984, that is the least any state should have provided for such a family. For some families this will mean that they will receive from the welfare system more than they would if they worked at the current minimum wage. Many in private industry will, of course, object to such a proposal since it will reduce the number of people who are forced to work, often at highly undesirable jobs, for such low wages. Others will object on the grounds that such a policy will undermine the work ethic. But our society does not have jobs for all, particularly for people with few skills; because of the rapidly changing nature of work, most experts predict we will lose still more unskilled jobs between now and the turn of the century. Aren't we really placing these people in a Catch-22 situation? We want everyone to work for their keep, but there are not enough jobs, particularly steady jobs with the possibility of advancement, that pay wages above the poverty level. Perhaps we should accept the fact that there may be a group of people, in this case women and children, who for a variety of reasons may need governmental support on a short-term or even on a long-term basis and that, for their own well-being and the well-being of the larger society, they should be maintained at a decent, livable standard of living, one that will not make them pariahs, one that will enable them to feel that they are part of the world around them. As we have seen, for most this will mean a short period of dependency until they reorganize their lives, until their children enter school, until they are retrained and can take a job with a future.

Doreen Johnson, the New Hampshire mother of eight whose husband left her because he "just couldn't live without Sandy," wrote to me some months after our interview:

> Recently I decided to start my own business in Private Home Health Care. . . . In nine months I have tripled the yearly salary [that I was making] when you interviewed me. *I'VE FINALLY MADE IT!!* I still don't get child support—but I don't need it either now and that's emotionally good for me. I feel wonderful. All of a sudden I'm growing again and love the challenge. I've lost weight and my health is the best it's been in 30 years. My family is very proud of me and say so.

After her marriage broke up, Doreen Johnson experienced a period of several years during which she personified the new poor. Her income dropped precipitously along with her self-esteem. She found that her skills could earn her very little money and that she could not count on her husband for any child support. During this period of time she needed help—food stamps, fuel assistance— but now she is on her feet again, doing better than she could have ever imagined. We must have programs that will help women, like Doreen, that will tide them over until they can put their lives together again, that will not permit their children to go hungry or make them feel like outcasts.

We must also develop imaginative programs to offer both short-term and longer-term welfare recipients a way out of AFDC. One such program has already been developed. In October 1983, the Massachusetts Department of Public Welfare inaugurated its Employment and Training CHOICES Program, known as ET. ET is a voluntary program that offers AFDC recipients career planning, education, and job training, as well as help in finding and securing a job. From October 1983 to February 1985, the ET program trained and placed over thirteen thousand welfare recipients in jobs. There are three extremely important components to the program: (1) Those who go into training receive a day-care voucher from the state for up to one year or until they arrange for long-term day care with payment based on a sliding scale; (2) they keep their Medicaid benefits for fifteen months after going into the program; (3) because the workers are placed through the Division of Employment Security, the employers do not know they are welfare recipients, and they are therefore not stigmatized on the job.

For the thirteen thousand people who have been trained and placed in jobs, the average salary is $5 an hour or $9,700 a year, not enough for a family of four to manage on without substantial difficulty but significantly more than the average yearly Massachusetts AFDC grant of $4,300 plus food stamps and Medicaid. Nearly 30 percent of the workers earn more than $5 an hour, not unexpectedly those who work in traditionally male occupations such as machine trades, construction, and professional/managerial jobs. But the largest number of workers, again not surprisingly, has been trained in clerical and service work.

One such woman is Ann Reilly, a twenty-two-year-old mother who lives with her three-year-old son in the largely working-class community in South Boston. Ann has five brothers and sisters; she is the third oldest. Her father is a security guard, and her mother also works, although she didn't when the children were younger.

Ann became pregnant at the age of seventeen during her last year of high school. She dropped out but then decided to attend a special school for pregnant girls, and she was able to graduate in June as she had originally planned. After the baby was born, her boyfriend denied paternity so that, according to Ann, he would not have to pay child support. Ann took him to court; the jury found in her favor and he was told to pay $60 a week; but Ann says he rarely did. She claims she hated him so for denying paternity that she would not let him see his son for a long time; he sees him now "once in a while," but "he's not too much of a father."

When the baby was born, they began receiving AFDC. She recalls: "At first it was easy 'cause I was living with my mother, but when he was a year old I felt I had to go out on my own and then I had to take under-the-table jobs to get through the month." At that time she was receiving $315 a month, $3,780 a year. In September 1984 she placed her son in day care and in October she entered an ET training program.

> Ever since the tenth grade I've wanted to be a secretary. I don't know why, but that's what I always wanted to do. The training program lasted 16 weeks and taught you typing, filing, word processing, punctuation and job development—you know, how to behave, how to go on an interview, how to dress. I was more ambitious than some and went out on several job interviews. When I got this job the other women were so happy for me! We all went out and celebrated!
>
> I love my job. I am a secretary/receptionist and I do a variety of things—payroll, bank statements, typing, filing. I work for six different people and they are all fantastic.

Ann currently earns almost $12,000 a year. She says the difference in income is incredible, that it is wonderful to be able to buy things for her son; but the best part is feeling good about herself. She says simply but with obvious pride: "I'm the only one of six kids who graduated and I graduated three times—from junior high school, high school, and from the training program. I'm the only success, and it's because I'm determined. I've got a lot of determination."

ET has enabled Ann and thousands of others to earn a decent living, to gain self-confidence. Moreover, in its first eighteen months, it has saved the Commonwealth of Massachusetts approximately $22 million.

There is no question that helping people to be self-sufficient is cheaper for society in the long run. Spending money for preventive health care, day care, education, and training programs not only saves lives but also saves money. It is far cheaper to make sure people are well-fed than to treat malnutrition; it is far cheaper to immunize children against infectious disease than to treat them once they are sick. The United States is acting in an incredibly shortsighted way when it cuts essential programs and permits the number of poor people to increase dramatically, then treats them so shabbily that they opt out of society. We will, of course, pay in the long run—in escalating crime, in massive alienation, in wasted lives, and in dollars as well.

The question of whether we can afford a family policy such as the one I have outlined must be addressed. I believe we can. First, the billions of dollars we currently spend on subsidizing the poor, on care for the illnesses that result from poverty, on crime, and on the other direct results of poverty could be spent far more profitably on prevention and on appropriate programs that train people for real jobs. While the financial outlay may be significant at first, eventually many of those who now require help would be working and paying taxes, some of them providing the very services that are so necessary for the society at large.

Second, the United States at present has a lower tax rate than many other industrialized countries and spends considerably less on social welfare. We have the resources; it is clearly a matter of determining our priorities.

Third, any country that can afford to spend $300 billion on arms each year, the largest peacetime arms buildup in the history of the world, can afford to provide a minimum standard of living for its citizens. As President Dwight D. Eisenhower so eloquently stated in 1953:

Every gun that is made, every warship launched, every rocket fired signifies, in the final sense, a theft from those who hunger and are not fed, those who are cold and not clothed. The world in arms is not spending money alone. It is spending the sweat of its laborers, the genius of its scientists, the hopes of its children. . . .[11]

We cannot afford to spend such incredible sums on armaments and to neglect the fundamental well-being of our citizens.

And finally, the United States has a greater maldistribution of wealth and income than other industrialized countries. It is estimated that, for the last twenty-five to thirty years, the richest fifth of the population has owned approximately three-quarters of the nation's wealth, and the bottom fifth approximately 2 percent.[12] If we look at income, we see a similar pattern: In 1968 the highest fifth of the population earned 33.8 percent of the total income, while the lowest fifth earned 7.4 percent.[13] By 1984 the highest fifth had gained considerable ground, earning 42.9 percent while the lowest fifth had lost ground, at 4.7 percent.[14] One of the results of a family policy such as the one I have outlined would be some modest movement toward a more equitable distribution of the nation's economic resources.

What we must keep in mind is that these problems are not insoluble. There are models—from other countries and from our own—for imaginatively helping people to help themselves. We know the essential services mothers and children need in order to be productive, contributing members of society. We have the resources. I believe we even have the will.

Finally, women must find ways of helping other women, of reaching out, of enabling one another to develop new strategies to create a society that will embrace all of its people. In my interviews with women of varying ages, backgrounds, and life experiences in different parts of the country, several central themes have emerged: the pain of being poor in affluent America; the commitment to childrearing, no matter how difficult life may be; and the concept of "sharing and caring." Whether it was an Atlanta mother of six or a Brooklyn mother of four or a Maine mother of two, the theme these women stressed was the need to help one another—friends, family, and even neighbors they barely knew. Woman after woman emphasized that the poor mother cannot make it alone, that she must help and be helped, and that often she must reach out to lend someone a hand without any specific knowledge of when another person will reach out to her.

Magdalen Daniels, a community worker in San Francisco's Tenderloin, echoes these views. The Tenderloin is a fifty- to sixty-block area that is in transition from a red-light district to a neighborhood that houses older people (it has the highest proportion of social security recipients in the city); poor people (more than 50 percent of Tenderloin residents receive either state or federal income assistance); and a polyglot of racial and ethnic groups. During the 1970s and early 1980s the number of South East Asians living there increased 850 percent, the number of children nearly 150 percent.[15]

Few services are available to meet their needs, but Daniels feels that women's skills are particularly important in improving the area. She says that women instinctively "network," that they are used to "sharing recipes, sharing shopping tips, sharing knowledge about the underground of society." She states that women are more willing than men to share ideas, that they are more "relationship-oriented," and that these qualities are essential for neighborhood change and empowerment.

It is, however, not only among the poor that one sees "sharing and caring." Mothers all over suburban America share car pools, watch each other's children, gather around when there is serious illness or a death in the family. And even legendary rivals are able to console or to congratulate one another in time of defeat or triumph. At the end of the 1985 French Open tennis tournament, a fiercely fought match in which Chris Evert Lloyd defeated Martina Navratilova for the first time since 1982 in a major, so-called Grand Slam tournament, the two women walked off the court, their arms around each other in sadness and in joy. It was a memorable moment not only for the winner but for all of us; these two women were saying that self-interest and pride and competition and incredible fame and money need not separate us, that we can still reach out to understand and share one another's feelings.

Jean Baker Miller suggests that women have developed a different reality from men's, in part because they have been excluded from traditional male routes of gratification:

> Male society, by depriving women of the right to its major "bounty"—that is, development according to the male model—overlooks the fact that women's development *is* proceeding, but on another basis. One central feature is that women stay with, build on, and develop in a context of attachment and affiliation with others. Indeed, women's sense of self becomes very much organized around being able to make and then to maintain affiliations and relationships.[16]

Carol Gilligan concurs, stating that "women's sense of integrity appears to be entwined with an ethic of care, so that to see themselves as women is to see themselves in a relationship of connection. . . ."[17]

A relationship of connection. That is what so many of the women I spoke with were describing—a relationship of connection with their children, with their families, with other women in similar circumstances. We must all feel that "relationship of connection," that "ethic of care," and work together to build a society in which families are strong, one in which individuals' essential needs are met, and one in which we are all enriched by our sense of affiliation with each other.

What we must recognize, above all, is that the poor are not a separate breed. They need what we all need: the opportunity to feel part of our society; to love and care for one another; and to participate in meaningful, decently paid work. These goals are not beyond our reach. We have but to commit ourselves to their fulfillment.

AFTERWORD

Since the original publication of *Women and Children Last*, the U.S. has become even more polarized around the issue of poverty and the social policy appropriate in dealing with the severe problems of the poor. The notion that the so-called "War on Poverty" of the 1960s was a failure and that, by providing benefits, federally sponsored programs—particularly Aid to Families with Dependent Children—in actuality create dependency and encourage the poor to reject the work ethic and other mainstream American norms is not only a central tenet of conservative analysts and politicians today but it has become accepted by many Americans.

The widespread use of the term "underclass" has contributed significantly to the difficulty in formulating a coherent, effective, and achievable social policy. While the term has been used to characterize individuals who, in the words of William Julius Wilson, "lack training and skills and either experience long-term unemployment or are not members of the labor force, individuals who are engaged in street crime and other forms of aberrant behavior, and families that experience long-term spells of poverty and/or welfare dependency,"[1] it has also become virtually synonymous in the language of many analysts and in the minds of many Americans with inner-city poor people, most specifically African-Americans. The term has also become associated with families that are headed by women, with teenage pregnancy and childbearing, with drug and/or alcohol abuse, and with people who live in high-crime areas. All too often the term "underclass" is used to describe and disparage the behavior, values, and norms of poor people rather than to analyze the economic status, level of educational attainment, adequacy or inadequacy of housing, or the opportunities available to that group. The term, in short, has been used as the quintessential "blaming the victim" technique. Implicit in the usage is the belief that if only the underclass did not engage in such "self-destructive," "aberrant" behavior they could live good lives like the rest of us.

The other critical problem with the widespread use of "underclass" is that it has increasingly come to represent the poor in general. While studies indicate that the vast majority of impoverished people are temporarily poor rather than persistently poor, that millions of poor people move in and out of poverty, that millions of poor people are members of the labor force, do not engage in "street crime and other forms of aberrant behavior," or experience "long-term spells of poverty and/or welfare dependency," the term "underclass" is used to stigmatize millions of poor Americans, to brand them unfit, unmotivated, unwilling, or unable to do their part to achieve their piece of the American Dream.

This is not to say that there are not millions of poor Americans who are undereducated, who live in deplorable housing in equally deplorable neighborhoods, or, even worse, who are among the vast numbers of homeless, who have few if any prospects for work in our increasingly technology-driven society, who are involved with drug and/or alcohol abuse, and who participate in one way or another in the underground economy. But these are not the majority of poor Americans, and thinking they are makes the task of helping impoverished people to lead useful, productive, rewarding lives seem virtually unachievable.

One of the most destructive stereotypes about the poor is that they do little to help themselves and rely almost entirely on the welfare system for their survival. It is important to stress that during 1989 in nearly half—48.9 percent—of all poor families at least one member worked full-time or part-time, and that in 16.2 percent of poor families at least one member worked full-time year-round. Even among female-headed families, in which all of the familial responsibilities rest on the single parent, 41.6 percent of the householders worked in 1989 and 8.8 percent worked full-time year-round.[2]

Yet another all-too-common stereotype is that the vast majority of those living in poverty in the U.S. are people of color. It must be stressed that even though the poverty rate for whites is indeed lower than that for other groups, the majority of poor people living in poverty in the U.S. are white. In fact, two-thirds of all Americans living below the poverty line in 1989—65.9 percent—were white.[3]

In order to understand the conditions under which poor Americans live we must recognize that over a third of the poor are categorized by the Bureau of the Census as the "poorest of the poor." These are individuals whose income is below half of the poverty threshold. In 1989 38 percent of the poor were individuals or in families whose income was less than half of the poverty line; for a family of four this meant a yearly income of less than $6,338.[4]

In addition to the 31.5 million Americans officially living in poverty, another 11.1 million are termed the "near poor"—that is, those with incomes greater than the relevant poverty threshold for their family size but below 125 percent of that level. For a family of four in 1989, this meant an income under $15,843.[5]

The "welfare system," otherwise known as Aid to Families with Dependent Children (AFDC), remains one of the key factors in keeping poor families below the poverty line. The late 1980s and early 1990s have brought federal cutbacks, recession, lower-than-projected tax income, a reluctance to raise taxes even on the very rich, and, consequently, austerity to states across the country. Many have responded with drastic cuts in social programs such as day care for children from low-income families, health clinics for the poor, and AFDC benefits. Nationwide, from 1970 to 1990 the purchasing power of welfare income, after adjusting for inflation, fell by almost 40 percent.[6] No state today provides benefits up to the poverty line ($12,675 in 1989 for a family of four), a threshold that virtually everyone agrees is too low to meet basic human needs. The states that provide the highest benefits are New York, Connecticut, and Alaska, which provide, respectively, 85.3 percent, 82.5 percent, and 82.1 percent of the federal poverty line for a family of three. At the other end of the spectrum are Alabama, Mississippi, and Texas, which provide 14.3 percent, 14.6 percent, and 22.3 percent respectively.[7] In March 1991 Michigan reduced AFDC payments by 17 percent; California withheld a cost-of-living increase to welfare recipients in 1991, and Governor Pete Wilson proposed a further cut of 8.8 percent in AFDC benefits. According to one lawyer who works with a legal aid group in Sacramento, "Poorer families are singled out for special attack in this budget. No other group has been asked to suffer as much as needy families with children."[8]

Studies such as the one conducted by the Community Service Society of New York (*Living in Poverty: Coping on the Welfare Grant*) indicate how inadequate the welfare budget really is. In 1990 a single mother with three children in New York City received a maximum of $312 per month as a shelter allowance. During that same year the vacancy rate for apartments renting below $300 monthly was 1 percent.[9] In part because they must pay rent higher than the allotted amount, recipients are forced to develop a system of rotating payments in order to get through each month. They are forced to "borrow" from food money to pay the rent, "borrow" from money for utilities to buy food, and so forth. While this system may work for a short time, living at the economic margin all too often eventually means going hungry or losing utility service or becoming homeless. As the report states,

> Indeed, given the extreme inadequacy of public assistance income in New York State, poor families on welfare "make it" only because they maintain a range of coping mechanisms and survival strategies based on indigenous social networks and institutions. . . . The extended family network, admittedly under great stress, remains the single most important pillar of self-reliance among the poor.[10]

The major piece of welfare legislation in recent years was the 1988 Family Support Act, which was hailed by some as a "historic change in the lives of millions of poor people in America." The bill's central provision requires single parents on welfare whose children are over the age of three to obtain jobs and work their way off of welfare. If they are not able to find jobs, they are required to enroll in educational and job-training courses that will prepare them for jobs. To smooth the transition, single parents are entitled to day-care assistance and continued eligibility for Medicaid benefits for the family for one year. In addition, the legislation requires all states to extend AFDC benefits to two-parent families in certain limited circumstances. Although some began earlier, all states were required to implement the Family Support Act by October 1, 1990.[11]

This legislation has hardly brought about a "historic change in the lives of poor people in America." It has provided federal support for state education, training, and job-placement efforts through the Job Opportunities and Basic Skills (JOBS) program. State and local fiscal problems are, however, making it exceedingly difficult for the states to match federal funds; consequently, programs serve only a fraction of the eligible population. While the Family Support Act mandates that states guarantee child care for JOBS participants and other AFDC parents enrolled in approved training, education, and employment activities, and while many states have taken steps to improve child care for AFDC recipients, in the vast majority of states, according to the Children's Defense Fund, "there are enough child care slots only for a fraction of AFDC children needing care."[12] Even the provision that requires all states to offer AFDC to limited categories of two-parent families with at least one parent unemployed only reaches a negligible number of poor two-parent families. Moreover, many welfare advocates question the law's requiring single parents to obtain jobs or, if jobs are not available, to enroll in educational and job-training programs. They argue that AFDC recipients should have the same rights as other parents to decide to enter the labor force or remain at home with their young children. Other critics point out that many jobs for which AFDC recipients are trained pay little more than welfare benefits, particularly when child care and Medicaid benefits are included, and therefore workers may gain little in monetary terms.

In recent years, while the real value of welfare benefits and the quality of education and other human services have been declining, repeated efforts have been made to attach the receipt of benefits to approved social behavior. In 1988, for example, Wisconsin implemented a Learnfare program that required teenagers whose parents are on welfare, as well as teen parents, to attend school. If the young person dropped out of school or had more than two unexpected absences a month, the family would lose approximately $100 from its monthly welfare checks. During the 1988 school year, the families of approximately 2,200 teenagers lost welfare benefits in an average month. As one critic has stated, the program "punished terribly vulnerable and stressed parents whose already inadequate income does not meet basic family needs like food and rent."[13]

In 1991 the governor of Wisconsin presented a plan to the state legislature to cap welfare payments to unwed teenage mothers regardless of how many children they have and to pay larger grants to those who marry. Proposed legislation in Wyoming would have the state pay childbirth expenses for all women who put their babies up for adoption, and a Kansas state legislator has proposed that the state pay $500 to any mother on welfare who uses Norplant, a new, long-lasting contraceptive that is surgically implanted.[14] An editorial in *The Philadelphia Inquirer* suggested that because of growing poverty among blacks, welfare mothers should be offered incentives to use Norplant. The editorial was so widely denounced by both the newspaper's readers and staff as racist that the newspaper later printed an apology.[15]

During the same year the Bush administration extended this punitive philosophy toward welfare recipients by suggesting that welfare benefits be contingent upon the children having been immunized against measles. The underlying assumption is that the immunizations are available, that the federal and state governments do not have special responsibility to make essential health services truly accessible to the poor, and that it is fundamentally the parents' fault if the children are not protected. This attitude is exemplified with particular clarity by the serious problems that poor families face in obtaining adequate health care.

Since the mid-1980s the health status of our poorest citizens has deteriorated further. In December 1990 a *New York Times* headline read "Sick at Their Heart, Cities Become Medical Disaster Area for the Poor." The article began, "While Americans elsewhere are living longer, healthier lives, residents of the inner cities inhabit islands of illness, epidemics and premature death. After decades of gradual improvement, the health of the urban poor took a turn for the worse in the late 1980s and has now reached critical condition."[16]

This critical condition is perhaps best symbolized by the U.S. infant mortality rate. In 1989 for every 1,000 live births in the

U.S., 9.7 babies died in the first year of life. The U.S. thus ranked twentieth in the world, behind countries such as Singapore, Ireland, Spain, and Hong Kong. But among black babies, the statistics are even more shocking. In 1989 the infant mortality rate among black babies was 17.6, while the rate among white babies was 8.5. In 1990 the U.S. infant mortality rate dropped to 9.1 per 1,000 live births. According to experts, the decline, while surely welcome, was mainly the result of medical intervention, specifically the introduction of new drugs to premature infants in their first hours of life, rather than gains in public health or social programs.[17]

One of the important causes of infant mortality is low birthweight (less than 5.5 pounds), and here too the U.S. rate is excessively high. In 1988 6.9 percent of all babies were born at low birthweight, while 13 percent of black infants were born at low birthweight.[18] One of the primary causes of low birthweight is inadequate prenatal care. In 1988 only 75.9 percent of women received care starting during the first trimester of pregnancy, the same rate as in 1979. Again, women of color are far more likely than white women to receive late or no prenatal care.[19]

Teenage pregnancy and teenage parenthood remain critical issues during the final decades of the twentieth century. A study sponsored by the Alan Guttmacher Institute and published in 1986 found that the rate of teenage pregnancy in the United States was higher than in twenty-seven out of thirty industrialized countries. Among younger teenagers—those seventeen and under—the U.S. rate was higher than that of any industrialized country except Hungary.[20]

The study examined in detail five countries thought to be reasonably similar to the U.S. and found that in 1981 the birthrate— the number of live births per 1,000 women aged fifteen to nineteen—was nearly double that of England and Wales, twice the Canadian rate, more than double the French rate, nearly four times the Swedish rate, and almost six times the rate of the Netherlands. If we consider only white teenagers in the U.S., their rate of teenage pregnancy is still double that of France, over one and a half times that of Canada and England and Wales, three times that of Sweden, and over five times that of the Netherlands.[21]

In 1988 both the number of births to teens and the teen birthrate increased—the teen birthrate for the second year in a row. The increase was the greatest for fifteen- to seventeen-year-olds: from 31.8 to 33.8 births per 1,000. Nearly two-thirds—65.9 percent—of all U.S. births to teenagers in 1988 were to unmarried women. Among teens of Hispanic origin, 59.2 percent were to unmarried women; among African-American teenagers over 90 percent—91.5 percent—were to unmarried women. While longitudinal studies indicate that some women who begin parenting during their teenage years can live full, productive lives and avoid the trap of poverty, women who begin childbearing in adolescence are likely to remain poor throughout their twenties. Among women aged twenty-five to twenty-nine surveyed in 1986 who first gave birth during their teenage years, one out of three was living in poverty. Among mothers of the same age who delayed childbearing until their twenties, one out of six was living in poverty.[22] Moreover, early childbearing leaves young mothers not only at great risk of poverty but also at significant risk of having low birthweight babies, of their babies dying during the first year of life, and of their children having greater health problems later in life.

Children's health continues to be endangered by the gaps in immunization in this country. The U.S. Public Health Service estimates that only 70 to 80 percent of all children are fully immunized, with certain groups in the population having rates lower than 50 percent. Black and Hispanic children, particularly those in inner-city neighborhoods, have the lowest levels of immunization. Measles provides an excellent example of the consequences of the federal and state governments reducing their immunization efforts. In 1983 the U.S. had brought the number of cases of measles down to an annual low of 1,500. By 1988, after a significant decline in the number of children immunized, a measles epidemic struck several communities across the U.S.[23] In 1989 the annual number of cases had risen to 18,000 and in 1990 to an incredible 25,000 cases.[24]

Hunger has continued to plague low-income families, particularly children. The Community Childhood Hunger Identification Project (CCHIP), which conducted a nationwide study from February 1989 to August 1990, estimates that 5.5 million children in the U.S. under age twelve—one child in eight—are hungry. The study also found that an estimated additional six million children under twelve are at risk of hunger because their families are experiencing food-shortage problems and that, in comparison to non-hungry children, hungry children are

> more than three times as likely to suffer from unwanted weight loss; more than four times as likely to suffer from fatigue; . . . more than twice as likely to have frequent headaches; almost twice as likely to have frequent ear infections; [and] almost three times as likely to suffer from concentration problems. . . .[25]

Of the "hungry households" surveyed by the CCHIP, almost half—49 percent—were headed by women and 76 percent were nonwhite. Although 46 percent of the hungry households had some wage income, the average income of hungry households was 77 percent of the official poverty line. Of these families, only 54 percent were recipients of Aid to Families with Dependent Children, 70 percent were participating in the Food Stamp Program, and 45 percent were participating in the Special Supplemental Food Program for Women, Infants and Children (WIC). While 95 percent of "hungry households" with school-age children were participating in the School Lunch Program, only half—48 percent—were participating in the School Breakfast Program.[26]

The intervening years since the original publication of *Women and Children Last* have witnessed selective but vigorous efforts on behalf of U.S. family policy. In 1988 the 100th Congress rejected a parental leave bill that called for unpaid leave for the parents of a newborn or newly adopted child. It would have affected only 5 percent of all businesses and 40 percent of all workers (the firms affected would have been those with fifty or more employees). Senator John H. Chafee, a Republican from Rhode Island, estimated that the cost would have been $160 million per year, which averages out to one cent per day for each covered employee.[27]

In 1990 the U.S. Congress passed important child care legislation, the Child Care and Development Block Grant, which provided new funds to help families with child care costs and to help states improve the supply and quality of child care services. Congress also reauthorized Head Start to expand in order to serve all eligible children by 1994. But, as the Children's Defense Fund has stated, "the 1990 legislation is only a beginning toward building a strong child care system that serves all families."[28]

In April 1990 the federal minimum wage was increased for the first time in nearly a decade. The minimum hourly wage was raised from $3.35 to $3.80 and again on April 1, 1991, to $4.25. Although this was important legislation, it has two major flaws: the minimum wage still does not lift families out of poverty, and a new loophole allows employers to pay teenagers regardless of previous work experience a "training wage" of 85 percent for up to 90 working days.[29]

The question of how to provide a decent standard of living for America's poor families remains a topic of debate. A family policy with benefits for all, regardless of income, maximizes the likelihood of passage of relevant legislation and minimizes both the cutback of benefits and stigma to the recipients. But clearly the policies necessary for middle-class families will not be sufficient to help poor women and children overcome the pernicious effects of poverty. A combination of universal entitlements and targeted programs for poor families is therefore urgently needed.

The universal entitlements necessary for all families include comprehensive, accessible, affordable maternal and child health care, preferably within a comprehensive health care system for all Americans; paid parental leave at the time of the birth or adoption of a child; first-rate, widely accessible and affordable child care and after-school care; stronger child support legislation; and a higher minimum wage for all workers. In addition, the U.S. should seriously consider children's allowances for all families regardless of income. Such payments are widely used and extremely popular in comparable industrialized countries and help to reaffirm a society's commitment to the well-being of all of its children.

Among the programs urgently needed for low-income families are both housing subsidies and the construction and rehabilitation of low-income housing; the expansion of food stamp assistance and increased funding for WIC (the supplemental Food Program for Women, Infants, and Children); and finally, of course, welfare reform. Every state should pay benefits up to the poverty line and should offer training programs and employment counseling to those recipients who choose to take advantage of them. Above all, we must recognize that life is too complex for families to go it alone.

As we entered the final decade of the twentieth century, many were hopeful that the greed-driven 1980s were behind us and that the winding down of the Cold War would stimulate the transfer of resources from armaments to the "Peace Dividend" to provide much-needed money for domestic programs. What we have witnessed instead has been an enormously costly war with Iraq on the international front, an incredibly expensive bailout of the savings and loan industry, an ongoing preoccupation with the federal deficit, and an economic recession on the domestic front. The early 1990s have also witnessed a continuingly obscene gap in income between the very rich and the poor. In 1989 the richest 20 percent of the U.S. population received 46.8 percent of national income, a significantly greater share than in 1979 or 1969, while the poorest 20 percent received only 3.8 percent, a significantly smaller share than in the comparable years in the two previous decades.[30] The distribution of wealth is even more inequitable. As Bennett Harrison and Barry Bluestone, professors of political economy, have pointed out, "the American Dream began to unravel" during the 1970s and has since taken a "great U-turn" toward inequality.[31]

In order to move toward greater equality, in order to provide our families adequate services and a minimum standard of living, in order to provide our children basic necessities and a start in life worthy of this great nation, we must redistribute our resources in a far more equitable fashion. To accomplish that task, we must first raise taxes, particularly on the wealthy and on corporations. The U.S. tax rate is far lower than that of other comparable industrialized countries. While the U.S. collects only 30 percent of gross domestic product in taxes, Sweden collects 57 percent, Denmark 51 percent, Norway 46 percent, France 44 percent, Italy 38 percent, West Germany 38 percent, Great Britain 37 percent, Canada 33 percent, and Japan 31 percent.[32] To those who say that the United States cannot afford to improve the quality of life and life chances for its poorest citizens, I suggest that we do indeed have the resources if we only have the will.

It is all too easy to lose heart in these difficult times. We must remember, however, that social change is a long, hard process, one that is characterized by advances and retreats, success and failure. I do believe that the vast majority of Americans genuinely want a more humane society, one in which each citizen can live a decent, productive life, one in which each family, no matter its configuration, can nurture its members and contribute to the wider world. We must continue to organize across class, race, gender, and age lines to achieve these goals, for it is only through recognizing our common needs, through recognizing our interdependence, through working together, that we can bring about urgently needed political, economic, and social reform.

NOTES

FOREWORD

1. *The State of America's Children 1991* (Washington, DC: Children's Defense Fund, 1991), 5.

INTRODUCTION

1. Walter Lord, *A Night to Remember* (New York: Bantam, 1956), 1.

2. Ibid., 2–3.

3. Ibid., 34.

4. Ibid., 82–83.

5. "Facts on Working Women" (Washington, DC: U.S. Department of Labor, Women's Bureau, September 1990): 1–4.

6. Jason DeParle, "Poverty Rate Rose Sharply Last Year As Incomes Slipped," *New York Times* (27 September 1991).

7. *The State of America's Children 1991* (Washington, DC: Children's Defense Fund, 1991), 24–25.

8. U.S. Bureau of the Census, Current Population Reports, Series P-60, No. 168, *Money Income and Poverty Status in the United States: 1989 (Advanced Data from the March 1990 Current Population Survey)*, U.S. Government Printing Office, Washington, DC, 1990, 2.

9. *Money Income and Poverty Status in the United States: 1989*, 9.

10. Ibid., 7–9.

11. *The State of America's Children 1991*, 143.

12. Anna Quindlen, "Hearing the Cries of Crack," *New York Times* (7 October 1990).

13. *The Public Health Memo* (Albany, NY: State University of New York School of Public Health, Winter 1991).

14. Lorraine V. Klerman, *Alive and Well? A Research and Policy Review of Health Programs for Poor Young Children* (New York: National Center for Children in Poverty, 1991), 30.

15. *The Public Health Memo*.

16. Dorothy Roberts, "The Bias in Drug Arrests of Pregnant Women," *New York Times* (11 August 1990).

17. Sara Rimer, "Drugs and the System and a Family Divided," *New York Times* (16 January 1991).

18. Joseph B. Treaster, "Drop in Youths' Cocaine Use May Reflect a Societal Shift," *New York Times* (25 January 1991).

19. Michel Marriott, "Raid Notwithstanding, Campus Drug Use Seems Less," *New York Times* (26 March 1991).

20. Joseph B. Treaster, "Cocaine Epidemic Has Peaked, Some Suggest," *New York Times* (1 July 1990).

21. Gina Kolata, "Old and Weak: Crack Users' Image Falls," *New York Times* (23 July 1990).

22. Terry Williams, *The Cocaine Kids* (Reading, MA: Addison-Wesley, 1989).

23. Mireya Navarro, "Shootings Jolt Children to New Views of Guns," *New York Times* (1 August 1990).

24. Rene Sanchez, "A Generation Born of Violence Creating a Brutal Legacy," *Washington Post* (27 January 1991).

25. Ibid.

26. Seth Mydans, "Homicide Rate Up For Young Blacks," *New York Times* (7 December 1990).

27. Klerman, *Alive and Well?*, 31.

28. *The State of America's Children 1991*, 65.

29. Klerman, *Alive and Well?*, 31.

30. *The State of America's Children 1991*, 109–111.

31. *Homeless Families: Failed Policies and Young Victims* (Washington, DC: Children's Defense Fund, 1991), 4.

32. Ibid., 5–8.

33. Jonathan Kozol, *Rachel and Her Children: Homeless Families in America* (New York: Crown, 1988), 100.

—1—
WHO ARE THE POOR?

1. Barbara Ehrenreich and Frances Fox Piven, "The Feminization of Poverty," *Dissent* 31 (Spring 1984): 162–170.

2. Robert Fleming, "Young Trouble: Survival Lesson from Teen Mom," *New York Daily News* (9 April 1984).

3. U.S. Bureau of the Census, Current Population Reports, Series P-60, No. 149, *Money Income and Poverty Status of Families and Persons in the United States: 1984* (Advance Data from the March 1985 Current Population Survey), U.S. Government Printing Office, Washington, D.C., 1985, 1–3.

4. Robert Pear, "U.S. Poverty Rate Dropped to 14.4% in '84, Bureau Says," *New York Times* (28 August 1985.)

5. *Money Income and Poverty Status of Families and Persons in the United States:1984*, 26–29.

6. Alvin L. Shorr, "Redefining Poverty Levels," *New York Times* (9 May 1984).

7. Michael Harrington, "The New Gradgrinds," *Dissent* 31 (Spring 1984): 171–181.

8. Ibid.

9. Leonard Beeghley, "Illusion and Reality in the Measurement of Poverty," *Social Problems* 31 (1984): 322–333.

10. Ibid.

11. Ibid.

12. Paul Brady, "Steel Claw," on Tina Turner, "Private Dancer," Capitol Records, 1983.

13. "The Canadian Fact Book on Poverty—1983," The Canadian Council on Social Development (Toronto: James Lorimer & Co., 1983), 2–3.

14. Bureau of Labor Statistics, telephone communication.

15. Beeghley, "Illusion and Reality."

16. Robert Pear, "Rise in Poverty from '79 to '82 Is Found in U.S.," *New York Times* (24 February 1984).

17. Ibid.

18. Robert Pear, "Is Poverty a Condition or Is It a Definition?" *New York Times* (1 September 1985).

19. "Poverty Rate Shows Disappointing Drop; Income Inequality Widens," Press Release, Center on Budget and Policy Priorities, 27 August 1985.

20. Greg J. Duncan, *Years of Poverty, Years of Plenty: The Changing Economic Fortunes of American Workers and Families* (Ann Arbor: Institute for Social Research, The University of Michigan, 1984), 34.

21. *Money Income and Poverty Status of Families and Persons in the United States: 1984*, 3.

22. Duncan, *Years of Poverty*, 3.

23. Ibid., 41.

24. Ibid., 51.

25. Ibid., 48.

26. Ibid.

27. Ibid., 50.

28. Ibid., 24–25.

29. Diana Pearce, "The Feminization of Poverty: Women, Work and Welfare," *Urban and Social Change Review*, February 1978.

30. *A Growing Crisis: Disadvantaged Women and Their Children* (Washington, D.C.: United States Commission on Civil Rights, Clearinghouse Publication 78, 1983), 2.

31. *Money Income and Poverty Status of Families and Persons in the United States: 1984*, 3.

32. *A Growing Crisis*, 2.

33. U.S. Bureau of the Census, Current Population Reports, Series P-20, No. 398, *Household and Family Characteristics: March 1984* (Washington, D.C.: U.S. Government Printing Office, 1985), 1.

34. U.S. Bureau of the Census, Current Population Reports, Series P-20, No. 381, *Household and Family Characteristics: March 1982* (Washington, D.C.: U.S. Government Printing Office, 1983), 3.

35. Duncan, *Years of Poverty*, 10.

36. Robert E. Tomasson, "A Lower Divorce Rate Is Reported," *New York Times* (9 January 1985).

37. Duncan, *Years of Poverty*, 21.

38. *A Growing Crisis*, 7.

39. *Children in Poverty*, Prepared for the use of the Committee on Ways and Means by the Congressional Research Service and the Congressional Budget Office (Washington, D.C.: U.S. Government Printing Office, 1985), 57.

40. "Births Among Teen-Agers Down in 70's," *New York Times* (7 November 1984).

41. Kay Johnson, Sara Rosenbaum, and Janet Simons, *The Data Book: The Nation, States, and Cities* (Washington, D.C.: Children's Defense Fund Adolescent Pregnancy Prevention: Prenatal Care Campaign, 1985), 7.

42. *Children in Poverty*, 57.

43. *Household and Family Characteristics: March 1984*, 4.

44. *A Growing Crisis*, 11.

45. Ibid., 10.

46. "Births Among Teen-Agers Down in 70's."

47. *A Dream Deferred: The Economic Status of Black Americans* (Washington, D.C.: The Center for the Study of Social Policy, 1983), 31.

48. Robert Pear, "Rate of Poverty Found to Persist in Face of Gains," *New York Times* (3 August 1984).

49. Kenneth B. Noble, "Jobless Rate Declines Slightly to 7.2%," *New York Times* (9 March 1985).

50. *A Children's Defense Budget: An Analysis of the President's FY 1984 Budget and Children* (Washington, D.C.: Children's Defense Fund, 1983), 81.

51. Ibid., 124.

52. Ibid., 134.

53. Ibid., 149.

54. Kathleen Teltsch, "Analysts Say Cuts in Aid Hurt Young," *New York Times* (1 September 1985.)

55. "Congress Study Finds Reagan Budget Curbs Put 557,000 People in Pov-

erty," *New York Times* (26 July 1984).

56. Alton Slagle, "Working Moms Hurt by Ron's Cuts: Study," *New York Daily News* (18 September 1984).

57. "Study Says Blacks Have Lost Ground," *New York Times* (6 October 1984).

58. Michael Goodwin, "Recovery Making New York City of Haves and Have-Nots," *New York Times* (28 July 1984).

59. Ibid.

60. *A Dream Deferred*, 4.

61. *Money Income and Poverty Status of Families and Persons in the United States: 1984*, 1.

62. *A Dream Deferred*, 10.

63. Ibid., 9.

64. Ibid., 5.

65. Ibid., 11–13.

66. Ibid., 15.

67. Ibid., 20.

68. John Herbers, "Income Gap between Races Wide as in 1960, Study Finds," *New York Times* (18 July 1983).

69. *Falling Behind: A Report on How Blacks Have Fared under the Reagan Policies* (Washington, D.C.: Center on Budget and Policy Priorities, 1984), 2–4.

70. "Poverty: Not for Women Only," Alliance Against Women's Oppression Discussion Paper No. 3, September 1983; see also Linda Burnham, "Has Poverty Been Feminized in Black America?" *The Black Scholar*, Vol. XVI, No. 2, March/April 1985.

71. Duncan, *Years of Poverty*, 23.

72. Carol Gilligan, *In a Different Voice: Psychological Theory and Women's Development* (Cambridge, Mass.: Harvard University Press, 1982).

—2—
THE NEW POOR

1. Barbara Ehrenreich and Karin Stallard, "The Noveau Poor," *Ms.* (July–August 1982): 217–224.

2. Anita Shreve, "The Working Mother As Role Model," *New York Times Magazine* (9 September 1984): 39–43.

3. Jane Gross, "Against the Odds: A Woman's Ascent on Wall Street," *New York Times Magazine* (6 January 1985): 16–27, 55, 60, 68.

4. Segment on the CBS evening news, February 18, 1985.

5. Nancy Chodorow, *The Reproduction of Mothering: Psychoanalysis and the*

Sociology of Gender (Berkeley: University of California Press, 1978), 3.

6. Ibid., 11.

7. Alice Schwarzer, "Simone de Beauvoir Talks about Sartre," *Ms.* 12 (August 1983): 87–90.

8. Dianne S. Burden and Lorraine V. Klerman, "Teenage Parenthood: Factors that Lessen Economic Dependence," *Social Work* (January–February 1984): 11–16.

9. Ibid.

10. Gloria Naylor, *Linden Hills* (New York: Ticknor & Fields, 1985), 58.

11. *Children in Poverty*, 200.

12. Murray A. Straus, Richard J. Gelles, and Suzanne K. Steinmetz, *Behind Closed Doors: Violence in the American Family* (Garden City, N.Y.: Anchor Press, 1980), quoted in *Inform*, published by the Maine Commission for Women (January–February 1984).

13. Lenore E. Walker, *The Battered Woman* (New York: Harper & Row, 1979), 20.

14. Ibid., ix.

15. Straus et al., *Behind Closed Doors*.

16. Walker, *The Battered Woman*, 43.

17. *Inform*.

18. Ibid.

19. Walker, *The Battered Woman*, 51.

20. Ibid., 49–50.

— 3 —
WOMEN AND WORK

1. Bettina Berch, *The Endless Day: The Political Economy of Women and Work* (New York: Harcourt Brace Jovanovich, 1982), 4.

2. Alice Kessler-Harris, *Out to Work: A History of Wage-Earning Women in the United States* (New York: Oxford University Press, 1982), 4.

3. Ibid., 7.

4. Ibid., 12–13.

5. Ibid., 29.

6. Berch, *The Endless Day*, 34.

7. Kessler-Harris, *Out to Work*, 36.

8. Ibid., 50.

9. Christopher Lasch, *Haven in a Heartless World: The Family Besieged* (New York: Basic Books, 1977), xx.

10. Ibid., xxi.

11. Kessler-Harris, *Out to Work*, 50.

12. Ibid., 70–71.

13. Ibid., 72.

14. Berch, *The Endless Day*, 41.

15. Ibid.

16. Barbara Ehrenreich and Frances Fox Piven, "The Feminization of Poverty."

17. Berch, *The Endless Day*, 46.

18. Kessler-Harris, *Out to Work*, 181.

19. Ibid., 185–188.

20. Barbara Mayer Wertheimer, *We Were There: The Story of Working Women in America* (New York: Pantheon, 1977), 309–310.

21. Ibid., 310.

22. Berch, *The Endless Day*, 49.

23. Kessler-Harris, *Out to Work*, 219.

24. Ibid., 224.

25. Ibid., 253.

26. Ibid., 255.

27. Ibid., 256.

28. Ruth Milkman, "Organizing the Sexual Division of Labor: Historical Perspectives on 'Women's Work' and the American Labor Movement," *Socialist Review* 10 (January–February 1980): 95–150.

29. Ibid.

30. Ruth Milkman, "Female Factory Labor and Industrial Structure: Control and Conflict over 'Woman's Place' in Auto and Electrical Manufacturing," *Politics and Society* 12 (1983): 159–203.

31. Milkman, "Organizing the Sexual Division of Labor."

32. Ibid.

33. Ibid.

34. Ibid.

35. Wertheimer, *We Were There*, 30.

36. Angela Davis, *Women, Race and Class* (New York: Vintage Books, 1983), 5.

37. Ibid., 6.

38. Wertheimer, *We Were There*, 32.

39. Ibid., 111.

40. Ibid., 110.

41. Kessler-Harris, *Out to Work*, 47.

42. Ibid., 53.

43. Wertheimer, *We Were There*, 228.

44. Gerda Lerner, ed., *Black Women in White America: A Documentary History* (New York: Vintage Books, 1973), 227.

45. Ibid., 227–228.

46. Kessler-Harris, *Out to Work*, 238.

47. Ibid., 279.

48. William Serrin, "Experts Say Job Bias against Women Persists," *New York Times* (25 November 1984).

49. Berch, *The Endless Day*, 12–13.

50. Serrin, "Experts Say Job Bias against Women Persists."

51. Ibid.

52. Serrin, "Experts Say Job Bias against Women Persists"; U.S. Department of Labor, Bureau of Labor Statistics, unpublished tabulations from the Current Population Survey, 1983 annual averages.

53. U.S. Bureau of the Census, Current Population Reports, Series P-60. No. 149, *Money Income and Poverty Status of Families and Persons in the United States: 1984* (Advance Data from the March 1985 Current Population Survey), U.S. Government Printing Office, Washington, D.C., 1985, 2.

54. Nancy S. Barrett, "Obstacles to Economic Parity for Women," *The American Economic Review* 72 (May 1982): 160–165.

55. Rosabeth Moss Kanter, *Men and Women of the Corporation* (New York: Basic Books, 1977).

56. William Serrin, "Labor Pact at Yale," *New York Times* (24 January 1985).

57. Nancy F. Rytina, "Earnings of Men and Women: A Look at Specific Occupations," *Monthly Labor Review* (April 1982): 25–31.

58. Serrin, "Experts Say Job Bias against Women Persists."

59. Rytina, "Earnings of Men and Women."

60. Mary Lindenstein Walshok, *Blue-Collar Women: Pioneers on the Male Frontier* (Garden City, N.Y.: Anchor Books, 1981), xvii–xviii.

61. Ibid., 69.

62. Ibid., 76.

63. Ibid., 78–79.

64. For additional material about Gwen Johnson, see Ruth Sidel, *Urban Survival: The World of Working-Class Women* (Boston: Beacon Press, 1978), 9–26.

65. Frances Fox Piven and Richard A. Cloward, *Regulating the Poor: The Functions of Public Welfare* (New York: Vintage Books, 1971).

66. William Serrin, "Jobs Increase in Number, But Trends Are Said to Be Leaving Many Behind," *New York Times* (15 October 1984).

67. Ibid.

68. Kenneth B. Noble, "Jobless Rate Up as Women Seek Work," *New York Times* (2 February 1985).

69. Serrin, "Experts Say Job Bias against Women Persists."

70. Serrin, "Jobs Increase in Number."

71. Tamar Lewin, "A New Push to Raise Women's Pay," *New York Times* (1 January 1984).

72. Carol Lawson, "Women in State Jobs Gain in Pay Equity," *New York Times* (20 May 1985).

73. "U.S. Court Upsets Pay Equity Ruling for Women," *New York Times* (5 September 1985).

— 4 —
WELFARE:
HOW TO KEEP A GOOD WOMAN DOWN

1. Walter I. Trattner, *From Poor Law to Welfare State: A History of Social Welfare in America* (New York: Free Press, 1974), 11.

2. Ibid.

3. Andrew Billingsley and Jeanne M. Giovannoni, *Children of the Storm: Black Children and American Child Welfare* (New York: Harcourt Brace Jovanovich, 1972): 22.

4. Trattner, *From Poor Law to Welfare State*, 17.

5. Ibid., 16.

6. Ibid., 51.

7. Ibid., 52.

8. Ibid., 51.

9. Ibid., 52–53.

10. Ibid., 55.

11. Ibid., 56.

12. Billingsley and Giovannoni, *Children of the Storm*, 34.

13. Lela B. Costin and Charles A. Rapp, *Child Welfare: Policies and Practice* (New York: McGraw-Hill, 1984), 162.

14. Ibid.

15. Ibid., 163.

16. Ibid.

17. Ibid.

18. Ibid.

19. Frances Fox Piven and Richard A. Cloward, *Regulating the Poor*, 116.

20. Ibid., xiii.

21. Ibid.

22. *A Children's Defense Budget: FY 1984*, 80.

23. Costin and Rapp, *Child Welfare*, 176.

24. *A Children's Defense Budget: FY 1984*, 81.

25. *Children in Poverty*, 189.

26. *A Children's Defense Budget: FY 1984*, 81.

27. *Below the Bottom Line: A Study of Poverty in Massachusetts*, Massachusetts CAP Association (December 1982): 38.

28. Ibid., vi.

29. Ibid., vi–vii.

30. *A Children's Defense Budget: FY 1984*, 81.

31. Ibid., 82.

32. Ibid., 83.

33. Ibid., 85.

34. *Children in Poverty*, 192.

35. Ibid., 212.

36. Ibid., 203.

37. Ibid., 214.

38. *A Children's Defense Budget: FY 1984*, 87.

39. Ibid., 86.

40. John R. Block, Secretary of Agriculture, interviewed by Leslie Stahl on *Face the Nation*, February 3, 1985.

41. Richard Sennett and Jonathan Cobb, *The Hidden Injuries of Class* (New York: Knopf, 1973), 191.

42. Ibid.

43. Maya Angelou, *I Know Why the Caged Bird Sings* (New York: Bantam, 1973), 40.

44. Carol B. Stack, *All Our Kin: Strategies for Survival in a Black Community* (New York: Harper Colophon, 1975), 32.

45. Stack, *All Our Kin*, 42.

46. Greg J. Duncan, *Years of Poverty*, 72.

47. Ibid., 77.

48. Ibid., 91.

— 5 —
BUT WHERE ARE THE MEN?

1. Ntozake Shange, *For Colored Girls Who Have Considered Suicide When the Rainbow Is Enuf* (New York: Bantam, 1980), 53–54.

2. Barbara Ehrenreich, *The Hearts of Men: American Dreams and the Flight from Commitment* (Garden City, N.Y.: Anchor Press, 1983), 20.

3. Ibid., 121.

4. Emile Durkheim, *The Division of Labor in Society* (Glencoe, Ill.: Free Press, 1964; originally published in 1893).

5. Peter Brown and Robert Rans, "Material Girl," on Madonna, *Like a Virgin*, Sire Records, 1984.

6. Joyce Everett, "Patterns and Implications of Child Support and Enforcement Practices for Children's Well-being," Working Paper No. 128 (Wellesley, Mass.: Wellesley College Center for Research on Women, 1984).

7. Ibid.

8. Ibid.

9. "Child Support Frequently Not Paid," *New York Times* (8 July 1983).

10. Everett, "Patterns and Implications of Child Support."

11. Glenn Collins, "Why Fathers Don't Pay Child Support," *New York Times* (1 September 1983).

12. Ibid.

13. Ibid.

14. Robert Pear, "Reagan Signs Bill Forcing Payments for Child Support," *New York Times* (17 August 1984).

15. Thomas Keefe, "The Stresses of Unemployment," *Social Work* 29 (May–June 1984): 264–268.

16. Paula M. Rayman, "The Private Tragedy Behind the Unemployment Statistics," *Brandeis Quarterly* 2 (July 1982): 2–4.

17. M. Harvey Brenner, "Estimating the Effects of Economic Change on National Health and Social Well-Being," study prepared for the use of the Subcommittee on Economic Goals and Intergovernmental Policy of the Joint Economic Committee (Washington, D.C.: U.S. Government Printing Office, 1984): 3.

18. Ramsay Liem and Paula Rayman, "Health and Social Costs of Unemployment," *American Psychologist* 37 (October 1982): 1116–1123.

19. Ibid.

20. Keefe, "The Stresses of Unemployment."

21. Steven Greenhouse, "Former Steelworkers' Income Falls by Half," *New York Times* (31 October 1984).

22. Damon Stetson, "City Survey Finds Unskilled in Bind," *New York Times* (4 September 1983).

23. Tom Joe and Peter Yu, "Black Men, Welfare and Jobs," *New York Times* (11 May 1984).

24. Ibid.

25. James Barron, "Urban League Cites Pressures on Black Men," *New York Times* (1 August 1984).

26. "Curbing the High Rate of Black Homicide," *NASW* (National Association of Social Workers) *NEWS* (September 1984): 3–4.

27. Ronald Smothers, "Concern for the Black Family: Attention Now Turns to Men," *New York Times* (31 December 1983).

28. Elliot Liebow, *Tally's Corner: A Study of Negro Streetcorner Men* (Boston: Little, Brown, 1967), 210.

29. Ibid., 84.

30. Michael Harrington, *The New American Poverty* (New York: Holt, Rinehart & Winston: 1984), 20.

31. Eleanor Holmes Norton, "Restoring the Traditional Black Family," *New York Times Magazine* (2 June 1985): 43, 79, 93, 96, 98.

32. Liebow, *Tally's Corner*, 132.

33. Ian Robertson, *Sociology* (New York: Worth, 1981), 304.

34. Segment on CBS Sunday morning news, February 10, 1985.

— 6 —
DAY CARE: DO WE REALLY CARE?

1. Pamela Roby, "Young Children: Priorities or Problems? Issues and Goals for the Next Decade," in *Child Care—Who Cares? Foreign and Domestic Infant and Early Childhood Development Policies*, Pamela Roby, ed. (New York: Basic Books, 1973), 125–126.

2. Marion Blum, *The Day-Care Dilemma: Women and Children First* (Lexington, Mass.: Lexington Books, 1983), 2.

3. Ibid., 5–18.

4. Ibid., 19–23.

5. Ibid., 67–76.

6. Ibid., 41.

7. *Child Care: The States' Response: A Survey of State Child Care Policies, 1983–1984*, White Paper prepared by Helen Blank (Washington, D.C.: Children's Defense Fund, 1984), 7.

8. Lela B. Costin and Charles A. Rapp, *Child Welfare*, 473.

9. Ibid.

10. Virginia Kerr, "One Step Forward—Two Steps Back: Child Care's Long American History," in *Child Care—Who Cares?*, 160.

11. Ibid., 161.

12. Ibid., 162.

13. Ibid.

14. Ibid., 163.

15. Ibid., 165.

16. Ibid.

17. Ibid., 166–167.

18. Ibid., 167.

19. Costin and Rapp, *Child Welfare*, 478.

20. Ibid., 478–479.

21. Ibid., 479.

22. For additional material on Maria Perez, see Ruth Sidel, *Urban Survival*, 93–106.

23. Mary Dublin Keyserling, *Windows on Day Care* (New York: National Council of Jewish Women, 1972), 1–3.

24. Ibid., 3.

25. Ibid., 120.

26. Ibid., 119.

27. Ibid., 64.

28. Ibid., 123.

29. Ibid., 155.

30. Ibid., 135.

31. Ibid.

32. *Child Care: The States' Response*, 13.

33. *A Children's Defense Budget: FY 1984*, 133.

34. *A Children's Defense Budget: An Analysis of the President's FY 1985 Budget and Children* (Washington, D.C.: Children's Defense Fund, 1984), 161–162.

35. Dana E. Friedman, "Employer-Supported Child Care: How Does It Answer the Needs and Expectations of Workers?" *Vital Issues* (a service of the Center for Information on America) 32 (1983): 1–6.

36. *A Children's Defense Budget: FY 1985*, 161.

37. Ibid., 162.

38. Ibid., 163.

39. *Child Care: The States' Response*, 10–11.

40. Glenn Collins, "More Corporations Are Offering Child Care," *New York Times* (21 June 1985).

41. Ibid.

42. Friedman, "Employer-Supported Child Care."

43. Ibid.

44. Ibid.

45. Sheila B. Kamerman, "The Child-Care Debate: Working Mothers vs. America," *Working Woman* (November 1983): 131–135.

46. Fred. M. Hechinger, "Blacks Found to Benefit from Preschooling," *New York Times* (11 September 1984).

47. Ibid.

48. Ibid.

49. Fred Hechinger, "Society's Stake in Preschool Teaching of Poor," *New York Times* (9 October 1984).

— 7 —
THE IMPACT OF POVERTY ON
HEALTH AND WELL-BEING

1. Ruth Sidel, *Urban Survival*, 94.

2. Ibid., 72.

3. "Sickle Cell Anemia," March of Dimes Birth Defects Foundation Public Health Information Sheet, October 1981.

4. Sidel, *Urban Survival*, 84–86.

5. "Heart Disease Tied to Poverty," *New York Times* (24 February 1985).

6. *Health of the Disadvantaged: Chart Book II* (Washington, D.C.: U.S. Department of Health and Human Services, 1980), 53.

7. Minako K. Maykovich, *Medical Sociology* (Sherman Oaks, Calif.: Alfred Publishing Co., 1980), 123–125.

8. *Health of the Disadvantaged*, 50.

9. E. Richard Brown, "Medicare and Medicaid: Band-Aids for the Old and Poor," in *Reforming Medicine: Lessons of the Last Quarter Century*, Victor W. Sidel and Ruth Sidel, eds. (New York: Pantheon, 1984), 72.

10. *A Children's Defense Budget: FY 1985*, 83.

11. Ibid., 83–84.

12. "Life Expectancy at New U.S. High," *New York Times* (12 February 1985).

13. Helen Rodriguez-Trias, "The Women's Health Movement: Women Take Power," in *Reforming Medicine*, 109.

14. Ibid.

15. "The Depo-Provera Debate," *Network News*, newsletter of the National Women's Health Network (March–April 1983) 8: 8–10.

16. Philip M. Boffey, "Panel Advises against Sale of Contraceptive," *New York Times* (27 October 1984).

17. "The Depo-Provera Debate," 9.

18. Boffey, "Panel Advises against Sale of Contraceptive."

19. Sybil Shainwald, "Prescription for Your Health," *Network News*, 6.

20. Lawrence Lader, "Women Angry, May Gain," *New York Times* (20 January 1984).

21. Dr. Walter A. Ruch, letter distributed by Planned Parenthood Federation of America, spring 1984.

22. Ibid.

23. *A Children's Defense Budget: FY 1985*, 94.

24. Richard J. Meislin, "U.S. Asserts Key to Curbing Births Is a Free Econ-

omy," *New York Times* (9 August 1984).

25. Nadine Brozan, "Birth-Control Rule: Clinics Ponder Effects," *New York Times* (29 January 1983).

26. "U.S. Drops Efforts for Notice of Child's Birth Control Use," *New York Times* (1 December 1983).

27. Rodriguez-Trias, "The Women's Health Movement," 116.

28. For a fuller discussion of this issue, see Rodriguez-Trias, "The Women's Health Movement," 116–122.

29. Maykovich, *Medical Sociology*, 125.

30. *Health of the Disadvantaged*, 80.

31. Ibid., 81.

32. Ibid., 84.

33. Quoted in Edwin M. Schur, *Labeling Women Deviant: Gender, Stigma, and Social Control* (Philadelphia: Temple University Press, 1983), 202.

34. Ibid., 199.

35. Peter Conrad and Rochelle Kern, eds., *The Sociology of Health and Illness: Critical Perspectives* (New York: St. Martin's Press, 1981), 244.

36. Physician Task Force on Hunger in America, *Hunger in America: The Growing Epidemic* (Boston: Harvard University School of Public Health, 1985), xiii.

37. Ibid., 4.

38. "Free Meals for Hungry Rising in U.S.," *New York Times* (7 September 1983).

39. Hunger Watch—New York State, *Part I: Profile of "At-Risk" Populations and Service Agencies* (February 1984): 37.

40. Ibid., 8.

41. Ibid., 17.

42. Ibid., 19.

43. Ibid.

44. Ibid., 34.

45. Ibid., 20.

46. Anna Lou Dehavenon, "The Tyranny of Indifference and the Re-Institutionalization of Hunger, Homelessness and Poor Health: A Study of the Causes and Conditions of the Food Emergencies in 1,506 Households with Children in East Harlem, Brooklyn and the Bronx," study prepared for the use of the East Harlem Interfaith Welfare Committee, 8 May 1985, 2, 9.

47. Robert Pear, "U.S. Hunger on Rise Despite Swelling of Food Surpluses," *New York Times* (20 July 1983).

48. *A Children's Defense Budget: FY 1985*, 100–102.

49. Marion Burros, "Nutritionists Assess Federal Meal Plans," *New York Times* (20 July 1983).

50. Ibid.

51. Agnes C. Higgens, "Nutritional Status and the Outcome of Pregnancy," *Journal of the Canadian Dietetic Association* 37 (January 1976): 17–35.

52. Richard L. Naeye, William Blanc, and Cheryl Paul, "Effects of Maternal Nutrition on the Human Fetus," *Pediatrics* 52 (October 1973): 494–503.

53. Higgens, "Nutritional Status."

54. *A Children's Defense Budget: FY 1985*, 97.

55. Ibid.

56. "Iron Deficiencies in Infants May Have Link to Economy," *New York Times* (30 April 1984).

57. *A Children's Defense Budget: FY 1985*, 99.

58. Robert Pear, "U.S. Reports Decline in Infant Mortality Rate," *New York Times* (16 March 1983).

59. "Life Expectancy at New U.S. High."

60. "Black and White Infant Deaths: A Widening Gap," *Clearinghouse Review*, National Clearinghouse for Legal Services, Inc., 18 (July 1984): 260–265.

61. "Life Expectancy at New U.S. High."

62. Pear, "U.S. Reports Decline in Infant Mortality Rate."

63. *A Children's Defense Budget: FY 1985*, 82.

64. Ibid., 85.

65. Ibid., 82–83.

66. "Measles in U.S. Rises Sharply," *New York Times* (9 September 1984).

67. "Lead Poisoning Kills!" *The Auricle*, Howard University Hospital (July 1983): 3–14.

68. Philip Shabecoff, "E.P.A. Offers Rules to Tighten Curbs on Gasoline Lead," *New York Times* (31 July 1984).

69. Thomas J. Cottle, *Children in Jail* (Boston, Beacon Press: 1977), 35–36.

— 8 —

THE SPECIAL PLIGHT OF OLDER WOMEN

1. Robert N. Butler, Preface, U.S. National Institute on Aging, *The Older Woman: Continuities and Discontinuities* (Washington, D.C.: U.S. Government Printing Office, 1979), 1.

2. Carroll L. Estes, Lenore Gerard, and Adele Clarke, "Women and the Economics of Aging," *International Journal of Health Services* 14 (1984): 55–68.

3. Ibid.

4. Meredith Minkler and Robyn Stone, "The Feminization of Poverty and Older Women," unpublished manuscript.

5. Estes et al., "Women and the Economics of Aging."

6. Butler, *The Older Woman*.

7. U.S. Bureau of the Census, Current Population Reports, Series P-60, No. 149, *Money Income and Poverty Status of Families and Persons in the United States: 1984* (Advance Data from the March 1985 Current Population Survey), U.S. Government Printing Office, Washington, D.C., 1985, 26.

8. Minkler and Stone, "The Feminization of Poverty and Older Women."

9. "Study Finds Elderly Women More Susceptible to Poverty," *New York Times* (24 September 1984).

10. *Money Income and Poverty Status of Families and Persons in the United States: 1984*, 13–14.

11. "Not Even for Dogcatcher: Employment Discrimination and Older Women," Gray Paper No. 8 (Washington, D.C.: Older Women's League, 1982): 1–23.

12. Ibid.

13. Teresa J. Arendell, "Women at Risk: The Economic Effects of Divorce and Their Gender Base," paper presented at the annual meeting of the American Public Health Association, November 1984.

14. "The Disillusionment of Divorce for Older Women," Gray Paper No. 6 (Washington, D.C.: Older Women's League, 1980): 1–19.

15. Ibid.

16. Estes et al., "Women and the Economics of Aging."

17. Ibid.

18. Jane Perlez, "Senate Approves Pension Measure to Benefit Women," *New York Times* (7 August 1984).

19. Ibid.

20. Ibid.

21. *Inequality of Sacrifice: The Impact of the Reagan Budget on Women* (Washington, D.C.: Coalition on Women and the Budget, 1984), 64.

22. Charlotte Muller, "Income Supports for Older Women," *Social Policy* 14 (Fall 1983): 23–31.

23. Ibid.

24. Ibid.

25. Ibid.

26. *Inequality of Sacrifice*, 65.

27. Estes et. al., "Women and the Economics of Aging.

28. James R. Storey, "Policy Changes Affecting Older Americans during the First Reagan Administration," paper presented at the annual meeting of the Gerontological Society of America, November 19, 1984.

29. Material presented by Scott Geron at the annual meeting of the Gerontological Society of America, November 19, 1984.

30. New York State Department of Health, "Nutritional Assessment of the Elderly," unpublished paper, May 1982.

31. Estes et al., "Women and the Economics of Aging."

32. Elaine M. Brody, "A Million Procrustean Beds," in *Growing Old in America*, Beth Hess, ed. (New Brunswick, N.J.: Transaction Books, 1980), 251.

33. Ibid., 245.

34. "The Color Line in Old-Age Care," *New York Times* (29 January 1984).

35. Pamela G. Hollie, "Nursing Homes Seek Affluent," *New York Times* (15 September 1984); see also Charlene Harrington, "Public Policy and the Nursing Home Industry," in *Readings in the Political Economy of Aging*, Meredith Minkler and Carroll L. Estes, eds. (Farmingdale, N.Y.: Baywood, 1984), 144–154.

36. Hollie, "Nursing Homes Seek Affluent."

37. Ernest Becker, *The Denial of Death* (Free Press: New York, 1973), ix.

38. Eva J. Salber, *don't send me flowers when I'm dead* (Durham, N.C.: Duke University Press, 1983), 83.

39. Ibid., 84–87.

— 9 —
WHAT IS TO BE DONE?
LESSONS FROM SWEDEN

1. *Toward Equality: The Alva Myrdal Report to the Swedish Social Democratic Party* (Stockholm: Prisma, 1971), 89.

2. Sheila B. Kamerman, Alfred J. Kahn, and Paul Kingston, *Maternity Policies and Working Women* (New York: Columbia University Press, 1983), 31.

3. *Some Data About Sweden 1983–1984* (Stockholm: Skandinaviska Enskilda Banken, 1983), 14.

4. Ibid., 39.

5. Rita Liljestrom, Gunilla Furst Mellstrom, and Gillan Liljestrom Svensson, *Sex Roles in Transition: A Report on a Pilot Program in Sweden* (Stockholm: The Swedish Institute, 1975), 9.

6. Elisabet Sandberg, *Equality Is the Goal* (Stockholm: The Swedish Institute, 1975), 11.

7. Ibid., 12.

8. Ylva Ericsson, paper presented at the conference, "Women and Labour Market Policy," Cornell University, Ithaca, New York, October 5–7, 1983.

9. Berit Rollén, "The Working Family," paper presented at the seminar, "The Working Family: Perspectives and Prospects in the U.S./Canada and Sweden," New York, May 16, 1984.

10. Ibid.

11. "Equality between Men and Women in Sweden," *Fact Sheets on Sweden* (Stockholm: The Swedish Institute, December 1983).

12. Ibid.

13. Rollén, "The Working Family."

14. Ericsson, "Women and Labour Market Policy."

15. Ibid.

16. Rollén, "The Working Family."

17. Bertil Ekdahl, "Child Custody Rules in the Context of Swedish Family Law," *Social Change in Sweden*, Swedish Information Service (November 1984): 1–9.

18. *Some Data about Sweden 1983–1984*, 19.

19. Sören Kindlund, "Family Policy in Sweden," paper presented at the seminar, "The Working Family: Perspectives and Prospects in the U.S./Canada and Sweden," New York, May 16, 1984.

20. Ibid.

21. Ibid.

22. Ibid.

23. Ibid.

24. Jan Trost, "Parental Benefits—A Study of Men's Behavior and Views," *Current Sweden* (Stockholm: The Swedish Institute, June 1983): 1–7.

25. Ibid.

26. Ibid.

27. Edgar Borgenhammar, "Health Services in Sweden," in *Comparative Health Systems: Descriptive Analyses of Fourteen National Health Systems* (University Park: Pennsylvania State University Press, 1983), 470–487.

28. Ibid.

29. *Yearbook of Nordic Statistics 1983* (Stockholm: Nordic Council, 1984), 61.

30. Ibid., 68.

31. Edgar Borgenhammar, "The Health Care Sector in the Future," unpublished paper.

32. "Legislation on Family Planning," *Fact Sheets on Sweden* (Stockholm: The Swedish Institute, August 1982).

33. Ibid.

34. Ibid.

35. Ibid.

36. "Child Care Programs in Sweden," *Facts Sheets on Sweden* (Stockholm: The Swedish Institute, October 1982).

37. Ibid.

38. Ibid.

39. Ibid.

40. Ibid.

41. Kindlund, "Family Policy in Sweden."

42. *Time to Care*, report prepared for the Swedish Secretariat for Futures Studies (Oxford: Pergamon Press, 1984), 2.

43. Ibid., 1.

44. Ibid.

45. Ibid.

46. Ibid., 41.

47. Ibid., 3.

—10—
A CALL FOR A U.S. FAMILY POLICY

1. Marian Wright Edelman, ''Democracy Is Not a Spectator Sport,'' commencement address, Hunter College, June 1, 1983.

2. Nadine Brozan, ''Rate of Pregnancies for U.S. Teen-Agers Found High in Study,'' *New York Times* (13 March 1985).

3. Janet Poppendieck, personal communication.

4. Sheila B. Kamerman et al., *Maternity Policies*, 145.

5. Ibid., 15.

6. Ibid.

7. Ibid., 23.

8. Ibid., 4.

9. Kay Johnson et al., *The Data Book*, 7.

10. Ibid., 23.

11. Dwight D. Eisenhower, speech to the American Society of Newspaper Editors, April 16, 1953.

12. Winifred Bell, *Contemporary Social Welfare* (New York: Macmillan, 1983), 66.

13. *Children in Poverty*, 167.

14. *Money Income and Poverty Status of Families and Persons in the United States: 1984*, 11.

15. Magdalen Daniels, ''Tenderloin Fact Sheet,'' unpublished paper.

16. Jean Baker Miller, M.D., *Toward a New Psychology of Women* (Boston: Beacon Press, 1976), 83.

17. Carol Gilligan, *In a Different Voice*, 171.

1. William Julius Wilson, *The Truly Disadvantaged: The Inner City, The Underclass, and Public Policy* (Chicago: University of Chicago Press, 1987), 8.
2. U.S. Bureau of the Census, Current Population Reports, Series P-60, No. 168, *Money Income and Poverty Status in the United States: 1989 (Advanced Data from the March 1990 Current Population Survey)* U.S. Government Printing Office, Washington, DC, 1990, 12.
3. Ibid., 9.
4. Ibid., 13.
5. Ibid.
6. Peter Applebome, "Growing Fiscal Problems Put Squeeze on Social Programs in Many States," *New York Times* (4 September 1990).
7. *The State of America's Children 1991* (Washington, DC: Children's Defense Fund, 1991), 153.
8. Robert Pear, "A Double Dose of Pain for the Poor," *New York Times* (7 April 1991).
9. Patricia Simpson, *Living in Poverty: Coping on the Welfare Grant* (New York: Community Service Society, 1990), 13.
10. Ibid., 5.
11. William K. Stevens, "Welfare Bill: Historic Scope but a Gradual Impact," *New York Times* (2 October 1988).
12. *The State of America's Children 1991*, 31.
13. George Gerharz, "Wisconsin's Learnfare: A Bust," *New York Times* (29 January 1990).
14. Isabel Wilkerson, "Wisconsin Welfare Plan: To Reward the Married," *New York Times* (12 February 1991).
15. Tamar Lewin, "A Plan to Pay Welfare Mothers for Birth Control," *New York Times* (2 September 1991).
16. Elizabeth Rosenthal, "Health Problems of Inner City Poor Reach Crisis Point," *New York Times* (24 December 1990).
17. Philip J. Hilts, "U.S. Reports Drop in Infant Deaths," *New York Times* (6 April 1991).
18. *The State of America's Children 1991*, 61.
19. Ibid., 62.
20. Elise F. Jones, *et al.*, *Teenage Pregnancy in Industrialized Countries* (New Haven: Yale University Press, 1986), 1.
21. Ibid., 25–36.
22. *The State of America's Children 1991*, 93–95.
23. Ibid., 63.
24. Ibid., 55.
25. *Community Childhood Hunger Identification Project: A Survey of Childhood Hunger in the United States* (Washington, DC: Food Research and Action Center, 1991), ix–x.
26. Ibid., 18.
27. Irvin Molotsky, "Fewer Businesses Affected by Parental Leave Bill," *New York Times* (28 September 1988).
28. *The State of America's Children 1991*, 37.
29. Ibid., 29–30.
30. *Money Income and Poverty Status in the United States*, 5.
31. Bennett Harrison and Barry Bluestone, *The Great U-Turn: Corporate Restructuring and the Polarizing of America* (New York: Basic, 1990), 136.
32. "Economic and Financial Indicators," *The Economist* 316 (1990): 91.

INDEX

243

☐ **ADDICTIVE DRINKING**
   The Road to Recovery for Problem Drinkers and Those Who Love Them
   Clark Vaughan

A recovered addictive drinker himself, Clark Vaughan leads you through the disagreement and confusion concerning addiction treatment and answers questions no counselor could answer before.

   318 pages   ISBN: 0-14-006969-0

☐ **MENOPAUSE**
   Rosetta Reitz

Growing out of Rosetta Reitz's own search for answers, this book tells how to deal positively with all the physical and psychological changes that menopause brings.   *276 pages   ISBN: 0-14-005120-1*

☐ **HOW TO STAY HEALTHY ABROAD**
   Dr. Richard Dawood

Dr. Dawood's team of medical specialists provide detailed, practical information on the prevention and treatment of a full range of health problems encountered by travellers.   *506 pages   ISBN: 0-14-010692-8*

☐ **NO MORE MENSTRUAL CRAMPS AND OTHER GOOD NEWS**
   Penny Wise Budoff, M.D.

The one essential health guide for women of all ages, *No More Menstrual Cramps* reports that menstrual pain has a specific physical cause and that safe, non-narcotic remedies are available.

   312 pages   ISBN: 0-14-005938-5

☐ **ACUPUNCTURE FOR EVERYONE**
   Dr. Ruth Lever

Dr. Lever explains simply and clearly what the acupuncturist does and why, using case histories to show how acupuncture can be used to prevent and heal many common medical problems.   *218 pages   ISBN: 0-14-008834-2*

FOR THE BEST IN PSYCHOLOGY, LOOK FOR THE

☐ **PSYCHOSYNTHESIS**
Roberto Assagioli, M.D.

More than a theory, psychosynthesis is a practical route to personal growth encompassing, among other approaches, meditation, encounter groups, and inner-imagery.　　　*324 pages　　ISBN: 0-14-004263-6*

☐ **BIOENERGETICS**
Alexander Lowen, M.D.

The revolutionary therapy that uses the language of the body to heal the problems of the mind, bioenergetics has a liberating and positive effect on emotional, physical, and psychic distress.　　*352 pages　　ISBN: 0-14-004322-5*

☐ **THE DIVIDED SELF**
R. D. Laing

A unique study of the human situation, *The Divided Self* makes madness and the process of going mad comprehensible and offers a rich existential analysis of personal alienation.　　　*218 pages　　ISBN: 0-14-020734-1*

☐ **THE PENGUIN DICTIONARY OF PSYCHOLOGY**
Arthur S. Reber

Clarifying approximately 17,000 terms from psychology, psychiatry, and related fields, this comprehensive reference book resolves many of the difficulties raised by psychological terms, distinguishing between a term's correct use and misuse over time.　　　*848 pages　　ISBN: 0-14-051079-6*

☐ **REDISCOVERING LOVE**
Willard Gaylin, M.D.

Using insights gleaned from great romantic writers, philosophers, and psychologists, Dr. Willard Gaylin explores the very essence of love and shows how we can recapture it in our everyday lives.

288 pages *ISBN: 0-14-010431-3*

☐ **KNOW YOUR OWN I.Q.**
H.J. Eysenck

The famous book describes clearly what an I.Q. (Intelligence Quotient) is, how it can be applied, and what its shortcomings may be, then enables readers to estimate and confirm their own rating through eight sets of problems.

192 pages *ISBN: 0-14-020516-0*

☐ **DEPRESSION AND THE BODY**
The Biological Basis of Faith and Reality
Alexander Lowen, M.D.

An eminent psychiatrist presents his revolutionary plan for conquering depression by activating dormant life forces and training mind and body to respond as a finely tuned instrument. *318 pages* *ISBN: 0-14-021780-0*

☐ **LIVING THROUGH MOURNING**
Finding Comfort and Hope When a Loved One Has Died
Harriet Sarnoff Schiff

With understanding and wisdom, Harriet Sarnoff Schiff explores the complex feelings friends and relatives must cope with when someone dies and details the gradual process of grieving, offering aid to anyone facing the loss of a loved one. *300 pages* *ISBN: 0-14-010309-0*

☐ **THE FARTHER REACHES OF HUMAN NATURE**
A.H. Maslow

Written by one of the foremost spokesmen of the humanistic, or "Third Force," psychologies, this wide-ranging book is a synthesis of Maslow's ideas on biology, synergy, creativity, and cognition.

408 pages *ISBN: 0-14-004265-2*

☐ **RELIGIONS, VALUES, AND PEAK-EXPERIENCES**
Abraham H. Maslow

One of the foremost spokesmen for the Third Force movement in psychology proposes that spiritual expression is both central to the "peak-experiences" reached by fully functioning persons and a rightful subject for scientific investigation. *124 pages* *ISBN: 0-14-004262-8* **$4.95**